T0330955

ROUTLEDGE LIBRARY EDITIONS: AGRIBUSINESS AND LAND USE

Volume 18

PLANNING FOR AGRICULTURAL DEVELOPMENT

PLANNING FOR AGRICULTURAL DEVELOPMENT

J. A. MOLLETT

Routledge
Taylor & Francis Group

LONDON AND NEW YORK

First published in 1984 by Croom Helm Ltd

This edition first published in 2024
by Routledge
4 Park Square, Milton Park, Abingdon, Oxon OX14 4RN

and by Routledge
605 Third Avenue, New York, NY 10158

Routledge is an imprint of the Taylor & Francis Group, an informa business

British Library Cataloguing in Publication Data
A catalogue record for this book is available from the British Library

ISBN: 978-1-032-48321-4 (Set)
ISBN: 978-1-032-46992-8 (Volume 18) (hbk)
ISBN: 978-1-032-47015-3 (Volume 18) (pbk)
ISBN: 978-1-003-38422-9 (Volume 18) (ebk)

DOI: 10.4324/9781003384229

Publisher's Note
The publisher has gone to great lengths to ensure the quality of this reprint but points out that some imperfections in the original copies may be apparent.

Disclaimer
The publisher has made every effort to trace copyright holders and would welcome correspondence from those they have been unable to trace.

Planning for Agricultural Development

J.A. MOLLETT

CROOM HELM
London & Canberra

©1984 J.A. Mollett
Croom Helm Ltd, Provident House, Burrell Row,
Beckenham, Kent BR3 1AT
Croom Helm Australia Pty Ltd, 28 Kembla St.,
Fyshwick, ACT 2609, Australia

British Library Cataloguing in Publication Data

Mollett, J.A.
    Planning for agricultural development.
    1. Developing countries – Agriculture
    2. Developing countries – Economic policy
    I. Title
    338.1'09172'4   HD1417

    ISBN 0-7099-1784-8

Library of Congress Cataloguing in Publication Data

Mollett, J.A., 1923-
    Planning for agricultural development.

    Bibliography: p.
    Includes index.
    1. Agriculture and State – Developing countries.
2. Agriculture – Economic aspects – Developing countries.
I. Title.
HD1417.M64   1984   338.1'8'091724   83-40192
ISBN 0-312-61401-2

Printed and bound in Great Britain

CONTENTS

CONTENTS

TABLES AND FIGURES

Tables

Figures

TABLES AND FIGURES

PREFACE

There is a new consensus in the air, i.e. that
both developing countries in their domestic
policies and the international community in its
global actions must give higher priority to agriculture. Even those who in earlier days in the
name of "modernisation" have advocated policies
of import-substituting industrialisation are now
fervent supporters of higher priority for agriculture, since the developing countries have
become net importers of food as a result of
neglect of agricultural production and this
directly competes for foreign exchange with the
claims for industrialisation. Here is one area
in which today the 'conservatives' who believe in
agriculture as a comparative advantage of developing countries and a necessary foundation for
industrialisation can fully agree with the
'radicals' of the "dependency school" who advocate
avoidance of undue reliance on foreign supplies
and proclaim the need for food security.
    Within this higher priority for agriculture
the necessity of which is now so well established
and widely agreed, there is again unanimity that
the capacity for improved agricultural performance
is crucially a matter of management, and of realistic planning properly implemented at the grass roots
level. That precisely is the area of this book.
I believe it gives information and advice which
could be immensely valuable to those concerned
with decision-making in agricultural development
at any level; they should have this book by their
side for reading and frequent reference. Being a
shortened and revised version of a previous AID
reference work, it is systematically and deliberately directed towards practical advice for planners
with little attempt to discuss theoretical aspects.

Considerable attention is given to planning
experience in many countries. I believe that all
that is exactly what is needed today. In the cause
of economic development and a better future world
order, one would wish that this book receives wide
circulation and careful study.

I have known the author for a number of years.
I first met him personally in connection with my
work as a UN staff member and later as consultant
to the UN Food and Agriculture Organization in Rome
where he worked for some 16 years from 1963 to 1979
and was closely associated with their main regular
publication on 'The State of Food and Agriculture'.
This is an indispensable volume for those working
in the field. But I had already been aware of his
distinguished academic contribution before 1963.
He was particularly well known for the international
and national courses in agricultural planning and
project analysis which he had been directing at FAO
Headquarters and in the Caribbean, India, Indonesia,
Nigeria, Philippines and Uganda. That experience
is now utilised and made available in this book to
those who did not have the chance to attend these
courses.

The term "applied knowledge" is often vaguely
and ambiguously used. But here we have a clear
example of "applied knowledge" - a book efficiently
organised in terms of content, approach, quality
and style for the purpose for which it was designed:
to be applied by those concerned with agricultural
development throughout the Third World, but not
excluding even those in better-off countries. There
is a power for good in this book. May it be widely
- and wisely - used!

H.W. Singer
Emeritus Professor and Fellow of the Institute of
Development Studies, University of Sussex.

ACKNOWLEDGEMENTS

This work is primarily a revision, condensation and
updating of Managing Planned Agricultural
Development, a reference book prepared for the
Agency for International Development (AID) under
Contract No. AID/csd-3630 August 1976. The Project
Director was Albert Waterston with Wayne Weiss,
Assistant Director and John L. Wilson, Project
Associate. They were assisted by a large staff in
the preparation of research materials and the
writing of early drafts. The main audience was
taken to be "agricultural managers" in developing
countries.
        AID has indicated that it supports the revision
of this major work as "it would promote development"
and it is on this basis that the current draft is
authorised - and justified. Any errors or mis-
judgements are, of course, the sole responsibility
of the author.
        In addition to the AID material, use has been
made of FAO's series of training courses in agricultural planning and project analysis. Particular
reference should be made to a lecture given by
P.E. Naylor on "Formulation and appraisal of agricultural projects in developing countries" given at
the Regional Training Course in Agricultural
Project Analysis held in New Delhi, India, 2-28
November, 1970.
        Considerable secretarial assistance has been
gratefully received from the staff of the Institute
of Agricultural Economics, University of Oxford, as
well as encouraging support from the Institute
itself. The final typing was in the very competent
hands of Mary Barnett.

INTRODUCTION

This text is written as a guide to agricultural
policy makers, planners and project managers in
developing countries, particularly for those in the
areas of programme formulation and implementation.
Elements from successful agricultural and rural
development plans have been selected, synthesised
and presented in a form suitable for inclusion in
new plans.

It should also be helpful to those students
working on all the various aspects of planning
agriculture as well as established practitioners of
the art. No extensive background knowledge is required although some training in economic analysis
is assumed.

The work is divided roughly into three parts.
The introductory section consists of five chapters,
and covers the purpose and scope of this book, the
link between agricultural and overall planning,
various aspects of agricultural planning (including
the usual components and deficiencies of plans, time
horizons and scope of plans, and regional planning),
and it concludes with a brief look at the preparation of a plan and objectives for agricultural
development.

The main section consists of nine chapters:

6. The stocktaking and diagnostic survey is based
    on a six-fold classification and sequence which
    is both simple and comprehensive.

7. Demand and supply projections covering domestic
    demand for food and agricultural raw materials,
    foreign demand, and projections of output and
    supply.

8. <u>Setting targets and allocating resources</u> covering targets and projections, kind and number of targets, and the move from projections to targets.

9. <u>The choice of strategies</u> dealing in passing with the nature of strategies and the need for them, but giving most attention to the various types of strategies. Also deals with constraints on the choice of strategy.

10. <u>Policy and policy instruments</u> one of the longest and most important chapters, presenting in some detail the following aspects of agricultural policy: inputs and their place in development programmes; incentives and price policy; credit; marketing; employment, mechanization and technology; land reform; and characteristics of different types of policy measures.

11. <u>Projects</u>, with Chapter 10, providing the key to the entire work. It begins by examining the various types of projects (experimental, pilot, demonstration, production) and then moves on to project identification and preparation. Project implementation takes up most of the remainder of the chapter, which includes a section on project evaluation.

12. <u>Financing agricultural plans</u> covers sources of financing and the role of institutions in this important area.

13. <u>Organization for planning</u> highlights administrative constraints and problems in agricultural development, and looks at ways of organising the sector.

14. <u>Monitoring, reporting and control</u> in which this generally neglected subject is examined.

The third and supplementary section contains ancillary chapters on:

15. <u>Research, extension and training</u> which attempts to pinpoint the role of agricultural planners in seeking better use of resources in these three areas.

and

16. <u>Consultancy services</u> which asks why they are
    still needed, how best to use them and how to
    obtain them.

Throughout the text there are numerous practical
examples, figures and tables to underline the main
points. There are no footnotes. Each chapter
begins with a summary which, it is hoped, will be
useful. The bibliography is relatively short but
selective.

PLANNING FOR AGRICULTURAL DEVELOPMENT

Chapter 1

INTRODUCTION

Summary
     This is a reference book for those who are or
     expect to be engaged in planning agricultural
     development. It is based on planning experience
     in many countries. An attempt is made to pro-
     vide a systematic guide to management practice
     in this important field.

The purpose of this book is to provide those engaged
in all the various aspects of planning agricultural
development in the developing countries with a useful source of reference. One of the reasons why
agricultural planning has often been disappointing
in these countries is the wide gap which frequently
exists between planning done by farmers and by
central government planners. This book attempts to
help bridge that gap. Even when national plans are
relatively sound, their results may be poor because
central planners include only what must be done to
achieve the various targets, without indicating in
sufficient detail how, by whom and when things will
be done.
     Planners fail in this way because systems of
communication are often weak between them and the
technical ministries, departments and agencies, between national, regional and local governments and
between private and public sectors of agriculture.
In addition, farmers are often not kept well-
informed by publicly-financed media.
     Another reason for the serious gap between plan
and performance is the lack of suitable administrative procedures and institutional organization, at
all levels of government, to manage agricultural
development. Thus actual expenditure on agricultural projects in developing countries tends to lag
far behind official commitment of loans and grants,

1

leading inevitably to failed targets and frustration. The shortage of skilled managers and other trained personnel, especially at regional and local levels, is an important element of this problem which so often bedevils the most determined attempts of governments to develop their agriculture.

Agricultural development is taken to be an intra-sectoral activity which includes all services necessary to its promotion. It is a key element of rural development which is a multi-sectoral activity covering, in addition, infrastructure (schools, clinics, roads, power, communications, etc.) and welfare services (disease control, programmes for improving nutrition, higher adult literacy, family planning, etc.). The main aim of agricultural development in the poorer countries is higher farm output while for rural development it is the improvement of material and social welfare. The first provides the basis for the second since agriculture largely generates the income required for sustaining rural improvement. Attempts to achieve agricultural development outside the framework of a programme for rural betterment often fail to benefit a majority of farm families but it need not be so. This situation, and problems involved in a multi-sectoral approach, make it desirable to limit the scope of this work mainly to agricultural development. Wherever possible, however, attempts are made to deal with this subject in terms of its impact on rural welfare.

As a result of the agricultural planning attempted in many developing countries in recent years, there is now a considerable body of theoretical and applied knowledge available to provide for improved management of agricultural development. This work attempts to synthesize much of this material and present it as a systematic aid to good management practice. Theoretical or normative works have been compared with actual planning practice and experience to arrive at the comparative analysis which provides the basis of this book.

It is concerned not only with the preparation and the provision for implementation of plans, and their general management, but also with improving decision-making in all the various aspects of managing plans, programmes and projects.

This work can be regarded only as a first step toward improving the capacities of agricultural managers in the widest sense of the word. It cannot hope to satisfy all the various demands of these managers as they attempt to face the different problems met at national, regional and local levels. Nevertheless the systematic approach adopted should be of some relevance.

Chapter 2

THE LINK BETWEEN AGRICULTURAL AND OVERALL PLANNING

Summary
       Ideally, an agricultural plan should be pre-
pared within the framework of a national
development plan but relatively few are.
Nevertheless, implicitly, assumptions about the
past, present, and probable future performance
of the national economy, and its relationship
to agriculture development, are generally part
of the fabric of a sector plan. Even planning
confined mainly to agriculture can produce useful results.

Planning within an Overall Framework
Although it is hard to find a national development
plan with a programme for agriculture that is carefully integrated with other sectoral programmes, or
with the general framework of the plan, overall plans
almost always include a plan for agriculture. In
addition, many countries have prepared agricultural
programmes without any reference to the national
development plan. Most professionals in agricultural planning dislike agricultural programmes
prepared outside the framework of the national plan.
They tend to take the position that such programming
must be done within "the framework of development
planning for the whole economy", or some similar
reasoning.
       The arguments for this point of view are force-
ful. Development in agriculture and in other
sectors is clearly interdependent and mutually
supporting. Some kind of balance is required in
inter-sectoral growth if the allocation of scarce
resources between these sectors is to be accomplished efficiently and if agricultural goals are to
conform to national goals.
       These arguments are sufficiently compelling for

4

most developing countries to include their agricultural programmes in national development plans. But,
unhappily, since national plans are frequently
ignored to a greater or lesser extent by budgetary
authorities, technical ministries, departments and
autonomous agencies, these plans are frequently not
carried out. Moreover, whenever countries fail to
meet plan targets, they almost always have the
greatest shortfalls in agriculture. This has happened not only in poor countries such as India and
Pakistan but also in others such as Spain, the
U.S.S.R. and several countries in Eastern Europe.
In poor countries where agriculture dominates the
economy, failure to attain agricultural targets
largely explains their failure to grow in accordance
with their general plan targets. So that, not
surprisingly, where the annual rate of increase in
agricultural output has been low, the corresponding
rate of national economic growth has also been poor,
and vice versa.

Obviously, one solution to this problem is to
improve the whole process of national planning. But
the problems involved have, thus far, proved to be
too difficult and intractable for most poor countries to solve. Results achieved from overall
planning have frequently been so discouraging that
some authorities contend there is a crisis in planning. However, the problem may well be one of how
to plan in crisis - how to plan at a time of
increased political instability and economic uncertainty, when governments may not be able to exert
the required discipline to carry through their
medium-term comprehensive plans.

It is unnecessary for our purposes to resolve
this issue but its effect on agricultural planning
cannot be ignored. Disillusionment with overall
planning, particularly in Latin America, explains
why many countries in the region no longer prepare
national plans. In other regions, most countries
have national plans but few have the chance of being
implemented.

Where there are no overall plans or where those
which exist are not being implemented effectively,
the question arises whether it is possible, and if
so, whether it is desirable to prepare sector plans
for agriculture outside an overall framework. Some
authorities contend that even when no general framework exists, agricultural plans must be based,
implicitly if not openly, on assumptions regarding
the performance of the whole economy, with parameters for the expected growth of population,

national product, consumption, foreign trade,
industry and so on. The Food and Agriculture
Organization of the United Nations (FAO) has adopted
this approach (in the agricultural plan it prepared
for Nigeria for 1965-1980, and in others). But
aside from the fact that the methodology of forecasting economic change for periods as long as 10 or
15 years is still an uncertain quality, in developing countries, particularly, political instability
and economic hazards often make short shrift of such
forecasts as recent events in e.g. Nigeria, clearly
demonstrate.

Planning Outside an Overall Framework

It is not in doubt that optimal allocations of
resources to economic sectors, and to projects within each sector, can only be made within the framework of a plan for the whole economy. But the
record shows that many professionals in agricultural
planning appear willing to forego such an ideal
situation since they do their work outside an aggregative framework, either where existing national
plans are not operational, or where it is not considered feasible to prepare national plans which
have a reasonable chance of being put into practice.

Moreover, experience shows that, however undesirable in theory, in practice it is possible to
achieve considerable success where planning is
confined to the agricultural sector. As agriculture
in most developing countries still provides the
major part of national output and employs a large
part of the population, success here in the leading
sector is bound to generate a wide impact. Even the
World Bank, sometimes in cooperation with FAO, have
been preparing agricultural plans outside a general
planning framework in a number of countries.

All of which is not to say that it is desirable
to plan for agriculture outside a general development plan. But it is worth noting that where
agricultural development is part of an overall plan,
it often has a lower priority than industry or
infrastructure. This could be one reason why those
who wish for stronger development efforts in agriculture often consider it desirable to plan for
agriculture outside the general or macro-economic
plan. They may believe it is more likely agriculture will receive greater recognition in a sector
than an overall plan - where it is all too easy to
shift resources away from agriculture to other
sectors, often politically more powerful. To the
extent that agriculture receives an appropriate

share of resources and encouragement in an overall plan, total planning is undoubtedly superior to partial planning for agricultural development. But to the extent to which central planners are biased against agriculture, or in favour of other sectors, those who wish to see agriculture advance more rapidly may opt to stay outside the macro-economic framework, if that is possible.

Chapter 3

SOME ASPECTS OF AGRICULTURAL PLANNING

Summary
    Many agricultural plans do not have clearly
defined objectives or explain in sufficient
detail how they intend to reach their objectives or targets. The time horizon is particularly important in agriculture and planning
must take full account of this factor.
Typically there is an annual or operational
plan and a medium-term (5-year) plan, and,
sometimes, a perspective plan (15-20 years).
Continuity is important in planning and some
form of rolling plan is useful. There are end-
less variations in the scope of agricultural
plans reflecting wide differences in stages of
development, political philosophy and competence. It is useful to identify the main
features of the agricultural sector using a
system of classification which covers:
employment, size and type of holdings, kinds of
economic activity and output of its various
commodities. There will be some problems of
definition, and the classification system
adopted should be influenced by the structure
of a country's agriculture, stage of development and its political and social objectives.
To be realistic, an agricultural plan has to
give recognition to the varying ecological
needs of its different areas and this situation
provides the basis for some form of regional
planning. Reference is made to the methodology
involved in this kind of planning and other
related issues. Planners need to understand
clearly the close relationship between agricultural and rural development, inappropriate
strategies for agricultural development can
hinder rural welfare particularly if the needs

of the generally large number of poor, small
farmers and landless rural workers are neglected. A viable model for rural development is
presented.

Most countries have some kind of agricultural plan,
whether or not it is part of a national development
plan. Such plans vary considerably from one country
to another because there is no widely-accepted set
of principles for ordering agricultural development.
If one believes that a plan for agriculture should
start with one or more attainable objectives.
indicate the resources available to achieve them,
explain how these resources are to be distributed
among specific projects, and state the strategies,
policies and institutional arrangements to be used,
then one will find few plans which meet these
criteria.
    Many agricultural plans do not have clearly
defined objectives unless it is to carry out a
bundle of projects which are often unrelated to each
other. Few of such projects are likely to have been
carefully prepared and their "cost-effectiveness"
estimated. Even where the objectives are clear, the
means for achieving them may not have been spelled
out in detail, quite simply because the required
analytical work has not been done. Some plans do
not indicate what resources are to be allocated to
each project in the programme, which may be because
there are not enough well-prepared projects. If
resources are, in fact, allocated to a sector only
in the aggregate, there is no knowing whether the
amount will be sufficient. Only when projects have
been prepared in some detail, and their location
determined, is it possible to estimate their cost
with reasonable accuracy. Another problem is that
plans which reckon to include all public investment
in agriculture may actually concentrate on only one
or two sub-sectors such as irrigation or land
settlement. Further, plans which claim to be comprehensive often exclude a large part of private
investment (probably due to the difficulty of
collecting these data).
    There are plans which attempt the impossible by
including a long list of projects which cannot all
be completed within the plan period. This practice
is defensible if the planners recognise that some
projects will give little or no return in the plan
period. But when no distinction is made between
such projects and those which are expected to yield
output and income in the period of the plan, it is

clear that the planners do not have a clear idea
of the limitations of the plan's time horizon.

Time Horizons of Plans

Since the agricultural plans of most countries are
part of their medium-term national plans, which
range from three to seven years, with a mode of
five, the time available in such plans is generally
too short for bringing about basic changes in agriculture. It is possible, however, to plan production of annual crops and crops from existing trees,
to carry out some projects for improving agricultural practices, to start and carry forward long-
term projects, and establish or reorganize institutional arrangements for improving agriculture. But
land reclamation and settlement projects, manpower
training and education projects for agriculture,
improvement of nutrition as well as large-scale
irrigation projects, take many years, and forest
projects may take decades, before they begin to
yield appreciable returns. The planting of such
tree crops as citrus fruits, coffee, coconut and
rubber, and the development of beef cattle breeds
are also well-known for their long gestation
periods.

It is essential, therefore, in planning for
agriculture to take a longer than medium-term look
into the future. How far ahead depends on the
agricultural changes desired. The development or
improvement of plantation crops like citrus, tea,
rubber, coconut and coffee, needs a perspective of
at least 10 years and for irrigation and soil conservation 15 to 20 years or even longer. Most
agricultural planners probably adopt a perspective
of only 10 to 15 years.

Yet, even a 10- or 15-year period is too long
for the formulation of plans of action for agricultural development. Aside from the shortage of basic
data required for long-term planning, so many
unforseeable changes in domestic and external conditions are likely to occur that a detailed plan for
10 to 15 years ahead is almost sure to be out-of-
date before too long. That is why planners recommend that long-term or "perspective" plans for 15
years or more provide only broad lines of desirable
agricultural development. The perspective plan need
not be couched in precise terms but should formulate
the strategy of agricultural development in terms of
the country's needs and technical possibilities in
particular fields, e.g. forestry, land development,
irrigation, agricultural education, and so on.

With such a perspective, it becomes possible to
define the general direction in which long-run
development should take place, in accordance with
the government's objectives. This strategy can then
be supplemented with projects and policies for
achieving development objectives for agriculture,
consistent with national development goals. But the
projects and policies need not, indeed should not,
be incorporated in the perspective plan for agriculture since the time horizon of such a plan is so
long that the perspective plan will undoubtedly have
to be revised, perhaps several times, in the light
of events. For this reason, it is generally recommended that the agricultural development be spelled
out in medium-term agricultural plans, leaving
details of the projects which extend beyond the
medium-term period for inclusion in future medium-
term plans. While each project needs to be studied
and prepared in detail, the timing and scale of its
inclusion into a medium-term agricultural plan
depends ultimately on unforeseeable factors which
may require it to be held back, brought forward or
even cancelled.

What matters is that the perspective and
medium-term plans be reviewed periodically and
adjusted to take account of changes brought about by
domestic and external events. This review of the
perspective plan can be made every few years, but
for medium-term plans it is usually an annual exercise, and may be done in one of several ways.

One method is to revise the entire medium-term
plan for agriculture every year for the remainder of
the plan period. This is both difficult and time-
consuming because it requires an amount of trained
personnel which few poor countries possess. A
second way is to prepare annual plans which take
account of progress made to date, allocate available
resources to projects as a basis for budgetary
appropriations, and set out specific instruments of
policy and other measures for achieving development
objectives. While this is an easier way of adjusting to unforeseen changes, it has a serious defect.
As the years pass, the annual plans tend to deviate
so substantially from the medium-term plan that it
no longer provides much guidance for the preparation
of annual plans. A third way is the introduction of
a so-called "rolling plan" where an additional year
is added to the length of the medium-term plan at
the end of each year, after making appropriate
adjustments required due to changed circumstances in
the year just passed. The medium-term plan will

thus provide a look ahead at each year's end for an undiminished period. This approach has the additional advantage of providing a medium-term plan with up-to-date benchmarks for annual plans, which have to be prepared anyway to make the medium-term plan operational. If the "rolling forward" technique is applied every few years to the perspective plan, the latter can also be updated to provide guidelines for rolling the medium-term programme forward each year.

Using perspective, medium-term and annual plans is an ideal solution to the time-horizon problem. The perspective plan permits a look far enough ahead to identify in broad outline the main directions of agricultural development. The medium-term plan spells out in greater detail than the perspective plan interim goals which must be achieved in the medium-term to attain the longer-run targets. And the annual plans make the medium-term plans operational by (a) reducing medium-term targets (which are usually stated in terms of the end of the medium-term plan period) to annual targets so as to allow allocations required for their achievement to be incorporated in annual budgets and (b) enumerating in sufficient detail the measures which will be adopted to achieve the plan's objectives. The three plans fit together like a nest of tables.

This approach to agricultural planning is largely associated with conventional macroeconomic planning which most authorities now agree requires the preparation of overall perspective, medium-term and annual development plans. The difficulty is that few low-income countries have ever succeeded, in practice, in formulating the three types of development plans and in integrating annual plans, where they exist, with annual budgets. Although some countries have, or have had, perspective development plans and almost all have, or have had, medium-term plans, very few have made these plans operational with annual plans closely linked with government budgets.

In practice, therefore, agricultural planning in developing countries has been largely limited to the preparation of only one medium-term plan, the duration of which has varied. Plans of shorter duration, usually for a year, are also frequently employed to translate the longer-term plans into action. This combination has proved to be workable.

On the basis of this experience, it would seem acceptable to prepare only one medium-term plan and an annual operational plan. While the longer-term

plan could cover a period of only five years in
countries which have few projects with long gestation periods, many countries are likely to find
plans for 10 to 20 years more suited to their needs.
Where time and talent exist, a rolling plan for the
first three years of the multi-annual plan, more
detailed than the rest of the plan, but less
detailed than the annual plan, could be given some
priority because it enables adjustment to be made
required by changed circumstances; in addition, the
multi-annual or medium-term plan as a whole might be
rolled forward every few years.

Scope of Plans
The scope of agricultural plans reveals as much
variation as their duration. Many countries prepare
what they term comprehensive sector plans for agriculture, but this does not necessarily mean that
each subsector receives equal attention. Plans for
forestry and, even more, fisheries are likely to be
less detailed than for crops and livestock. Nor
does private investment always receive the same
emphasis as public investment. At the other extreme
some plans make no attempt at a wide coverage and
limit the document to only one sub-sector, or even
one crop.
    Where possible, it is desirable to deal with
the whole sector but limitations of planning data,
trained manpower, finance and time may make partial
coverage inevitable. Although partial planning is
not as good as comprehensive planning in theory, it
sometimes works better in practice, particularly
where one or two sub-sectors dominate the agricultural scene. Partial planning should be avoided,
however, where the government is attempting to
diversify agriculture and to shift the emphasis away
from one or two commodities. Even so it is well to
be selective in emphasizing one sub-sector over
another.

1. Classification systems. For this purpose, as
well as for other reasons, a suitable definition of
the agricultural sector is essential, which pres-
cribes its limits and classifies or divides it into
appropriate components. There are four ways in
which this sector has generally been defined: in
terms of employment, holdings, kinds of activity and
output. Each definition has its problems.

a. Employment. The general concepts, definitions
and classifications on labour force, employment,

unemployment, under-employment, etc. recommended by
the International Labour Office (ILO) were elabora-
ted in the framework of an industrial society on the
basis of the existence of well organised establishments with employers, workers, fixed wages, fixed
hours of work, etc. They are difficult to apply to
agriculture where business is often done on a family
or household basis

The amount of agricultural work to be carried
out on a holding is irregular and may change from
day to day. It is also seasonal. There are times
when the work is intensive and others when it is
almost non-existent. For these reasons, the agricultural statistician is not so much interested in
measuring the volume of employment and unemployment
on a fixed date, or during a short period to time.
He or she is much more interested in quantifying the
total volume of work to be carried out on the holding, its distribution according to source of labour
inputs (family, non-family, regular, part-time or
spare time, etc.) and its relationship with size,
type and other characteristics of the holding.

The concept of time worked in agriculture is
much more difficult to define than in other fields
of activity. Such work includes working in the
fields, preparing goods for and taking them to the
market, buying and transporting farm inputs, record
keeping, etc. There is no fixed working place.
Distances between different sites of work may be
long and time-consuming. Care is thus needed to
include all the relevant periods of work and travel
when recording the time worked by the farmer, the
family workers and paid workers.

To take account of the wide variety of labour
used in farming, a useful concept is the 'man-year'
unit of work. This unit is defined as the amount of
agricultural work carried out by an able man during
a year, the year being defined as a number of hours
(e.g. 2800 hours) or days (e.g. 275 days). Appropriate adjustments are made for the labour of older
workers, women and children.

This kind of analysis requires data and expertise, however, which are not always available. To
avoid difficulties any planning exercise should
explicitly state how the agricultural labour force
has been counted.

b. Holdings. The size and type of holdings are
major characteristics investigated in agricultural
censuses. The concept of size of holding can be
defined in a number of ways according to the basis

of measurement. It can be measured in terms of area, output, livestock, trees, labour, etc. The concept of area to be considered could be:

- Total area: which may or may not be satisfactory according to the size of unproductive land
- Agricultural area: which includes meadows and pastures and may be more relevant when the holding includes both crops and livestock
- Crop area or arable land area: one or other of which could be particularly relevant if the size is to be correlated with the labour inputs

In censuses of agriculture, especially those carried out on a complete enumeration basis, practical considerations make it necessary to limit the enumeration to holdings above a certain limit of size. Further, most of the agro-economic surveys carried out, subsequent to a census, use as a frame the results of the census of agriculture and thus do not include holdings below the lower limit. This results in a situation in which the most vulnerable section of the agricultural population may not be investigated at all. To remedy this situation, planners should specify that some key question be introduced in the censuses of population to identify these small holdings which could then be investigated on a sampling basis. Planners will also find it helpful if holdings are divided into the following three sectors:

1. The Private sector which includes all holdings operated by individuals or households;
2. The Public sector which covers those holdings operated by a central or local government, either directly or through a special body;
3. The Collective sector which covers the holdings operated by a group of persons who, voluntarily, or by mandate of the governing authority, join together to exercise land rights in common. However, if a member of a collective receives a plot for his personal use, this plot will be part of the private sector.

Another classification of agricultural holdings is based on the degree of utilization of advanced techniques where holdings are sub-divided into modern, progressive and traditional. However, the definitions generally used are rather vague and are differently interpreted by the countries, which often use only the terms modern/traditional farming or commercial/subsistence farming.

c. Kinds of economic activity. Defining the agricultural industry by the kind of economic activity raises the problem of how to identify establishments which are engaged in a variety of agricultural enterprises. The two criteria set by the United Nations (U.N.) International Standard Industrial Classification (ISIC) to deal with this problem provide that (1) the farming units included in a given activity group must account for the bulk of the output of these units and (2) the group must contain most of the farming units which produce most of the class of foods and services which characterize the activity concerned.

The best-known example of a classification system which groups farming (and other) establishments by their economic activity is the abovementioned U.N. system. The ISIC arranges economic activities into four sub-divisions: (1) Major Divisions, (2) Divisions, (3) Major Groups, and (4) Groups. There are 10 Major Divisions in the ISIC of which Major Division I covers agriculture, hunting, forestry and fishing. This Major Division is sub-divided as follows:

Division 11 Agriculture and hunting
           111 1110 Agricultural and livestock production
           112 1120 Agricultural services
           113 1130 Hunting, trapping and game propagation

Division 12 Forestry and logging
           121 1210 Forestry
           122 1220 Logging

Division 13 130 Fishing
               1301 Ocean and coastal fishing
               1320 Fishing not otherwise classified

d. Output. The most common way of defining the agricultural sector is by the output of its various commodities. A typical classification system uses five sub-sectors: (1) Crops, (2) Livestock and livestock products, (3) Forests and their products, (4) Game, and (5) Fisheries.

These sub-sectors may, in turn, be divided into branches and sub-branches. As shown in Figure 3-1, there are a number of possibilities for choosing the basis for this division. Crops, for example, may be divided into major or minor crops, for export or domestic consumption, for sale or subsistence. The dividing line between the various categories is not always clear-cut, for example, oil-producing plants fall into "food and beverage" as well as "industrial raw material" branches.

Figure 3-1 <u>Classification of the Agricultural Sector</u>

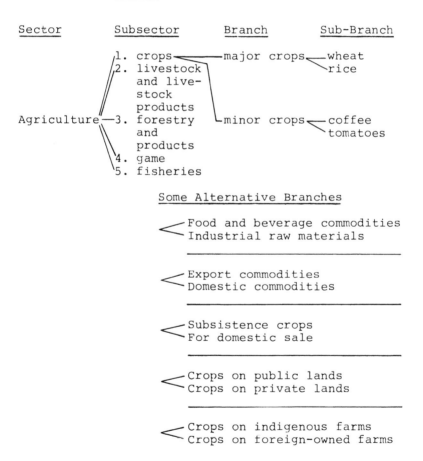

2. Which classification system to use. The classification system eventually adopted should be determined by the structure of a country's agriculture,
its stage of development and its objectives. Each
country must adapt the system to its own situation.
Thus where impact of an agricultural plan on the
balance of payments is important, it should be
possible to distinguish between export- and
domestic-oriented activities. If the main effect is
a general increase in output and international comparisons are not important, then a commodity classification may be adequate. However, if there is an
interest in income distribution, or levels of living
of specified groups of farmers then a system based
on economic activity is needed because it will
provide for farms to be classified according to
size, character, technology and production organisation (besides facilitating international comparison).

As indicated earlier, the ISIC system not only
provides for farms of different kinds, technology
and organization to be identified, it also permits
classification by output of commodities. A system
based on economic activity, like the ISIC, can,
therefore, meet planning requirements where objectives include the improvement of particular groups
of farms, increased output, or both.

Of course, much depends on the quality and
coverage of a country's statistical services in
deciding which classification system to choose.
Ideally, statistics should conform to the needs of
agricultural planning rather than the other way
around. One must make the best use of whatever data
are available, however frustrating this may be.

Territory covered by Agricultural Plans

1. The need for regional planning. A national agricultural plan cannot be realistic unless it takes
adequate account of the varying ecological requirements in the different areas of the country.
Temperature, rainfall, humidity, soil and water
resources, drainage, topography and altitude, all
condition the methods used to increase crop and
livestock production. Some regions are more potentially productive than others; some with easy access
to markets have had a head start, while others
perhaps less accessible lag behind. Regions with
irrigation are able to take advantage of new high-
yielding varieties of grain, for example, while
those wholly dependent on rainfall may not be able

to. Moreover, if disparities among regions are to
be reduced, the needs of the poorer regions will
increase. Each region is, therefore, likely to have
its own development requirements, and within each
region there may well be considerable diversity.

Ideally, therefore, a national agricultural
plan should include plans for all the regions. But
this is a difficult task especially if the national
plan is attempting to deal with agriculture in comprehensive terms. This situation helps to explain
why such plans are usually couched in broad terms,
with few details given about the problems and needs
of specific areas.

2. Putting the plan on a regional basis. Within
recent years, however, countries with and without
national plans have been turning increasingly to
regional planning for agriculture. This has partly
come about from growing political awareness in the
less-favoured regions of the vital role that the
central government plays in the allocation of investment, and the consequent need for organisations
in the poorer regions to exercise more pressure on
the central authorities. Paradoxically, national
and sector planning has encouraged this political
development, as one result of such central planning
is that well-endowed regions often get the lion's
share of infrastructure and other substantial
investment projects - leading to a widening of
regional disparities.

Experience shows that regional planning for
agriculture has taken three main forms. The first
is a national plan for agriculture composed of sub-
plans for all the regions in a country, coordinated
in line with national development objectives and
strategies. France, Israel and the U.S.S.R. are
good examples of countries where this kind of
planning is followed. The second type covers one or
several selected regions within a country. This
approach is sometimes adopted by less developed
countries which do not have the resources to carry
out a comprehensive programme. They prefer to concentrate their effort in one or a few regions where
total additional returns are likely to be higher
than if the same resources were spread more thinly.
India led the way with its intensive Agricultural
Development Programme in the 1960's under which one
district in each State was selected for a concentrated approach to development. The third kind of
regional plan for agriculture is one which is part
of a comprehensive plan for a specific region as in

Brazil's Northeast and in the south of Italy, or
where it is considered desirable to develop national
resources located in a given region e.g. a river
basin for irrigation or other purposes as with the
Aswan Dam development in Egypt.

3. The methodology of regional planning. There is no
widely accepted theory which identifies the key
elements in regional development. Nevertheless
regional planners would probably agree that the
following propositions are helpful. Regional development (1) largely depends on the extent to which
a region's export capabilities expand, (2) requires
the mobilisation of government and individuals to
take advantage of development opportunities as they
arise, and (3) is most effective within the framework of an integrated regional or sub-regional plan.
    The argument in favour of developing the
export base assumes that a region has a comparative
advantage in one or more agricultural or manufactured products, or in both, which can be expanded by
the establishment of specialised marketing organizations, improved credit and transport facilities,
a trained labour force, and complementary industries.
The need to mobilize government and individuals
assumes that ability to recognise, evaluate and act
on investment opportunities, as well as willingness
to accept risk and adopt innovations, is frequently
lacking in undeveloped regions.   And the notion
that economic development must take place within an
integrated regional or sub-regional system derives
from the belief that only then can planners obtain
a proper understanding of where development arises,
and how it is diffused through the regional or subregional economy.
    The model which is most widely accepted among
regional planners may be stated in two propositions:
(1) Growth and development are initiated in a
limited number of urban "growth centres" or "growth
poles"; and (2) is then diffused from these centres
to their respective hinterlands by growth-inducing
innovations and market mechanisms. The model
necessarily requires the concentration of resources
on urban development, at least in the early stages
of regional development. Those who hold to the
growth centre or pole model contend that theoretical and empirical findings show that regional growth
and development tak place most effectively through
the articulated development of a system of urban
centres, arranged in a hierarchy from small agro-
urban towns through several intermediate types to

the metropolis. Growth impulses are transmitted
from the metropolis to the rural areas, with the
larger centres retaining activities of greater scale
and capital-intensity, and smaller centres developing activities which can be performed at lower scale
for more local markets, or in which the capital-
labour ratio is low; and with all centres diffusing
growth to their hinterlands. The city is regarded
as the "engine" of regional development and is the
link between the regional and national economy.
Agriculture tends to be more efficient, commercial
and prosperous in the vicinity of cities and becomes
less so as the distance from urban centres increase,
until in the less accessible marginal areas agriculture is characterised by backward, subsistence
systems. An essential element of this model is the
provision of a good network of roads and transport
facilities for providing efficient distribution of
goods and services required for rural development.
   Most countries which have made an attempt at
regional development have relied on growth centre
strategy. Regional planners in these countries
have tried through various means to create external
economies and linkages at selected urban locations.
The usual approach has been through a government-
sponsored industrial development plan. Frequently,
the plan is directed toward strengthening existing
towns and cities that are considered to be strate-
gically located or on the threshold to sustained
growth. In some cases, new towns are constructed,
especially in areas lacking cities and towns of any
significant size. After identifying the locations
to be developed as growth centres, a government
usually devises a public investment plan and economic incentives for the private sector, designed to
guide industrial investment toward these centres.
The plan may include provision for direct public
investments in industry, industrial estates, other
infrastructure and social programmes, as well as
low-interest loans, grants, tax abatements and subsidies to private investors.
   Italy has had one of the longest experiences
with growth centre planning. Between 1950-57, the
Cassa per il Mezzogiorno, the organization established by the Italian government to raise the economic
level of the poor southern part of the country, proceeded on the assumption that agriculture was the
key to reducing the economic gap between the poor
South and the richer North. When it became apparent
that industry would not be self-generating from an
improved agricultural base in the South, a three-

pronged programme was substituted for the agricultural strategy in 1957.

The first element of the programme was a set of compensatory measures designed to offset the higher operating costs of firms locating in the South as compared to the North. These included exemptions from some taxes and duties, grants to small-and-medium-sized firms, low-interest loans, provision of risk capital, reduced transport fees and technical assistance. The second element was a series of investments in state-controlled regional firms, largely in the heavy industry sector. The third element was a growth centre strategy.

Spain has also had experiences with growth centres but the results obtained from regional development planning there as in Italy, have not been too encouraging. There have also been mixed results from several Latin American countries - Chile, Colombia, Peru and Venezuela - as well as in Israel, Ghana, India (with their Community Development Programme) and Nepal.

The relatively few poor countries which have begun to plan for regional development, and the mixed results they have obtained, tend to show that the state of regional planning is still in its early stages in such countries. Experience of economically-advanced countries in dealing with problems of backward regions suggests that attempts to restructure the regional organisation of an economy are likely to be extremely costly and only marginally successful. In less developed countries, where there is as yet little infrastructure and other heavy investment, opportunities exist to structure investment in ways which may prevent or at least reduce widescale regional inequalities.

Nevertheless, it is by no means clear that the way to start development of a region is by making some small town or large village grow rapidly by heavy investment of mainly industrial inputs along the lines advocated by the growth centre theoreticians. In fact, industries may not find it easy to expand in a new urban environment if there has been no prior agricultural growth. In such cases, they may find it difficult to establish linkages with the rural areas, and finish up as isolated out-stations of the modern sector in an unchanged rural environment.

4. Problems posed by regional planning. Despite its problems, some of which are outlined below, regional planning continues to hold the interest of govern-

ments.

a. Size and definition of a region. There is, for
example, the matter of the appropriate size and
definition of a region. In general, the appropriate
size is one which is not so small as to lead to undue fragmentation of national agricultural planning
efforts, yet small enough to enable rapid feedback
between farm units and regional planners. In the
Philippines, which consists of many islands, the
entire island of Mindanao was originally established
as a region (it was later sub-divided into four
regions). In Italy, the southern part of the
country was constituted a region; in Colombia it was
a valley which determined the Cauca Valley region
and the Gezira Region in Sudan was defined on the
basis of irrigation possibilities.
    It is thus apparent that a region may be de-
fined in different ways. Its boundaries may be
determined (1) geographically, e.g. a valley or
river basin, (2) demographically, for example, an
area inhabited by a specific population group, e.g.
a nomad tribe, (3) administratively i.e. one or more
political sub-divisions of a country and (4) functionally e.g. an area within the sphere of influence
of a particular urban centre.
    Since regional development usually includes a
variety of functional activities, which may be as
different as the construction of irrigation systems
and programmes for family planning, the most suitable set of boundaries for one purpose, may differ
very much from those for another. Consequently, the
definition adopted for a region is likely to be a
compromise which is better for achieving some objectives than others. In practice, the realities make
it necessary for most countries to define regions
by their political-administrative boundaries rather
than by what may be considered the more natural
boundaries. This is not always bad because the introduction of a new region adds new "relay points"
into the bureaucratic system and may cause serious
administrative delays. For these reasons, even if a
major development effort e.g. an irrigation area,
has contours that deviate so much from existing
political-administrative jurisdictions that new
regional boundaries seem necessary, the new region
should be built up from multiples or components of
existing jurisdictions.

b. Definition of needs and objectives. A second
problem in regional planning involves defining the

23

basic social and economic difficulties to be resolved. Everything depends on who tackles this issue.
If officials set the objectives and priorities, the
results may and are likely to be different than if
farmers set them. Too often, planners and other
officials look on the farmer as someone to be acted
upon instead of to cooperate with. They frequently
take a paternalistic, or even worse, a patronizing
view of the farmer and assume they know his business
better than the farmer does. Planners and advisors
must learn to listen to farmers so that they can
help to resolve problems as farmers see them. Even
when planners recognise the need to talk with
farmers, it is often difficult for them to give up
the idea completely that they know as well, or
better than, the farmer what his needs really are!
There is the added barrier that even if individual
officials understand the advantages of close
liaison with farmers, their senior officers in
central ministries, departments and agencies may
not.

c. Regional planning co-ordination. A third problem
relates to co-ordination of the various regional
plans. There is always the danger that competing
regional claims may get out of hand and exceed
available resources, or result in wasteful duplication of projects in different regions. The finance
with which the central government provides regions
is a powerful device for co-ordinating regional and
national development plans and objectives, but regional pressures for funds are often so great as to
upset the national strategy. Making sure that
objectives do not conflict does not necessarily require that either farmers or government abandon
their objectives. Rather, it may involve compromise
about priorities or timing.

d. Regional planning organisation. The need to
establish suitable systems for regional planning
raises a fourth problem: What kind of institutions
are needed to prepare and implement regional and
local plans? In most developing countries there are
few subnational planning entities. This means that
in most of these countries suitable regional and
subregional bodies must be devised and established
if effective planning is to take place.
    Whether regional plans have been prepared by
national or regional bodies has generally depended
on the stage of development of the region(s) concerned, the availability of regional planners, and

the size of the country. As a general rule, the earlier the stage of regional development, the greater the likelihood that regional plans were prepared by the central planning agency, or by a planning authority established for the purpose by the central government. Conversely, the more advanced the region, the greater the availability of regional planners; and the larger the country, the more likely that the plans were prepared by the regions themselves.

Since regional planning in most mixed-economy countries has been for economically backward areas, with special problems and shortages of financial and human resources, most regional planning has been conducted by central planning agencies, or by special authorities created by national governments. Frequently, regional plans have been prepared outside the regions, usually in the national capital, with little participation of the people in the regions. Aside from the fact that this approach has not been very successful, it is less likely to be used today when political awareness in the regions is increasing.

The institutional problem is one of finding the right structure and balance between centralised and decentralised authority, self-financing and decision making. Unless properly structured institutions are set up with the right balance there is a danger that the most logically consistent regional plans will not work in practice.

While every country will have to establish planning bodies suited to its own institutional arrangements and stage of development, in general, organisations at the local level should be simpler than those at the intermediate level, and intermediate bodies need be less complex than those at the regional level. For example, at the village level, programming (as distinguished from more professional "planning") committees may suffice, while at the intermediate level (e.g. a district), one or two planners in a small planning unit may be adequate. However, at the regional level, a regional authority, appropriately staffed with planning technicians, is likely to be essential for effective planning.

Special problems arise for federal governments. India is a good example. In that country, it has been found that the unit of organisation for the development of a river valley, which extends beyond a single state, should cover all the states through which the river valley runs. This unit of political organisation could not be the central Government of

India since it is too remote to deal effectively with the communities concerned with the river valley. Consequently, an organisation with jurisdiction smaller than the central Government but larger than a state government has to be devised.

While structural problems can be difficult, they are likely to be easier to resolve than questions relating to the degree of autonomy to be granted to regional planning units and the extent to which these units should be advisory or supervisory in carrying out regional plans. In some countries, these questions have been resolved by the establishment of a regional authority with considerable power and independence. These organisations are generally responsible to the central government, and have authority to act in lieu of regular central ministries, departments and agencies in the region over which they have jurisdiction.

Another kind of authority is advisory in nature, prepares regional plans but relies on regular government ministries, departments and agencies to decentralise responsibility for taking action to their regional representatives, and for the regional authority to coordinate their activities to insure well-phased implementation of regional plans. Unless the regional authority has the right to coordinate these activities, all questions must be referred for decision to ministries, departments, or agencies in the capital. Not only is this a time-consuming process, but it may yield the wrong answers because civil servants in the capital are not usually aware of the nature of the problems in different regions of the country.

The effectiveness of a regional authority often depends on the financial resources put at its disposal. Equally important is the way in which funds are allocated to it for implementing plans. The authority is likely to have the greatest independence in implementing plans if funds are allocated to it directly by the central government, and to have less freedom of action if it has to rely on transfers of funds allocated to the various ministries, departments and agencies for projects and programmes within its region for whose implementation it is responsible. The authority is likely to have the least independence if it must apply to the budget authority for funds every time it needs money for a project.

The location of the headquarters of the regional authority is also significant. To carry out its functions effectively, the authority should be based

in the region. Since it is usually more difficult
to staff an authority located in a region than one
located in the capital, there is a tendency for
regional authorities to establish themselves in the
capital. But this is a mistake, as the authority's
staff loses touch with regional problems, while the
people in the region tend to view the authority as
alien. In contrast, where the authority has been
established in the region at the start, the population of the region tends to view the authority as
its own, and the staff of the authority is in
position to take quicker action on problems than if
it were in the capital. Regional authorities
located in rural areas can also be adequately staffed if regional development is made sufficiently
challenging, and higher status, pay, living arrangements and wider opportunities for professional
training are offered to technicians than are available in the capital.

In some countries, proximity to the budgetary
authorities, the seat of power, or other government
entities with which the regional authority must
deal, may make it essential to have close and continuing contact with persons and entities in the
capital. In these circumstances, an office of the
regional authority, adequately staffed with individuals qualified to deal effectively with those
concerned, should be established in the capital. It
may even be necessary for the head of the regional
authority to spend much of his time in the capital
to assure that the region and the regional authority
concerned obtain what is required from those in the
capital. Even so, and with the assumption that a
suitably capable person will always be in charge of
the authority's technical staff in the region, the
headquarters of the regional authority should be
located within the region for the reasons given in
the preceding paragraph.

The relationship between the regional authority
and the local population and authorities may assume
a variety of forms. Where a regional organisation
exists, and where it represents the people, the most
suitable arrangement is to put the regional planning
authority in the existing organisation. If this is
done, there is greater likelihood than otherwise
that regional and local plans will come close to
representing prevailing views at regional and local
levels.

In contrast, a central government may create a
regional authority as an arm of the central government in a region to be developed. SUDENE in north-

eastern Brazil is an example. With this approach, however, there is a greater probability than in the preceding approach that there will be difficulties in communication between the authority and the people.

A third variety of regional authority includes representatives of both the central government and regional farmers. This pattern has the advantage of establishing a communication link between local and central government representatives. Crete and Israel have adopted this approach.

Since the first and third approaches seek to relate the people in the regions and local areas directly with the central government, they are preferable to the second. But regardless of which approach is adopted, the regional authority must still take measures to insure adequate participation of producers in defining the basic objectives to be achieved by the planning process.

While each country should create regional planning authorities in a form suitable to its needs, successful regional planning depends on the degree to which regional plans are formulated and implemented with the participation of farmers in the regions or sub-regions concerned. To the extent that such participation occurs, farmers are likely to be amenable in helping carry out the plans.

e. Lack of regional information. Planning at the national level has been seriously hampered in most developing countries by the scarcity of reliable statistical and other information. Indeed, the lack of adequate data on such basic series as the size and growth rate of national populations, production, investment, consumption and employment has frequently cast doubt on supply and demand projections, as well as parameters included in national planning models. The fact that regional and local statistics in most poor countries are generally much worse, where they exist, than national data, makes it particularly difficult to plan effectively at regional and local levels in these countries. The lack of good data on land use, water resources and manpower constitute an especially great handicap. Even in countries where political subdivisions are defined as agricultural regions, as in India, serious deficiencies in data impede effective planning; and the situation is usually worse when an agricultural region or subregion does not conform to administrative boundaries. Whereas sector planning for agriculture has frequently relied on data from a few experimental farms as conventional yardsticks for estimating inputs and outputs, regional and sub-regional planning must obtain field data from actual farms in each area to prepare accurate estimates. This implies that new approaches to the collection of relevant agricultural statistics are required for effective regional and subregional planning.

The data gap therefore is a fifth problem confronting those who would expand regional and local planning. The magnitude of this problem, and the fact that it will take much time to resolve, makes it evident that regional and local planning will have to proceed at a lower level of technical sophistication than prevails at national levels and that, for the time being, mathematical formulations of regional and local planning models are likely to be of little practical value in most poor countries. Moreover the more one descends the hierarchy of jurisdictions, the more modest requirements should become for comprehensive planning. Nevertheless, as regional planning in such countries as China and Tanzania has shown, there is no reason for postponing the start of regional planning until adequate data become available. Some specialists become so preoccupied with the data problem that they all but counsel postponement of regional planning until what they consider to be adequate data are produced.

In the longer run, steps must be taken to set up suitable systems for the collection of data which employ uniform units of measurement to allow intra- and inter-regional combination and comparison of data on a continuing basis and for clearly defined regional and local areas.

Consideration should be given to the preparation of a multi-annual statistical collection plan, including a system of financing its implementation, which sets forth the types of data to be collected and the priorities to be given to each. Since the task of carrying out such a plan is likely to be beyond the capacity of existing central statistical organisations in most developing countries, attention also needs to be given to the reorganisation and expansion of the central statistical office, as well as to the possibility of dividing the task between it and regional statistical organisations in a manner which would promote the most efficient use of scarce manpower and statistical equipment.

f. Training regional planners. Since regional planning is still in its infancy in most developing countries, regional skills and expertise are in

short supply. If regional planning is to expand to
the extent required, means of training those needed
for the purpose will have to be devised. This is no
easy matter and constitutes a sixth problem for
regional planning.

Because of the variety of skills demanded,
training for regional development must be problem-
oriented. This implies a multi-disciplinary
approach. While much has been written about the
need for a comprehensive approach to development
problems, little as yet has found its way into
training materials and courses. The same is true
about planning "from the bottom up."

Another training constraint has to do with the
"labour-intensive" way in which planning, as a discipline, has been taught. Teachers in the field are
generally highly-trained specialists whose teaching
reaches only a few students each year. Moreover,
would-be planners are generally required to undertake a lengthy course of study to provide them with
the ability to formulate sophisticated plans, often
based on mathematical models. As a result, the
training of planners has proceeded so slowly that
there is still a great shortage at the national
level in developing countries, and even more, at
regional and local levels.

If regional planning is to expand at the rate
required to meet urgent demands, a more "capital-
intensive" approach to training regional planners
will have to be devised. If, for example, the
information which planning specialists have accumulated were incorporated in "programmed" form in
teaching materials, teachers in training centres in
the developing countries could use these materials
to train individuals within regions to prepare and
implement regional plans. Only by some such method
will it be possible to spread available knowledge
about regional planning as widely and as rapidly as
is required.

g. Need for a regional planning manual. If regional
efforts are to make a substantial contribution to
effective allocation of national and regional resources, the central government must establish basic
rules applying to regional planning which all
regions should follow. Governments sometimes have
complicated procedures and requirements, insist on
too much detailed information or do not define with
sufficient clarity the technical criteria which
regional planners must follow in preparing plans,
programmes and projects, with the result that

regional planning is uninformed and disorganised.
To provide regional, subregional and local planners
throughout a country with an understanding of what
needs to be done, and to have them follow the same
basic rules, a central government should prepare and
disseminate a simply written planning manual which
includes at least the following:

1. a statement of the national objectives for
regional, subregional and local planning;
2. a statement of national policies and
measures which have been or will be adopted to
achieve these objectives;
3. a statement of the emphasis to be given to
the different ecological regions (e.g. rainfed
vs. irrigated regions) by the central government, if the emphasis will differ among them;
4. a list of priorities for regional planning
from the national viewpoint, with an explanation of the rationale for these priorities;
5. the procedures to be followed by regional,
subregional and local planners in preparing
plans, programmes and projects, the data to be
included, and the form in which they are to be
presented;
6. the cost-benefit methodology to be followed
in preparing programmes and projects;
7. a requirement that plans be prepared with
two alternative assumptions about the size of
the plan, one with a higher cost than the other
(as specified by the central government), each
with a list of projects and programmes to which
priorities have been assigned (this to facilitate the addition of projects and programmes
(to the low-cost alternative) or their sub-
traction (from the high-cost alternative), as
the availability of financial resources dic-
tates);
8. an outline for a regional stocktaking and
diagnostic survey, like the one in chapter 6,
modified to meet the needs of each region.

Agricultural vs. Rural Development

1. The role of agriculture in rural development
While the primary objective of agricultural development is usually increased growth of agricultural
output, the main aim of rural development is the
improvement of the material and social welfare of
the rural population, always including poor farmers,
and sometimes, landless farm workers and others in

rural areas.

Although not usually intended, rich farmers tend to gain most from development efforts as they have easy access to education, credit, markets, irrigation and other facilities in contrast to those at the other end of the scale. This has led the World Bank and other donor agencies, and countries, to give increasing attention to the needs of poor, mainly small, farmers. Serious difficulties stand in the way of mounting such rural development programmes, however. The rural poor may be helped by these agencies in the provision of infrastructure and other services but it is difficult to make these facilities financially self-sustaining since, in most instances, in the short run, they contribute only marginally to economic development.

For rural development to be economically sound, it is essential to provide for a self-supporting agriculture which can generate enough surplus to finance social overhead facilities, and services, on a continuing basis. Central government may provide rural areas with water supply, drainage, roads, buildings and other facilities at little or no cost to local people but it cannot be expected to operate and maintain this rural infra-structure indefinitely, otherwise such a programme becomes little more than welfare or a "handout." Tanzania has been into this problem.

In many countries, governments have spent considerable sums to provide social infrastructure in rural areas, at the expense of allocations to improve farm production, and have ended up with schools without teachers, clinics without doctors and chronic unemployment and under-employment. In contrast, countries with rural development programmes which have given priority to farm production, and higher productivity, have been able to generate the resources needed to finance these social facilities, e.g. communes in China have constructed health and education facilities from their own savings.

Since a thriving agriculture is the key to self-sustaining rural development, a model is needed which, unlike the usual model for agricultural development, provides for benefits to a wide range and a substantial number of rural people. The elements of one such model are outlined below.

2. A viable model for rural development
a. Labour-using agriculture. Since poor farmers and rural workers generally suffer heavily from being

under- or un-employed, and have few capital resources, labour-using techniques must be employed as
much as possible in a programme for rural development - if the poor are to benefit most. While more
capital is likely to be used in some countries than
in others, the model requires that only relatively
small amounts of capital (including working capital)
is used per unit of employment and output. An agriculture using labour more intensively becomes a convenient way for promoting a more equitable distribution of the benefits of agricultural growth since
it necessarily requires that those who provide the
labour are paid for their contribution. At the same
time, larger or richer farmers, usually employing
more capital-intensive production methods can be
excluded from the benefits of labour-intensive
agriculture.

b. Small development works. Since even labour-
intensive agriculture is unlikely to provide year-
round full employment, "employment generating" minor
works with a high labour content (e.g. the construction of feeder roads, irrigation, etc.), as well as
social facilities, such as schoolhouses and clinical
buildings, should be carried out with under-employed
or seasonally unemployed rural labour. Farmers with
time to spare, at irregular intervals, are likely to
find it easier to contribute their labour to smaller
than to larger projects, because the larger ones
frequently require more formal work schedules. If
the projects are timed to provide for peak construction activity during the periods when agricultural
activities diminish, they can give substantial
amounts of employment, and increased income, to
farmers and other rural workers. To minimize housing and transport costs, productive activities
should be concentrated as much as possible in areas
with the greatest surplus labour. In addition,
local materials should be employed wherever possible
because their use provides employment and reduces
transport costs. The handicap of under-employment
of the labour force can be converted into an advantage by using local labour to create some of the
infrastructure needed in rural communities. In
China, peasants have constructed irrigation, flood
control, terracing, and other works and have re-
forested local areas. In Pakistan, rural populations at the thana and union levels have been used
in the Rural Public Works programme to construct
roads, bridges, embankments and other works. In
India, small capital formation projects have

provided supplemental incomes to small cultivators
and landless agricultural workers who worked on them,
and in Bangladesh, the First Five-Year Plan called
for emphasis on small and intermediate scale irrigation and drainage projects, and the installation
of low lift pumps and tubewells. These are low-
cost, labour-intensive activities which are expected
to reduce under-employment or seasonal unemployment
and provide water for food grain production.

c. Light industry. Small-scale light industry, with
low capital requirements, should be established in
rural areas to supplement employment opportunities
in agriculture. Specific kinds of light industry
are needed covering mainly the processing of farm
produce and the manufacture of selected inputs for
agriculture. Wherever it is economically feasible,
rural industry could also produce consumer goods as
well as building materials for capital construction
and infrastructure projects. Agro-industries of the
first kind will have the advantage of location if
established near their sources of raw materials,
while some of the second type have transport advantages when located near their markets (especially if
these consist mainly of farmers), and particularly
if their products are heavy. Many kinds of agro-
industries are, in fact, well suited to small- or
medium-scale production in rural areas.

d. Self-help as the foundation. To be self-sustaining, the model must rest on a foundation of local
self-reliance or self-help, which means that those
communities which benefit from rural development
must assume responsibility for finding a reasonable
proportion of the resources needed. The total
quantity available is likely to fall short of what
is needed, unless a proportion of the money (or
labour) required is raised from the countryside
itself. One way of meeting this problem is to
challenge local authorities and organizations to
provide some funds through matching grants, or other
incentives, to reward those jurisdictions which
gather what is considered to be an adequate amount
of funds, or labour, for rural development.
   While self-help should be a part of every
rural development project or programme, technical
and financial assistance by government is also
essential. It may be desirable to conduct educational programmes which teach farmers and their
families how to do things for themselves, and to
understand that rural development requires a

partnership between the rural people and the government. The people must be persuaded that the government will only help if the people in the community are prepared to fulfill certain obligations, e.g. to group into organisations which meet regularly, make regular savings deposits to create equity capital or undertake the maintenance of completed works.

What is a reasonable contribution for a community depends on the size of the population, the degree of economic backwardness, its growth potential and other relevant circumstances. In each situation criteria for judging success would include measures of the extent to which local or regional areas should be required to contribute to the support of rural social services. A second criterion should indicate the time and extent to which jurisdictions would have to take over the support of rural facilities, initially financed by the central government or other outside bodies; incentives might be provided for speeding up the agreed timetable.

Where areas are completely dependent on outside grants and loans, rural planning becomes a matter of drawing up shopping lists for outside funding without the hard choices which realistic planning requires. If the localities are to participate in the planning process, as good planning requires, it is likely that the quality and reliability of investment, as well as its management, will be improved.

Implicit in self-reliance is the concept of full participation by small farmers, through their own or other institutions where they feel they can freely express their views, and get a sympathetic hearing during the formulation of rural development plans. It is idle to expect farmers to help to implement plans which do not reflect their needs and objectives.

Self-reliance is becoming increasingly important as the basis for rural development. Kenya, Tanzania and other countries have emphasized "self-help" as integral parts of their rural development programmes. China has probably gone further than any other country in this direction.

e. Organization for rural development. The preparation and implementation of a programme of rural development is a long-term task which requires much planning and farmers' support. It must be evolved by the country concerned, as well as by its farmers; and, by the same token, it cannot be the result of short-term missions of international or national

lending agencies. These agencies can do much to
support rural development by financing components of
programmes, but it would be unreasonable to expect
them to provide the continuing, long-term effort
which viability requires. Only the country concerned can do that. The effort usually leads to
major changes in government organization and procedures because each ministry, department or agency
tends to concern itself only with its own functional
sector or sub-sector. A rural development programme
requires coordinated action among ministries,
departments and agencies which cuts horizontally
across the vertical organization typical of most
governments. Organizational structures should be an
outgrowth of a rural development programme instead
of preceding it, as sometimes happens. It is thus
essential to establish the organizational structures
required soon after the start of a rural development
plan, and to make them work well as quickly as
possible. This is because it usually takes a long
time to "institutionalize" the organizations as well
as the hierarchical relations among them.

For the model to be self-sustaining, therefore,
institutional and organizational arrangements must
be built into a rural development programme and
sufficiently well-structured to permit the activities covered by the first four elements in the model
to proceed on a continuing basis. These arrangements will necessarily vary from one country to
another, but they should include farmers' organizations as well as government, and (where pertinent)
private agencies and institutions. Too often, rural
development fails to become self-sustaining because
of weaknesses in this whole area of organization and
initiative.

f. Marketing or Development Centres. Rural development must be seen as part of wider national development. If it is to proceed beyond limited levels, a
way must be found to bridge the wide gap which
usually exists between the villages and the metropolis, usually the capital, which characteristically
dominates a less developed country in terms of population, economic activity, income growth, decision-
making and other development indicators.

A modern agriculture presupposes the existence
of markets where produce can be sold and where
agricultural inputs can be bought; and these markets
must be accessible to farmers because their occupation limits their mobility. This means different
things to different countries, depending on whether

the truck, the horse, the ox-cart, the wheelbarrow, the bicycle or human carriage is the common mode of transporting agricultural produce.

Most developing countries lack a national hierarchy of marketing and distribution centres. Rural farmers, most of whom are usually not within commuting distance of a major city, have to depend on the inadequate marketing and other poor facilities typical of village economies in less developed countries. Because the village market is small, the scale of farm operations tends to be too small to make the adoption of modern techniques practicable. Moreover, monopoly conditions in the villages keep produce prices low, thereby reducing farmers' incentives to adopt improved techniques and expand production. These conditions keep rural areas poor and underdeveloped, and impede development.

Even when development begins in rural areas, the impact seldom spreads beyond the immediate area around the primary city, and large parts of the country remain outside the growth area. Where several urban centres exist, absence of a hierarchy of regional distribution and collection centres may impede the integration of rural areas into the regional and national economies.

The establishment of an appropriate hierarchy of development centres is therefore the sixth and final element of a viable rural development model.

3. Applying the model. The six elements in the model together provide a workable basis for rural development as seen in such diverse countries as China, India, Israel, Malaysia and Pakistan. The precise form of the model will, of course, vary from one country to another, reflecting different conditions; with the timing of the various innovations in both agriculture and industry being of key importance.

Chapter 4

PREPARING AN AGRICULTURAL PLAN

Summary
Too much attention in planning is usually given
to plan formulation. This is understandable as
implementation, the next stage, is more difficult, but it makes the chances of a plan succeeding that much less. A plan can usefully be
divided into its main components: choosing
objectives, a stock-taking and diagnostic
survey, a set of targets, of policies, projects
and programmes, research and special studies
needed, public expenditure programme, manpower
training programme, institutional changes involved, consulting services, plan evaluation
and control. There is a definite sequence in
which these components should be undertaken,
unfortunately not always followed. A tentative
plan gradually takes shape through a process of
iteration or successive approximation.

Components of A Plan
Advisors on agricultural planning tend to concentrate more on the formulation, or preparation, of
the main elements of a plan than with the awkward
details of implementing it. In the sparse literature on agricultural planning there is relatively
little about how to devise appropriate strategies
and policies for putting a plan into action, how to
prepare a stock of suitable projects in sufficient
number to enable intelligent choices to be made
about them, how to encourage farmers to increase
their investment and output, or how precisely administrative procedures must be changed and adjustments
made to organizations and institutions - if sector
goals are to be achieved.
    There is, of course, a good reason for this
state of affairs. It is easier to formulate a plan

than to state, in sufficient detail, what action is
specifically needed to reach planning goals: how
things are to be done, who is to be responsible for
what, and to give the sequence and latest dates when
action must take place if the plan is to be implemented within the planning period.

This does not mean that plan formulation is
easy or less important than plan implementation. It
means that insufficient attention is usually given
to implementation. As a result, many plans have
little chance of being carried out in practice. The
two tasks are inseparable. If this was better
understood, plan formulation would be even more
difficult than it is now - but, at least, it would
be more realistic.

A good plan should have many more of its components concerned with implementation than formulation. The following list summarises 12 major components of an agricultural plan of which the first
four deal with formulation and the remaining eight
with implementation.

1. Development objectives for the sector
2. A stock-taking and diagnostic survey
3. A set of targets
4. Selection of a strategy from among available
alternatives
5. Policies for achieving programme objectives
and targets
6. Projects and programmes to be carried out in
agriculture, as well as in related sectors, to
achieve the plan's objectives and targets
7. Research and studies to obtain the technical
information needed for development of the
agricultural sector
8. A programme of public expenditure for
financing each year of the plan period, including the source of finance
9. A programme of manpower training
10. Improvements needed in organisations,
institutions and administration
11. Consultancy services required
12. A system of plan evaluation and control

Planning Sequence
The sequence in which the 12 components are given
has significance. Some things should be done before
others, even if only tentatively. The setting of
agriculture's development objectives, for example,
should precede the stocktaking and diagnostic survey
because a given objective may, and often does,

require specific information.

Setting the sector's objectives should also precede target fixing (since targets are really quantified objectives). Similarly, the implications of new projects and sub-programmes for organisation and administration should be thought out before organisational responsibilities are assigned and requirements for technical assistance determined. Unfortunately, this kind of sequence is not always followed.

In practice, sector surveys are often made and targets set before objectives are clearly defined. Economic policies and measures are adopted without reference to the requirements for achieving targets and new agencies established, or existing ones reorganized, before the tasks which must be carried out to implement the sector programmes have been properly identified.

Although some aspects of planning precede others, it would be a mistake to suppose that no deviation is permitted from the suggested sequence, and that each component must be dealt with consecutively in the order given, one at a time. Work on some components low in the list may have to begin before work on others higher up. Such is the nature of the planning process. Project identification and preparation, for example, may take two or three times as long as the preparation of the entire agricultural programme.

Usually, work must procede simultaneously on two or more components, with the emphasis changing from one component to another. This is because sector, like macro-economic, planning is a continuous process, with inter-related and mutually interacting elements. Each component must be coordinated with the others if the plan is to be consistent. Targets may have to be altered as planning procedes if, for example, the strategies or policies required to achieve them are politically not feasible. Projects may have to be reduced in number and size. Strategy may have to be modified in the light of rates of return realisable from available projects, and even objectives revised or discarded if, for example, investment funds prove to be insufficient. Conversely additional funds may have to be found to permit retention of objectives and projects which are considered of the utmost priority

In short, planning for agriculture starts with assumptions and speculations which may turn out to be untenable, and by iteration, or successive approximation, moves toward what is possible. The final form of the plan emerges at the end, and not surprisingly, at the beginning.

Figure 4-1 illustrates how the inter-relationships between components affect the order in which they may have to be considered.

Figure 4-1   Inter-relationship between Plan
             Components - an illustration

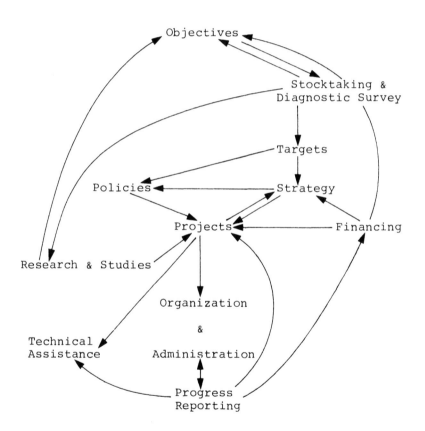

Chapter 5

OBJECTIVES FOR AGRICULTURAL DEVELOPMENT

Summary
     Responsibility for setting the objectives for
     agricultural development rests firmly with
     political leadership. Planners have the re-
     sponsibility of providing the politicians with
     alternative objectives, together with their
     relative benefits and costs in economic, social
     and financial terms. The general aim is to
     achieve national political and social objec-
     tives at minimum cost - in its widest meaning -
     and this cannot be left to foreign advisers or
     donor agencies. There are usually too few
     precise indicators pointing the way to the best
     set of measures to bring about national agri-
     cultural objectives. But few objectives are
     better than many, preferably expressed in
     concrete terms.

Who sets Objectives
Objectives chosen for agricultural development must
be considered provisional, subject to change.
Agricultural planners have the responsibility of
providing those who determine objectives with guidelines to help them make rational choices. Information given to the decision-makers, whoever they may
be, should include a wide range of data about the
main agricultural problems of the country and its
regions, feasible alternative solutions and estimates of resources needed and likely to be available
for this purpose. Such problems may include high
rural unemployment or underemployment, a greatly
skewed pattern of income distribution among farmers,
low levels of output and productivity, lack of
foreign exchange due to poor levels of income from
agricultural exports, etc. Information about such
problems is usually adequate in most countries for

preliminary objectives to be set.

Agricultural development carries a price which farm workers, farmers, land owners and urban dwellers pay in varying proportions. Future benefits must usually be paid with present sacrifices. Modernisation leading to improved output and incomes tends to destroy traditional ways. Because the choices to bring about basic changes in agriculture are heavily weighted with social, political and economic implications, responsibility for setting agricultural development objectives must rest with the nation's political leadership. The extent to which this leadership understands fully the implications of the objectives it selects, and accepts responsibility for them, is a good rule-of-thumb test of its commitment to the plan's realisation. If the government does not grasp how large is the scope, and how wide the implications, of their objectives - or if it evades responsibility for them altogether - there is little chance of the targets of the agricultural plan being achieved.

For their part, planners must realise that economic objectives should conform to social and political realities and aims, rather than the other way around. Planners frequently find it difficult to accept this situation as it may lead to higher costs, or lower returns, than if economic costs alone were paramount. This attitude misses the point since the main purpose of planning is not to maximise cost-effectiveness but to achieve social and political objectives at the lowest possible cost.

Just as objectives cannot be left to national planners to decide, they cannot be left to foreigners either. This is because the way in which development, and hence its objectives, is defined depends at least partly on a country's values, culture and heritage. Development in the richer countries has usually been equated with increases in per caput output and income, or growth with the structural changes which accompany modernisation of a traditional society. At first, a similar approach was adopted towards poorer countries but now development is taken there to be an attack on the worst manifestations of underdevelopment, namely poverty, unemployment and inequality.

Even this approach may be unsuitable. There are no absolute conditions which can measure objectively a state of development. Nor is there an accepted set of economic and social indicators which can trace the progress of a country from under- to full-development, although some indicators e.g.

infant mortality rates, are widely used as signs of
progress toward development. Underdevelopment must
be seen as a culturally-determined assessment of
what is an unsatisfactory quality of life. The
method of assessment is likely to differ between
rich and poor countries. Thus both rich and poor
are likely to agree that apathy, fatalism, back-
breaking labour and low levels of productivity are
all aspects of under-development, while other aspects such as the extended family, tribal and other
forms of communal land ownership, or illiteracy, may
be viewed as much more undesirable by rich than by
poor countries.

If, then, underdevelopment is a state of being
which can be defined only in a specific culture context, it follows that development has to be treated
in the same way. Development objectives must be
appropriate to that context, and established by the
society concerned. Objectives and programmes based
on foreign cultural values may generate change which
is incompatible with traditional institutions and
patterns of behaviour. In that event the changes
are likely to have only a temporary effect (while
the foreigner is around) or, if more permanent, may
have an unsettling influence on the traditional
society.

It is not always tradition or the "dead hand of
the past" which shapes a people's attitude. The
experience of a people may play as powerful a role
as tradition in shaping social, political and
economic attitudes. Foreigners may accept experience as a more rational determinant of attitudes
than tradition (e.g. the effect of huge losses in
the U.S.S.R.'s military and civilian population in
World War 2 in its attitude to national security)
and may even applaud attitudes based on experience.
But the point is that foreigners not having been
through the same experience may be unaware of it as
a determinant of a people's attitude, or, even if
aware of it, under-estimate its significance.

Every society should therefore set its own development objectives, including, of course, its agricultural objectives. Foreign advisers may have a
useful but supporting role to play in this process.

The Importance of Few and Clear Objectives

It is no simple matter to get an unambiguous statement of objectives. They should preferably be
concrete rather than abstract because vagueness
leads to confusion. An objective to raise rural
incomes to a level related specifically to incomes

in other sectors, for example, is preferable to one
which aims to increase rural incomes to levels "not
too far behind those in other sectors". Concrete-
ness helps in the setting of targets and in the
choice of appropriate means for realising them.

Political leaders are sometimes reluctant to
commit themselves to clearly-stated objectives which
may be seen as a threat to powerful interests. They
are also likely to wish to satisfy every important
group by fudging the issues, in which case planning
objectives becomes an exercise in public relations
rather than the real thing.

It is common, therefore, to find agricultural
plans with an abundance of objectives some of which
quite plainly are contradictory. A long list of
objectives is generally harder to achieve than a
short one because of the scarcity of resources.
Priority becomes harder to determine. Since the
problem is more often one of too many objectives
than the lack of them, one precept worth bearing in
mind is the desirability of having as few objectives
as possible.

The Difference between Ends and Means
A related principle is that ends, or objectives,
should be clearly distinguished from the means to
achieve them. There is often confusion on this
point. For example, where self-sufficiency in food
supplies is the objective, a high-yielding varieties
(HYV) programme may be the strategy, the use of
government subsidies for fertilizer the policy, and
the sale of fertilizer by co-operatives at subsi-
dised prices the policy instrument. (Figure 5-1
illustrates this relationship between ends and
means).

The HYV programme, the use of subsidies, or the
role of cooperatives to sell the cheaper fertilizer
should not be included as objectives because they
are the means for achieving self-sufficiency. Yet
plans still include such items as more efficient use
of land, more research, a higher level of double-
cropping as plan objectives instead of means to an
end. Land reform may be a key element of policy in
a strategy to increase rural employment and other
agricultural development objectives but it is still
a means toward achieving those ends. Where, in
fact, land reform has been carried out as an end in
itself, it has led to failure because complementary
measures to make the reform productive have simply
not been attempted.

Confusion between means and objectives only

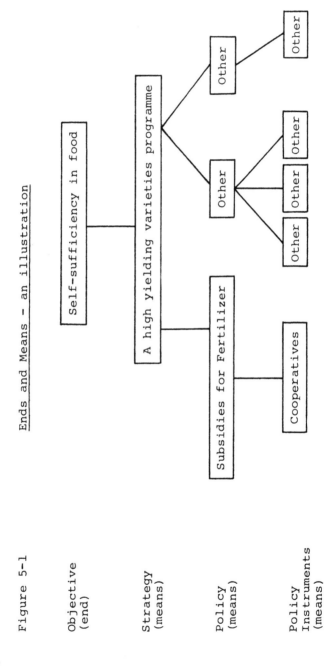

Figure 5-1

Ends and Means – an illustration

46

makes for uncertainty. For example, in Tanzania it has sometimes been unclear whether participation of the rural masses in planning and its implementation is an objective, or a means of increasing rural incomes. One does not necessarily lead to the other.

Other Distinctions Among Objectives
Social and political objectives are becoming a regular feature of agricultural programmes. Since objectives such as raising income levels in depressed rural areas may reduce the rate at which output may otherwise increase, in the short run at least, it is essential for the political leadership to indicate the extent to which it is willing to sacrifice growth of output and income to achieve equity objectives. Otherwise it is difficult to select appropriate strategies and policies.

Short-, medium- and long-term objectives should be clearly distinguished too. A realistic assessment of what can be done in the short- or medium-term can usually be based on recent performance, available resources, and the current level of administrative competence. The rest had best be left for the more distant future, broadly framed and indicating only the general directions in which to move.

Structural change in agriculture falls into the latter category because it tends to take many years to achieve. Such change involves items such as the shift to modern commercial agriculture, a greater diversification of output, a large reduction in the proportion of the population dependent on agriculture and a shift in dietary habits.

Although a short- or medium-term objective is frequently a necessary stage in the achievement of a long-term objective, it may be different from, and even opposed to, the long-term objective for the same variable e.g. farm employment. Because this may be an area of conflict, decisions may have to be made about whether the short-term objective e.g. creating farm employment, is to prevail at the cost of the long-term objective e.g. lowering the proportion of the labour force engaged in agriculture, or whether the latter objective has greater priority.

Objectives and the Stage of Development
Agricultural objectives naturally differ among countries. They also differ in the same country at different stages of development. In the earlier stages, agricultural objectives are broadly the national objectives because of the dominance of this

industry. Later, as agriculture contributes a relatively small share of the total output (GDP) there is sometimes a wide divergence between national and agricultural objectives.

The major objective in developed mixed-economy countries has been improvement of farm incomes, by preventing output from increasing beyond what the market will absorb, at prices considered remunerative for farmers. This objective in Western Europe and North America has meant that attempts must be made to reduce the gap between the lower farm and the higher non-farm incomes. Where developed countries are large exporters of agricultural products, this objective has had to be balanced against the need to maintain competitive prices in international markets (and by export subsidies).

Since agriculture contributes such a large proportion of GDP in the developing countries, and, in fact, plays an important part in financing early stages of industrial development (at least), it cannot hope to obtain equity with income levels of the advanced sectors of the economy as a primary objective. Instead, it directs attention to increasing agricultural production to become more self-sufficient in food supplies, to increase exports, improve relations, etc.

As a country gradually develops so there is a subtle shift in its agricultural objectives depending upon the particular characteristics of that country. It may, for example, continue to place heavy emphasis on agricultural exports where conditions especially favour this trend, or concentrate on import-saving and independence. Policy makers need to take account of this state of affairs and avoid a rigid and possibly out-dated approach to their analysis.

CHAPTER 6

THE STOCKTAKING AND DIAGNOSTIC SURVEY

Summary
    A stocktaking and diagnostic survey is needed
    early in the planning process to provide in-
    formation about the wide range of factors
    influencing agricultural performance. The
    scope of this survey should be limited and
    closely allied to plan objectives. An eight-
    fold classification is suggested which in
    addition to covering traditional kinds of data
    also includes such items as agro-industry,
    nutrition planning and information gaps. Good
    planning can be done with surprisingly few
    data, provided they are accurate, timely and
    relevant. Conversely, large amounts of in-
    accurate, untimely or only partially relevant
    information can be costly and of little help
    to planners. Great care is therefore required
    in setting up the survey. The survey team may
    well include foreign advisers whose role
    should be not only to assist in carrying out
    the survey to a high professional standard, but
    also in training nationals in this work. The
    latter may then provide the nucleus of an agri-
    cultural planning unit.

Agricultural planning requires knowledge about
recent progress in agriculture, the existing situation (especially the main problems impeding development), and the potentialities for achieving agricultural objectives. This information is needed for
re-assessing current investment and other development activities as well as for planning new measures,
and setting benchmarks against which to monitor
progress. Improvement in the way things are being
carried out can make as great a contribution to
development as the start of new ·activities. Analysis

of recent and current conditions may also reveal structural and institutional relationships, or policies, which have to be modified.

Knowledge of the recent past, and the present, is thus essential for defining the nature of the planning task and its limits. A stock taking and diagnostic survey, carried out early in the planning process, is a desirable way of providing the required information.

This survey is quite different from a basic research study. Although short-term research and a few fact finding, ad hoc studies (which can be completed quickly), are not necessarily to be excluded, a stocktaking and diagnostic survey should be, as its name implies, a broad-gauge inventory, and an assessment of largely existing information about the sector or sub-sector.

Its purpose is to prepare, collect and classify pertinent information needed to formulate an agricultural plan. The process by which the plan is prepared may therefore be seen as consisting of two main steps: the survey and then its conversion into an ongoing plan in the light of objectives set for the agricultural sector. Since the provision of information for preparing a plan is the justification for the stocktaking and diagnostic survey, the duration of the survey should be determined by the requirement for completing the formulation of the plan by a given date. In general, the survey should take no more than six months, while formulation of the plan usually takes longer, perhaps a year or more.

Information is never available in sufficient quantity and quality to meet all planning requirements, and the accumulation of data required for planning purposes is a never-ending task. Hence, those responsible for the survey must resist the temptation to produce new data which take much time to obtain. Instead, they should concentrate on the collection, analysis and projection of available data. At the same time, they must note the informational gaps which require longer term research, and study, so that provision may be made to fill these gaps with a programme of pre-investment and other research studies, which may require years to complete.

The data collected, the way they are arranged and analysed, and the choice of issues examined must be dictated by the plan's objectives. The survey is not intended to be a means for accumulating and analysing all available facts about the agricultural sector. What matters is not the quantity of data obtained but its relevance. Careful discrimination is needed in the selection and rejection of data to be acquired.

The scope of a survey should therefore be limited and the survey report developed around particular issues rather than discursive. The information in the report must be pointed and relevant, not merely of general interest and sufficiently detailed to be useful, but not so detailed that the report is too bulky for easy use as a reference.

A good way to begin is to outline the scope and emphasis of the survey, as well as the subsectors to be covered. As far as possible, the survey should provide separate information for each of the major regions in the country. An early task is the collection of all previous studies (and plans) of the agricultural sector, as well as all available indexes of aerial photographs, and topographic and other relevant maps for examination, comparison and analysis.

In many countries, there are surprisingly good opportunities to obtain regional or local plans, statistics, maps and other useful material from district and other area offices. Those conducting the survey should therefore arrange to visit these offices. It is also desirable, as soon as possible, to determine the subjects for which short-term field investigations will be required. This is not always easy to do unless gaps in information are known in advance, or become clear soon after the survey begins. But the later such studies start, the smaller the chances that they will be completed in time for use in preparation of the programme. Finally, it is important to set up a timetable, with deadlines, for each phase of the survey and to check progress at regular intervals. By "planning the planning" in this way, it is easier than it otherwise would be to take appropriate action when work falls behind schedule.

A stocktaking and diagnostic survey covers a wide range of subjects which may be grouped in different ways. Although they may be divided into separate classes for better understanding, the subjects are not really discrete. Proper analysis of the agricultural sector requires that it is seen as a system of functionally inter-related and inter-dependent elements, each of which contributes to the existing and potential level of performance of the sector. Thus, the survey should combine its parts in a form which constitutes an integrated whole, in which information, analysis and projections comple-

ment each other. What has been said about classification of the data therefore also applies to the
sequence to be followed in their collection and
analysis. While it is sensible to assemble and
analyse information included in a survey in accordance with some logical sequence, it is unnecessary
and not practicable to establish one sequence for
general use. With these reservations in mind, the
following eight-fold classification and sequence is
proposed as one possibility:

1. Basic Data
2. Inventory of Agricultural Resources
3. Agriculture's Role in the Economy
4. Present State and Potentialities of
   Agriculture
5. The Role of Agro-Industry
6. Demand and Supply Projections
7. Nutrition Planning
8. Information Gaps

An early task in the survey is the collection
of the available relevant data about agriculture.

1. Basic Data
The basic data should include information on the
production of major crops, the area cultivated in
each major crop, yields per unit of area, areas
sown but not harvested and areas of fallow, double-
cropped, irrigation and inter-cropped land. Information is also needed on livestock numbers,
production and yield per unit. Estimates should be
made of final demand for each major crop and livestock product, including consumption on farms.
Statistics should also cover trade in agricultural
commodities and the extent to which imports and
exports are involved; and on the size, character,
technology and organisation of farms, by groups.
As early as possible, it is important to
determine the realiability of the available data.
Such an assessment often requires an enquiry into
how the data are collected, their coverage, time-
liness, comparability and accuracy. Any weaknesses
in the data collection system should be carefully
noted and as far as possible, allowed for - prior
to recommending action for improving the whole
system.
If the agricultural plan is an aggregative or
macro-plan, prepared at the centre, the data required will be very different from that of a plan
which is basically the sum total of individual

regional, sub-regional and local plans, prepared within each of these localities. Since planning "from the bottom up" is an essential element of good planning, detailed local data will be needed in the formulation and implementation of sub-national plans. If information about farmers' priorities, objectives, attitudes and beliefs are to be considered, as well as those of traders, processors and others in the private agricultural sector then data will have to be collected in the field from other than official sources. And if policy and administration practice are to conform to the process of planning "from the bottom up" then information collected must be collated and organised with this in mind.

Implicit in "planning from the bottom up" is the need to obtain actual farm data, in each area for which a plan is to be prepared, on the relationship between inputs and output. In most developing countries, calculations of required inputs and their effects on output are based on data from a few experimental farms for which national or regional averages are calculated. Not only may these calculations never have been accurate for individual farms in some regions, subregions and localities in a country; they may have been made so long ago that they are no longer suited as yardsticks even in those areas in which they may have been appropriate originally. Where agencies for the collection and arrangement of the necessary data exist, reorganisation and administrative changes may be required; where they do not exist, the need for creating organisations suited to the collection and arrangement of such data will have to be provided for when the inventory of institutional resources is made.

2. Inventory of Agricultural Resources

Closely related to the collection and analysis of basic data, and in some respects an extension of it, is the taking of an inventory of currently used, and potentially available, resources for agricultural production, and an evaluation of the quantity and quality of these resources for increasing production in each major region of the country.

Some resources may as yet be unknown. An inventory may bring these to light and also reveal areas which might repay further investigation, even when resources are not available for immediate use, e.g. the possibility of increasing the amount of water for irrigation. An inventory may also discover which resources are only partially or ineffectively employed, and which are relatively scarce, and should therefore be carefully used. Common to all this is the need to learn enough about the available productive resources to allow the national effort to be concentrated on those which are most important for achieving development objectives.

The inventory and its appraisal should cover natural, capital, and institutional resources and manpower currently and potentially available for the production and distribution of agricultural commodities. In estimating future resources, forseeable changes in quality, e.g. of water, are as important as those in quantity.

A. <u>Natural Resources</u>. The preparation of a plan is much easier when there is an inventory of all land available for agriculture. For each major region, the inventory should include information on the physical features (topography, geology, soils, natural vegetation, and hydrology - both surface and sub-surface) which determine the land's capability for agricultural development. It should compare the potential uses of land in each major region with the way it is actually employed, making special note where the land is under-utilised or poorly utilised. Since the comparison of actual use with land capability may provide key information leading to the identification of agricultural projects, it is important that the comparison be made with this in mind.

In classifying the principal uses to which land is or may be put, distinctions should be made between cropland, pasture, forests, wasteland, or other uses in terms of acres, hectares or other appropriate units of measurement, as well as in terms of farm units. Wherever possible statistics should be supplemented with maps which facilitate reference to differences in physical land characteristics, as well as in meteorological, climatological, hydrological, geologic and geomorphic conditions. The inventory should also relate land capability to other pertinent factors, including population densities, types of land tenure systems used, proximity to markets and urban centres, as well as available transportation and other infrastructure.

Most physical data have traditionally been collected by aerial photographic or ground surveys. Now, the Earth Resources Technology Satellite (ERTS) system put into operation in 1972 has led to

a significant improvement over the older methods.
Through photographic maps, ERTS provides an inventory and monitoring of the earth's resources, the
details of which far exceed the capabilities of
aerial photographic or ground surveys. The advantages of ERTS are its cost-effectiveness and scope
of coverage. In one day, ERTS can scan over 6 1/2
million square kilometres and produce about 1,350
photographic images. Moreover, with a near-polar
orbit about 912 kilometres up in space, which is
sub-synchronised, ERTS can photograph any given
location on earth at the same time of day on conse-
cutive days over an extended period. This permits
a recording of seasonal changes to a degree not
possible before.

ERTS has been particularly accurate in crop
and vegetation identification, timber and range
resource surveys, and the construction of soil
association maps. With an accuracy level of 70-90%,
it has been able to identify, for example, corn,
soybean, winter wheat, rice, asparagus and cotton.
It has been able to detect field conditions for
areas as small as 10 acres.

ERTS makes it possible to map remote and previously inaccessible terrain, record villages and
cities, fields, forests and wastelands, distinguish
among crops, separate healthy from unhealthy crops,
locate geological faults and other features. The
data made available through satellite photography
surpass serial and ground surveys in providing information on land use, land classification, and
natural and other resources. However, data from a
satellite survey are complementary to traditional
surveys since they can indicate where more intensive
ground or aircraft surveys will be useful.

Where a country's objectives for agriculture
emphasize increased output, it may help to divide
all land available for agriculture within each farming area in accordance with its potential to
increase output. For example, the inventory can
divide all the available agricultural land into the
following three classes: (a) areas of immediate,
(b) of future, and (c) of low growth potential.

(a) Areas of immediate growth potential would include those where climate, soil and water conditions
are favourable for agriculture and where technology
needed to substantially increase output of at least
one major crop, already being grown, is available.
To the extent that problems existed which could
impede substantial increases in output, they would

have to be capable of resolution within a short
period, of say one year.

(b)   Areas of future growth potential would include
those with favourable climatic and soil conditions
which lack one or more of three elements essential
for an area of immediate growth potential.   The
first would be an adequate and controlled supply of
water; the second the technology required for substantially increasing production of a major crop or
crops, currently grown, or capable of being grown;
and the third would be the transportation needed to
bring the area(s) into the national economy.   Lands
which would otherwise be considered areas of
immediate growth potential would have to be classified as areas of future growth potential if the
missing element(s) could not be provided in a short
time, which might be defined for illustrative purposes as three years.

(c)   Areas of low growth potential would include
those with climatological, soil, topological or
other deficiencies without economic means for
correcting them.   Frequently, such areas have too
little or too much rainfall, or rainfall at the
wrong time; and have subsistence farms over a large
part of their territory.   For such areas, only major
technological breakthroughs, not foreseeable at the
time the inventory is taken, are required before
substantial increases in output are possible.
     As indicated, this three-fold classification is
appropriate if the objective is to increase all
agricultural output.   Frequently, however, plan
objectives call for increases in the output of a
specific crop.   In this case, the available lands
would have to be classified in accordance with their
potential for producing e.g. rice.   But if land were
divided without reference to a single crop, greater
variations would be possible, even in so homogeneous
a country as Bangladesh.
     If the plan objective is not mainly increased
output, an attempt should be made to classify the
available land areas accordingly.   For example, in
Tanzania, where the plan emphasizes the ujaama
village, the land area might be classified in
accordance with the potential for furthering the
ujaama concept through (1) villages which are likely
to be especially suited to organization into ujaama
units because they were settled with this purpose
in mind by government intervention; (2) village
units which might be somewhat harder to organize

because they were spontaneously settled by those who live there who were not especially oriented to the ujaama ideal; and (3) villages which would be hardest to change into ujaama villages because they were engaged in commercial agriculture, especially of perennial crops.

This kind of land classification differs from that for assessing the potentialities for increased output in that it refers more to the likely attitudes of producers than to the characteristics of the land on which they are located. However, if the potentialities for achieving agricultural objectives other than increased output can be related to specific land areas, classification of available agricultural lands would be useful. This would also be true if a plan's objectives called for raising the income of producers, say, the lowest 20% of income strata, in clearly-defined depressed regions. But if the poorer farmers tended to be dispersed in many areas among the more well-to-do farmers, there would be little value in classifying land area in accordance with its potentiality to achieve plan objectives. Instead, it would be better to classify producers in the various areas in accordance with the level of income, size of farm worked, farmers' relationship to the land (renters, squatters, owners, etc.), the kinds of crops produced, and the marketing system employed. Thus, for Mexico, where poor and rich areas tend to be separated, a classification of land in accordance with its potentiality for achieving plan objectives (whether for growth output or for objectives other than growth), is likely to be useful; in contrast, in India where poverty is endemic, a division of land area is likely to do little to help shape policy for dealing with the problem. Here, it would be better to classify producers in each region, subregion or locality in accordance with their levels of income, size of farm, crops grown, and so on.

Without division of the available agricultural land areas (or producers, where this is indicated) into some such grouping as those described above, resource allocations are unlikely to match the requirements of different agricultural areas or groups. For example, when land has been classified into the three classes mentioned, according to its growth potential for a specific crop, whose output the plan is attempting to stimulate, it becomes possible to allocate financial and other resources in a way calculated to (a) maximise output from areas of immediate growth potential, (b) insure the soonest possible conversion of areas of future growth to areas of immediate growth potential, and (c) maintain the socially minimal status of areas of low growth potential.

B. Capital resources. The inventory should describe and analyse investments in agriculture, as well as annual increases in the value of long-term improvements in each major region although, initially, the data available may be far from complete. Investments should, as far as possible, be divided into categories which distinguish, e.g. among buildings, water systems, irrigation works, drainage systems, fruit or other trees, etc. The value and kinds of machinery and equipment used in agriculture should be classified by kind, e.g. tractors, tillage and harvest machinery, hand tools, trucks and automobiles. Work animals and breeding stock should also be included among capital investments, and estimates made of circulating or working capital invested in such items as seed, fertilizer, spray materials, feed and the like.

The main private and public sources of financing agricultural investment and working capital should be identified and reviewed, including the extent to which farmers finance their own investments. If investment and working capital are shown to be constraints on development, the nature and extent of this problem should be fully analysed, too.

C. Institutional resources. It is also important to include in the inventory detailed accounts and evaluations of the national, regional and local institutions connected with agriculture: research, extension, training, the provision of short- and medium- and long-term credit, marketing and development. The nature, scope and method of operations of each of these institutions, and whether they are national, regional, public, private or mixed organisations should be described. This analysis should include an assessment of the ability of each major institution to carry out its present and likely future functions.

The organisation and role of the most important government ministries and departments concerned with agriculture should also be assessed. In many countries, the ministry or agency most concerned has failed to prepare, implement and manage effective agricultural development programmes. In some, other public and private entities (marketing boards,

commercial and public banks, cooperatives, etc.)
processors of agricultural products, importers and
exporters, etc. have performed some of these functions. The inventory should where possible describe
the organization and operations of the most important of these bodies in detail and evaluate their
effectiveness.

D. Human resources. The size, composition, distribution and recent changes in the agricultural labour
force should be estimated by major regions and related to demand. Labour force estimates should show
the composition (e.g. the number of owner-farmers,
sharecroppers, and wage workers), and the number of
the labour force employed, underemployed and un-
employed, as well as seasonal variations. Trends in
the composition and distribution of the agricultural
labour force should be estimated, as well as internal migration (among rural communities and to urban
areas) and external migration. The level of
illiteracy and education, as well as the levels of
nutrition of the agricultural population should be
noted, especially if there is reason to believe that
nutritional intake levels are below levels required
to obtain increased productivity and output. Indeed,
the inventory of human resources should be designed
to reveal the extent to which the human condition
acts as a constraint on, and can contribute to,
expanded output.

Estimates should also be made of the number of
technicians available for research, extension and
administration of agricultural projects and programmes. Present employment of technically-trained
personnel should be noted, as well as the fields in
which shortages of such personnel exist or are
likely to appear. For this purpose, it may be useful to estimate the number of different kinds of
technicians required for minimal or optimal results.
The numbers needed will vary according to the
situation. For example, the ratio of extension
workers to farmers will depend on such factors as
farmers' level of education, farming conditions, the
road network, the quality of the extension workers
and the techniques they use, as well as the financial resources and organisation for extension
services.

3. Agriculture's Role in the Economy
The collected basic data and inventory of resources
outlined above, will facilitate analysis of agriculture's role in the economy, which is the third

element in a stocktaking and diagnostic survey.
Such analysis is essential since planners must first
know what is actually happening before they can
project, and plan, agriculture's future role in the
economy.

If the agricultural plan is to be for a region,
the part played by agriculture in the region and in
the nation should be analysed; if the plan is for a
nation, this review should cover agriculture's role
in the national economy and in the major-producing
regions. Besides the present, the analysis should
cover a period in the recent past, the length of
which should be determined by the extent and timing
of changes in agriculture's role in the economy.
The rate of growth in agriculture, both on an aggregative and per caput basis, should be compared with
the corresponding rate of growth in other sectors
and of the economy as a whole. The net value of
agricultural production should be compared with net
output in other functional sectors, as a portion of
the gross national or domestic product, and its
share in the country's foreign trade noted. The
number of persons in the rural population, the
numbers dependent on agriculture (if this differs
from the rural population) and the agricultural
labour force should be compared with the urban population, total population, and the total labour force
(in the region and/or the nation), respectively; and
the level of income in agriculture should be compared with those in other economic sectors.

4. Present State and Potentialities of Agriculture
In addition to the natural, capital, institutional
and human endowments of the agricultural sector, the
level of development attained in the sector and in
each major region of the country, can provide important indications of possible directions for future
development. Unlike industry, where planning can
sometimes start from scratch, agricultural planning
is always conditioned by an existing production
system with certain capacities and resources. Part
of the stocktaking and diagnostic survey should
therefore include assessment of the existing capacities and resources of the sector, and its regional
distribution and utilization with: a descriptive
analysis of how the agricultural sector functions in
the various regions; the nature of the major production and distribution problems encountered; and
the opportunities available for meeting them.

Variations in the agricultural system should be
described and analysed. Attention should be given

to the major problems which limit efficient agricultural production. Since marketing weaknesses often plays a crucial role in holding back growth in production, the system should be examined with special care. Attention should also be given to the relative importance of demand and supply factors for determining future growth of the sector, including whether growth is inhibited by limited output or inadequate demand. If there is a high level of urban migration, the problem of how to meet the resulting increase in urban demand for food becomes a priority issue.

Some resources, like climate, have to be taken as given but others such as the amount of water available for irrigation, can vary over time. Feasible alternatives for increasing the resource base should be explored e.g. possibilities for using water more efficiently, or raising labour productivity or increasing yields by the introduction of new techniques. The relative merits of diversification, improvement and expansion of traditional exports, and production for import substitution should be assessed, including the probable effort and cost required for each proposed alternative.

It is also important to understand farmers' attitudes toward change and innovation. If, as seems likely, the poorest farmers have different attitudes to richer ones, a distinction should be made between the attitudes of the two groups. Answers are needed to questions which cast light on farmers attitudes, for example, how do farmers appear to respond to various incentives? Do their responses reveal an elementary desire for status or prestige? Do they respond to appeals to religious motivation, or the "better" ways of long ago?. Do they have pride in family or village? Are tribal loyalties strong? What kinds of stimuli for producing change are likely to be ineffective, or even worse, do more harm than good? Is agricultural change best introduced by one or two leading farmers or by a group (e.g. the tribe or village)?

The survey should describe and evaluate successful and failed attempts to introduce changes in agricultural and related practices, in the areas of the country covered by the survey. Successful attempts should be evaluated to determine the likelihood that they could be repeated in other areas of the country. The assessment should also indicate which existing social forms in each area are likely to support innovation and which are likely to undermine it. There are times when innovation has a

better chance of being accepted than at other times.
The assessment should therefore include suggestions
concerning what is likely to be the best timing for
attempts to introduce innovations. Since the "right
time" might refer to the time of the year (e.g. when
farmers are likely to have the time and money to try
something new) as well as the longer term, the
assessment should consider this aspect as well.

5. The Role of Agro-Industry
Agro-industry is so important that it deserves a
special section in the survey because it may stimulate the expansion of agricultural production, provide employment and raise rural levels of living;
and conversely, a lack of processing or other agro-
industry may impose constraints on a country's agricultural development. Indeed, agro-industry can
spell the difference between rural development and
stagnation.

This survey should include a description of
existing agro-industries, major kinds of agricultural inputs used, rural consumer goods produced and
agricultural commodities processed, as well as the
quantities involved. The description should also
indicate the character of existing agro-industries,
the extent to which production is in cottage
industries and/or separate plants and whether plants
are power-driven. For each major agro-industrial
group, the data should cover the extent to which
labour-intensive and capital-using techniques are
employed.

The distribution of agro-industries between
rural and urban areas should be indicated, as well
as the size of plants, the number of persons
employed and the extent to which agro-industries
draw workers from farm communities. Information
about how the industries are financed is also useful, as well as the extent to which they are integrated with farming and forestry.

Major problems confronting the most important
branches of agro-industry should be discussed,
including, for example, lack of adequate credit,
power or transport facilities; need for technical
information or advice for improving product design
and marketing; competition from products of larger-
scale, urban-based or foreign industry.

Possibilities for establishing small- and
medium-scale agro-industries, and the pre-requisites
for this, should be considered; in particular, the
possibility that the lack of adequate agro-industry
might be a bottleneck to further agricultural

development, and whether existing producer cooperatives, or other organizations, are equipped to set
up and operate agro-industries or whether new
organizations are likely to be needed. It might
also be useful to know whether there is scope for
joint ventures between farmers and private investors
and how such joint ventures might be organized and
financed.

Where relevant, attention could be given to the
role which trade associations play in coordinating
and otherwise influencing agro-industries and the
impact of these activities on the agricultural
sector. Finally, the survey should indicate what
public policies and programmes might be set up to
promote agro-industry and the extent to which
private investors, farmers and the public sector
might cooperate to maximum advantage in this enterprise.

6. Demand and Supply Projections
Demand and supply projections of agricultural products involve the use of methodological techniques
of some complexity. Some of these techniques are
still evolving. Chapter 7 provides a resume of the
present state of the art, its rationale and some of
its deficiencies. It provides benchmarks for agricultural planners who wish to use the techniques
outlined there. Here, only the difference between
projections and targets, as well as the relationship
between the two, are considered.

Projections versus targets. Production targets may
be set in any one of several ways. They may be
fixed on the basis of more or less detailed field
surveys, extrapolation of past production data,
estimates of future demand based on specific
nutritional standards (see next section), estimates
of the level of agricultural production required to
achieve aggregative targets in a national or regional development plan, or on purely arbitrary or subjective grounds. The most common way of arriving at
production targets is to base them on estimates of
future levels of consumption, despite the fact that
accurate projections depend on good statistics
which are often scarce. Even so, in the hands of
competent technicians, margins of error may be kept
within permissible working limits.

Production and supply projections, whether of
individual products or aggregates, are more subject
to uncertainty than demand projections. Nevertheless, supply as well as demand projections are

generally recommended for plans for agriculture
since practicable output targets must take account
of the kind and amount of agricultural commodities
which can be produced with available resources.

If the targets are to be chosen for their
economic, political and social viability, they
should be selected only after alternative projections have been made and evaluated to reveal the
feasible possibilities for action. Since each projection embodies its own assumptions, comparisons
may be made of the economic effects of the varying,
sometimes complementary, sometimes conflicting,
assumptions on which each projection is based,
thereby determining the most economic or otherwise
most acceptable variant. Projections thus serve as
a valuable tool in target-setting and are in fact
a first step in this exercise.

So closely allied are the procedures by which
projections are prepared and targets set, they can
be considered as parts of one procedure. Yet projections and targets are conceptually and opera-
tionally two radically different things. Projections are quantified forecasts of the likely response
of a multitude of producers and consumers to assumed
government policies and events, without any attempt
to influence the response which is being forecast.
In contrast, targets are a specific prescription for
the future which require the adoption of specific
policies and measures for their achievement.

Targets may be based on projections, but they
need not be the same as any projection. Projections
are useful for taking the spectrum of possible
options into account without resolving which projection is to be selected as an output target until the
different projections have been completed and compared. Conceptually, therefore, projections are a
way of exploring different variants before one
projection (which may be an amalgam of two or more
of the original projections) is selected as a programme target. Thus, the target is a result
arrived at after a variety of projections have been
considered. It follows, therefore, that operation-
ally, the preparation of projections precedes the
setting of targets, although in the process of
setting targets it may be necessary to amend or
supplement projections prepared earlier.

The projection of demand does not imply freedom
of consumer choice or the allocation of resources
through the market. A government may wish to stimulate the consumption of some commodities or bring
about a reduction in the consumption of others. It

would then set targets in the plan to produce a
different pattern of consumption or output than
what would have materialised if consumers had
followed their own inclinations. Even so, it is
desirable to project what consumers themselves want,
partly to determine the extent to which intervention
is needed to decrease or increase demand to conform
with development objectives.

7. Nutrition Planning
Closely associated with projection of demand for
food is a systematic approach to the analysis of
nutrition problems and their potential solutions.
The factors influencing food consumption and nutrition are depicted in figure 6-1. Although the
relative importance of each of these factors may
vary among countries and population groups, low
household incomes, insufficient food availability,
and high food prices are likely to be primary causes
of calorie-protein deficiencies.

Figure 6-1 Agricultural and Rural Development
            and Other Factors Influencing Food
            Consumption and Nutrition

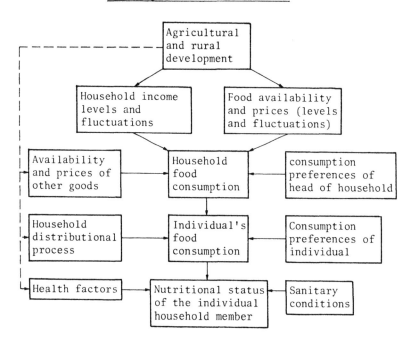

A systematic approach to nutrition problems can provide the framework for assessing costs and benefits of alternative programmes designed to alleviate them. The steps in such a problem are likely to include the following:

> (a) describe the national nutrition system, quantifying as far as possible all factors (see figure 6-1) that appear to influence the nutritional status of the population.
> (b) select target groups (e.g. young children, expectant mothers), goals and objectives
> (c) identify intervention points
> (d) compare the alternatives in terms of both the intervention points and the interventions themselves.
> (e) develop plans or projects for implementation.

Nutritional considerations may be incorporated at the sector or at the project/policy level. Ideally they should be incorporated at both.

Nutrition planning is still in its infancy and it does not help to take a dogmatic approach to the subject; a flexible approach is desirable. Institutional rigidities and vested interests may well deter an effective integration of nutrition and agriculture. But in most countries with significant degrees of malnutrition, some kinds of nutrition programmes, such as direct feeding schemes, will be needed for a long time to come. Only when extreme poverty has been eliminated and agricultural and rural development has a nutrition focus will this need for intervention programmes be eliminated.

8. Information Gaps

The preceding discussion has occasionally touched upon the scarcity of reliable data. For the sake of simplicity, it was generally assumed that the required data were available. In fact, great gaps in the information needed to carry out a stocktaking and diagnostic survey, as well as a plan for the agricultural sector, will surely be exposed as the survey proceeds. In many countries, even the most basic data required for planning do not exist.

While the conceptual framework for analyzing agriculture is reasonably satisfactory, the great weakness is in the scarcity of reliable empirical evidence. It is one of the most serious handicaps to consistent plan formulation and implementation.

In many countries, the only production data with much reliability involve major export commodities and those which are commercially produced. Censuses of agriculture are recent innovations. They are hampered by lack of maps, by small and the irregular fields in which crops are often grown, by the prevalence of mixed and successive cropping, by widespread subsistence production, and by the illiteracy of the producers from whom data must be obtained. It also takes a long time to obtain, assemble and check data from the large number of farms found in many countries.

Much of the basic data is likely to be little more than guesswork. What is available is often of questionable reliability. Attempts to compare data often rest on extremely weak foundations. The national income accounts, none too precise for most sectors, are likely to be least accurate for the agricultural sector.

To obtain the value added in agricultural production, it is necessary to know output quantities, prices obtained by farmers, paid out costs of raw materials and intermediate goods, non-cash costs (e.g., for seed and wastage), and depreciation allowances. None of these data are generally available.

Inventories of agricultural resources are hard to carry out in the absence of reliable statistics on natural resources (especially water supply), capital inputs (working capital), institutional facilities (as regards their limitations), and human resources (the extent of their under-employment). Determining prices of agricultural products in poor countries is extremely difficult because of price variations in both time and place. Projections of final demand are usually based on shaky statistics. In many countries, income elasticities are unavailable, so that expected increases in demand have to be estimated arbitrarily. There are often few dependable statistics on the quantities of foodstuffs being produced for commercial sale, which makes it difficult to relate output to capacity. The lack of good information about area and yields for each major crop, inputs, rainfall and prices, makes it a problem to forecast production; and similarly the paucity of reliable data on subsistence foods and stocks makes it almost impossible to forecast supply with any degree of confidence.

Basic economic data required for planning forestry are also often lacking. The planning of fisheries development presents special difficulties,

in particular because of the lack of knowledge about
the size, mobility and sustainable yield of the resource base.

In these circumstances, margins of error in the
available data are often so large that projections
based on them appear to be of doubtful value. Yet,
if agricultural planning were to wait for perfection
of the data, it could not begin for many years in
most developing countries. It is preferable to
begin the planning process as soon as possible by
assembling the information available and using it
with judgment, and appropriate qualifications, to
make the best possible decisions.

However, the more complex and detailed a plan,
the more information is needed. For this reason, it
may be desirable at early stages of development,
when data are scarce and unreliable, to begin the
planning process with a simple plan which is largely
confined to the provision of basic inputs and the
creation of key institutions. As information im-
proves, plans can gradually be made more complex. By
avoiding the formulation of plans which are too
elaborate for the available data to support, planners can produce realistic plans quickly.

Those who conduct the stocktaking and diagnostic survey are in a good position to evaluate the
extent to which data are available for plan formulation. They should therefore, consider this aspect
as part of their task, and include recommendations
concerning the complexity of the planning which the
data permit.

Many gaps in the data will be exposed during
the conduct of the survey; others will become
apparent in later stages. As part of the planning
process, a medium-term research and studies programme should be devised with a view toward filling
the most important informational gaps, in accordance
with an appropriate set of priorities and a suitable
timetable.

9. If the Survey Team Comes from Outside the Country

It is no exaggeration to say that the planning process will depend in large measure on the results
produced by the survey. If all possible sources of
data have been thoroughly combed, and the available
data assembled and analysed in ways which provide
planners with clearly defined issues, and alternative ways of dealing with them, the rest of the
planning process will be greatly facilitated.

It is therefore imperative that those who make
the survey be provided with carefully worked-out

terms of reference for its conduct, which embody precisely what is wanted and what is not. The terms of reference for each country must be specifically tailored to its own conditions and development objectives. They are bound to vary with a country's stage of development, type of agriculture, emphasis given to each agricultural subsector, and most important of all, whether the primary objective is growth in national output and incomes or, alternatively, equalisation of regional or income disparities.

The number of members of the survey team and the expertise required will also vary from one country to another, depending on the nature of the agricultural sector, the size of the country, and the complexity of the problems likely to be encountered.

Since the nature of the problems likely to be encountered, and their level of complexity, must be adequately gauged before a survey team is assembled, it is desirable to have one or two specialists (including the one who will lead the team) carry out a preliminary inspection trip in the country concerned to determine the nature and scope of the problems required in the agricultural sector. Such a trip, of about two weeks' duration, can do a lot to prepare the way for a survey team. Among other things, those who make the preliminary trip can determine the number and kind of experts who will be required, the likely duration of the survey team's stay in the field, and the availability of information about agriculture.

In this connection, and on the basis of the findings of the preliminary inspection trip, a request for information required by the survey team should be prepared as soon as possible after the trip and forwarded for action to the appropriate official of the country concerned. The request, which should be prepared with considerable care, should ask that the materials to be collected for the survey team be ready at least two weeks before the survey team is scheduled to begin work. A member of the team should be assigned to the place where the information is being assembled to inspect it at least two weeks before the survey team begins work, and to ask officials concerned to fill informational gaps as quickly as possible.

When a survey team has been assembled, and before it leaves for the field, briefings for its members should be conducted for at least one week, during which team members should try to familiarise

themselves with: the country and its problems; the
objectives of the survey; the functions of each team
member; his or her responsibilities and timetables;
administrative, reporting and consultation arrangements; etc. If this is done, the team will be prepared to begin work in the field at the appointed
time with little waste of effort and time. Thereafter, weekly meetings should be held in the field
and, to the extent possible, each team member
should report orally on the progress of his work,
problems encountered, successful practices employed
to achieve results, etc. In this way, each team
member will be kept informed about the work of his
colleagues and learn from their experience. The
weekly team meetings should be supplemented with
meetings between the team head or his deputy and a
team member where it appears that the team member is
in need of guidance or other assistance.

The choice of chief of the survey team should
be given considerable thought. Ideally, the person
chosen should combine technical, managerial, and
leadership abilities with tact, and the ability to
obtain the cooperation of government officials and
others whose acceptance of the team is essential to
its success. It is rarely possible, in practice, to
find one individual with all the required talents.
Even if one can be found, he or she can hardly be
expected to find the time required to do all the
things which must be done if the survey team is to
function satisfactorily. Therefore consideration
should be given to dividing leadership responsibilities between the team chief, a deputy chief and, if
need be, others. It is often desirable for the head
of the team to concentrate on policy and the team's
relationships with government officials, and others
whom the team must look for information and acceptance, and for the deputy head to concentrate on the
team's administrative tasks and the direct supervision of the team members' work. The actual
division of functions between the head and his
deputy will depend on the training and predilections
of the head of the team. But, depending on the
head's training and disposition (e.g. is he or she
primarily a technician or does his or her strength
lie in diplomacy?), he or she must be supported by
a deputy head or others on the team to the extent
required to insure that the team's outside relationships, policy formation and technical work each
receive the attention required for efficient operations.

10. The Survey as a Means to a Planning Unit

The stocktaking and diagnostic survey must be seen
as more than an exercise in gathering and analysing
data, important though this is. When properly
organised and conducted, the survey can also become
a means of promoting a new institution for improved
organisation and management of the agricultural
sector. Specifically, the survey should be considered as a means for on-the-job training and
establishing an effective agricultural planning
unit. These ends may be achieved by the assignment
to the survey team of individuals who either are or
will become senior staff members of an agricultural
planning unit. These individuals should participate
in the whole survey, including its design. While
the survey is being conducted, the members of the
survey team (if they are not the same as the senior
staff of the agricultural planning unit), should
train the members of the senior staff in the techniques of data collection, collation and analysis,
and make certain that they are involved in all
aspects of the survey. Indeed, the senior staff
should participate as full team members in discussions concerning all problems encountered in
carrying out the survey. If this is done, they
should be in an excellent position, after the
survey's completion, to carry on the continuing
planning activities in the agricultural sector. If
the main body of the survey team is composed of
other than the senior staff, one or two should stay
on for a year or two after the survey's completion
to help the staff of the agricultural planning unit
convert the data in the stocktaking and diagnostic
survey into an on-going agricultural plan and to
organise and put the agricultural planning unit on
a sound footing.

CHAPTER 7

DEMAND AND SUPPLY PROJECTIONS

Summary

Demand and supply projections, however crude or sophisticated, are an important feature of agricultural planning. Using different scenarios, they can indicate the extent of the effort required from domestic agriculture to help satisfy demand from home and abroad. Projections of demand are required for food and agricultural raw materials and for domestic and foreign markets. The main determinants of demand are population growth and changes in per caput income. Demand for food tends to expand in line with population growth and as incomes rise, expenditure for food rises too, but less than proportionately and this income response differs for individual foods. Estimating domestic demand for food thus tends to be difficult. A compromise has to be found between the various techniques of estimation and available data. There are likely to be special problems when estimating demand for agricultural raw materials as markets for their various end-users have to be assessed separately. And similarly for export demand, where estimation techniques are likely to vary according to the nature of the commodity and the provisions under which it is exported.

Projections of output and supply are technically much more difficult to make than those of demand. There is the uncertainty of farmers' response to changing prices, costs and technology, added to such factors as weather and crop diseases. Then, output depends so often on decisions of many millions of small- and medium-sized producers. Nevertheless, experience has shown that it is possible for

planners to provide useful estimates of future
output, under given assumptions of yield, area
planted, input of fertilizer, etc. Some of
their methods are outlined in this chapter.
Projecting supply takes account not only of
domestic output but also of imports, exports
and any changes in stocks. Once demand and
supply projections have been made, it is necessary to bring the two into balance. Some sort
of commodity balance sheet may be constructed
as a basis for determining what adjustments are
needed. They may require a considerable change
in the proposed agricultural programme or
possibly only minor alterations. In any event,
an element of flexibility should be a feature
of the plan eventually adopted.

1. Demand Projections

Demand projections are an integral part of agricultural planning, not only because demand influences
agricultural output, but also because it affects
internal and external trade, price stabilization
schemes, national stock policies and development
programmes for industry and other sectors.

Since the variables which affect the demand for
food may differ from those influencing demand for
agricultural raw materials, it is useful to separate
the projections; one for food, the other for raw
materials; and, for a similar reason, to project
demand for food and raw materials for domestic consumption separately from demand for these commodities in the export market.

A. Domestic demand for food. Many factors have an
important influence on the growth of demand for
agricultural commodities, including: (a) increases
in population; (b) changes in the distribution of
population, especially as a result of migration from
rural to urban areas; (c) changes in family size,
age and sex composition; (d) occupation; (e) growth
in per capita incomes; (f) changes in the distribution of incomes; (g) price changes; (h) shifts in
the pattern of consumption; (i) attempts to raise
nutritional levels; (j) improved marketing arrangements; (k) social class; level of education; and
climate.

The effect of each of these variables on future
demand is likely to differ from the effects of the
others. Some variables (like population growth and
changes in income per head) generally have a direct
and profound effect on the level and pattern of

future demand; others (e.g. changes in family composition and occupation) may have an indirect and
lesser effect; some have a greater effect in the
long- than in the short-run; some have a greater
effect in the short-run (e.g., seasonal price
changes); while others make an impact in both the
short- and the long-run.

Reliable data for measuring the impact of all
major variables affecting future demand are almost
never available. Moreover, some possibly important
variables (such as social class and climate) are
difficult to measure numerically and are therefore
often ignored in estimating demand. Although the
neglect of some factors may restrict the usefulness
of demand projections, there is usually no practicable alternative to the preparation of projections
on the basis of only two or three variables for
which reasonably good data are obtainable. Even
when data are available, it is advisable to estimate
first the influence of what are believed to be the
most important variables for determining demand before estimating the effect of the less important
ones.

In projecting the domestic demand for food in
low-income countries, the growth of population is
generally considered to be the basic variable, since
in many of these countries it is the high rate of
increase in population which is the source of the
greatest pressure on food supplies (it may account
for 80-85 percent of growth in food demand). And
since an increase in national income is generally a
major objective of development plans and programmes,
the second most important factor is usually considered to be the expected increase in per capita
disposable incomes.

As long as reliable data on the size of the
population and its rate of increase are available,
population presents no great problems since demand
for food tends to expand by the same percentage as
population (on the assumption that there is no significant change in the age structure of the population). But this is not true of income. As incomes
rise, expenditures for food rise, but less than
proportionately. However, since levels of consumption in less-developed countries are lower than in
the more-developed countries, the rate at which food
expenditures rise in poor countries when incomes
increase is generally higher than in rich countries.

The rate at which expenditures change as incomes rise is measured by the income-elasticity of
demand. The general formula for calculating the

the income-elasticity of demand may be expressed as

$$E_i = \frac{\Delta Q}{Q} \div \frac{\Delta Y}{Y} \text{ , where}$$

E_i = the income elasticity

Q = the original quantity consumed

ΔQ = the change in the quantity consumed after the change in income

Y = the original per capita income

ΔY = the change in the level of per capita income

For example, if an increase of 10% in per capita income is accompanied by an increase of 5% in consumption, the coefficient of income elasticity is 0.5, thus

$$E_i = \frac{\Delta Q}{Q} \div \frac{\Delta Y}{Y}$$

$$= \frac{10}{200} \div \frac{10}{100}$$

$$0.5 = .05 \div .10$$

Studies have confirmed that in many poor countries an increase in income of one per cent will lead to an increase in demand for food of between 0.3 and 0.5 per cent.

B. <u>Estimating domestic demand</u>. There are several different ways in which the influence of income on consumption may be measured. Some methods are simple, but the results obtained from them are not as useful for economic analysis as those obtained from more refined methods. But the more refined the function by which per capita income is related to per capita consumption, the more complex the computation is likely to be and the greater the data requirement. While the need for economic interpretation makes the more complex formulations preferable to the simple ones, paucity of good data may make it necessary for countries to settle for the simple techniques. Nevertheless, it is useful to know what the ideal models are, not only because they point up the crudity of existing techniques, but because they provide reference points for approximating the ideal in reality.

A simple way of estimating the impact of increased population and income on the demand for food is by the formula, $Y = a + bX$, where Y is the rate of increase in demand (or consumption of, or expenditures) for food, a is the rate of population growth, b is the coefficient of income elasticity of the demand for food, and X is the rate of growth in per capita incomes. If hypothetical numbers are substituted for the letters in the equation, it may be seen that the annual rate of increase in the demand for food, Y, would be 3 per cent if a were equal to 2.4 per cent, b to 0.3 and X to 2 per cent $[3 = 2.4 + (0.3 \times 2)]$.

As long as b remains unchanged, and a and X continue to grow at the rates assumed in the formula Y would increase at the compound rate of 3 per cent annually. At the end of five years this would yield an increase in the annual demand for food amounting to almost 16 per cent and in 10 years to 34 per cent.

The greater the disaggregation in estimating demand for food, the greater the possibility of error. Since agricultural foodstuffs are frequently substitutes for one another, it is difficult to project with reasonable accuracy the demand for one food in isolation. It is usually desirable, therefore, to first project demand for all food commodities, then for major commodity groups, e.g., cereals, and finally for the main individual foods, e.g., wheat. If this is done, it becomes easier to compare demand estimates for individual foods against estimates for broader groupings, and in relation to likely supply.

In the example given above, the income-elasticity of demand was assumed to be constant. While this may be true in the short run, over long periods of time, the elasticity coefficient is likely to change. A simple method of dealing with this problem is to divide the long-term projections into shorter sub-periods or different levels of income, for each of which a different elasticity is used. But if a long-term projection is made, functions which adequately reflect the changes in elasticity over time must be fitted to the data. The choice of the right function for projecting the total demand for food, groups of food or a specific food is ultimately a matter of judgement, based on information about the consumption habits of different parts of a population in the various regions,

and at different income levels in a particular
country. However, consumption in most developing
countries tends to follow similar patterns. This
makes it feasible to use the same set of functions
to project demand in most of these countries.

Thus, $Y = a + bX$ is generally appropriate only
for analyzing all expenditures for food over the
very short run, since it assumes that regardless of
the level of per capita income, demand or consumption will rise proportionally (e.g., a one-unit increase in income will be accompanied by a half-unit
increase in demand for or consumption of, food).
Taking Y as the dependent and X as the independent
variable, $Y = a + bX$ will be represented on a graph
as a straight line, moving upward diagonally from
left to right. This implies that the marginal
demand is constant. Similar results, which give
increments in demand in percentage rather than in
absolute terms, may be obtained with the logarithmic

Figure 7-1   The Logarithmic Demand Function

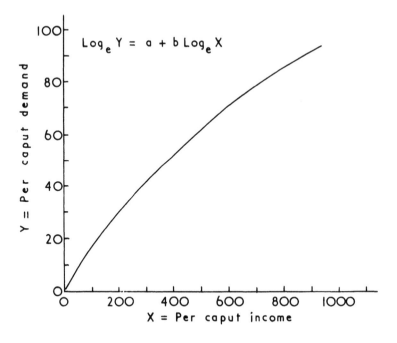

function, $Log_e\ Y = a + b\ Log_e\ X$ (Where Y is per capita consumption, b is the income-elasticity co-efficient and X is per capita income). With this function, the demand curve is represented by Figure 7-1.

Both equations imply a constant income elasticity of demand, i.e., a constant ratio between the percentage increase in per capita demand and per capita income, and both are appropriate for analyzing expenditures on food when, as is true of the very poor, demand is likely to remain far below the saturation point during the projection period.

However, in most poor countries, the income-elasticity coefficient is likely to decline as consumption increases long before the point of saturation, i.e. consumption increases at a declining rate as per capita income increases. In these circumstances, which apply to many individual foods, the simplest function used is the semi-logarithmic

Figure 7-2   The Semi-Logarithmic Demand Function

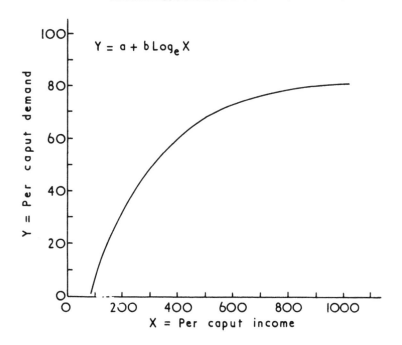

$$Y = a + b\ Log_e\ X$$

Y = Per caput demand

X = Per caput income

equation, Y = a + b log$_e$X. This function implies a
decline in the absolute value of the income-
elasticity coefficient represented by b/Y which is
proportional to changes in the quantities of food
consumed. (Figure 7-2)
    Where the total calorie intake is near the
saturation point, or where consumption of certain
foods (e.g., sugar, fats and oils), is already high
and likely to be stablilized soon, it is more appropriate to use the log-inverse function Log$_e$ Y = a -
b/X, to analyze consumption or expenditures. This
function implies a decline in the absolute value of
the income-elasticity coefficient (represented by
b/X) which is proportional to increases in per
capita income.
    Finally, where consumption of staple foods
(e.g., cereals and starchy roots) starts at low
levels when incomes are low, increases to a high
point, and thereafter declines as incomes continue

Figure 7-3   The Log-Inverse Demand Function

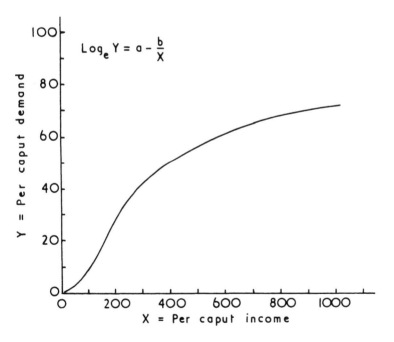

to rise, it is most appropriate to analyze food expenditures with the log-log-inverse function, $\text{Log}_e Y = a - b/X - c \log_e X$ (with the income-elasticity coefficient represented by $b-cX/X$).

Figure 7-4   The Log-Log-Inverse Demand Function

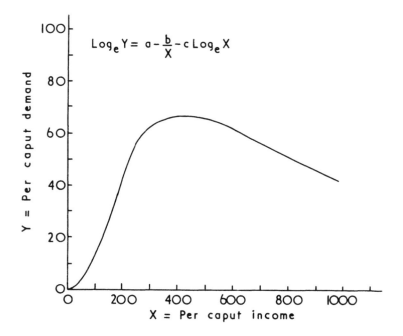

C. Constraints on the approach. The method just outlined makes measurement of the demand-increasing effects of population and income growth seem easier than it is. This is partly because it requires information, for the year(s) selected as the base period for the projection, which is not always available. If a year can be found which is "representative", in the sense that the influence of unusual factors is minimal, the base period may be one year. But if sharp and unusual fluctuations which are characteristic of agriculture makes the choice of one year inadvisable, it is preferable to use statistical averages for two or three years to smooth out the fluctuations.
    The statistics required for the base period include the size and composition of the population,

its distribution between rural and urban areas, per capita income and consumption of food in rural and urban areas, income and price elasticities of demand for food, and food exports by volume and value. To the extent that these data are unavailable or unreliable, the projected percentage increases in demand, when converted into absolute figures, are also unreliable.

The approach also ignores changes in real or relative prices which implies that supply will increase in proportion to demand. If prices are expected to increase because of short supplies or for other reasons, the stable price assumption must be modified and the demand estimates adjusted since the price elasticities often have a significant effect on demand. However, the concept of price elasticity is complex and much less is known about it than about income elasticity. The price elasticity of demand is the proportional decrease in demand for a commodity in relation to a given proportional increase in price or, conversely, the proportional increase in demand in relation to a given proportional decrease in its price. Thus, a price elasticity of demand of 0.5 means that a 1 per cent change in price will be associated with a change in demand in the opposite direction of 0.5 per cent. Useful data on price elasticities of demand are rarely available in less-developed countries in the quantity and form required to permit reasonably precise adjustments to be made. Calculation of reliable price elasticities requires the comparison of quantity and price data obtained from monthly or quarterly consumption surveys over a period of years. This shortcoming severely limits the reliability of demand projections in many countries. In the absence of dependable price elasticity data, planners usually assume, for good theoretical reasons, that prices will remain constant, even when they have reason to believe that prices will change over the period of the programme or plan.

This assumption may be justifiable when a commodity has no close substitutes, e.g., sugar, but not where, as for many foods, there are substitutes. In this situation the price elasticity for a specific food is likely to be higher than the corresponding income elasticity. In fact, available information shows that for low-income countries, price elasticities are generally higher than income elasticities for food. Even when information on the price elasticity of demand is inadequate, therefore,

there is something to be said for the planner to
make the best possible estimates of price changes,
where these seem likely to occur, and their probable
effect on consumption.

A third limitation concerns the use of per
capita income as a variable for estimating demand,
when it may not be suitable. This may be true, for
example, in countries which curb consumption to
increase investment. In these countries, a distinction needs to be made between per capita income
and disposable per capita income i.e., between the
national income divided by the total population as
against the actual amounts available per capita for
expenditures for foodstuffs.

Per capita income may also be an inadequate
measure of future demand where the distribution of
marginal increases of national income is greatly
skewed; and it may not reflect differences in urban
and rural incomes, or income variations among
regions. Adjustments in the calculation of future
demand have to be made for these factors if there is
reason to believe that they will seriously affect
the realiability of projections. Moreover, per
capita income is difficult to estimate in the subsistence part of an economy, because the value of
home-produced food consumed on farms has to be taken
into account as part of family income. Such estimates necessarily involve a considerable amount of
subjective judgement.

There is another constraint: income elasticities are not likely to remain constant for more than
a few years in a developing country. It is because
the percentage spent on food begins to decline after
a certain point as incomes rise (the widely accepted
principle known as Engel's Law), that account must
be taken of this tendency when coefficients of income elasticity of demand are calculated. Furthermore, the rate at which demand changes as incomes
rise often varies for different foods and may vary
between negative elasticities to those of 1.5% and
even higher. Consequently, available information on
the relationship between income and demand must be
analyzed, and curves fitted to the data to derive
appropriate income elasticity coefficients for
different foods.

This is not technically an especially difficult
task if the necessary data for different foods are
available, but they rarely are. Where the data are
lacking or inadequate, income elasticity coefficients based on the income-demand relationships
in other countries (many of which have been

estimated by the Food and Agriculture Organization of the United Nations (FAO) and other agencies) have been used, on the assumption that they are relevant in the country where they are applied.

Since income elasticities for total food requirements for a country are averages, they may differ greatly from the average for specific population groups or foods. Cultural, regional, climatic and psychological differences often account for considerable variations in consumption patterns and hence for differences in income elasticities. The most striking contrast is the variation between rural and urban groups. Not only do rural diets usually differ in some respects from urban diets, but the income elasticity of the demand for food is likely to be different in rural as against urban communities. Thus, where the overall income elasticity of demand for food is, for example, 0.4 the average is more likely to be as high as 0.5 for the rural part of a country and as low as 0.2 for the urban part. Furthermore, the rate at which demand elasticities change in response to changes in income is likely to differ in the farm and non-farm (or rural and urban) sectors.

Since a shift of rural populations to cities is a characteristic of developing countries, projections based on national income-elasticity of demand coefficients for food are likely to be less precise than projections of demand obtained from the consolidation of rural and urban estimates of demand based on separate rural and urban (or farm and non-farm) demand coefficients. Calculation of separate rural and urban income-elasticity coefficients not only requires data for each group, but also estimates of population changes in urban and rural areas during the period of the projection.

There are other problems, as already indicated, for as population increases, demand tends to expand by the same percentage for each kind of food. In contrast, as per capita incomes increase, demand for some commodities will rise more rapidly than for others and may even decline for a few. This change in the structure of demand as incomes rise is important for the planning of production since resourse requirements may vary for the production of different crops. The calculation of income elasticities of demand should therefore go beyond the determination of demand elasticities for the aggregate of food products and include some income coefficients for at least each of the more important foods consumed.

The calculation of income elasticities in less-developed countries involves a certain amount of compromise. The ideal way is through the accumulation of time series which relate changes in income to changes in total consumption of different foods over a period of several years. However, the scarcity of comparable data on incomes and consumption for a sufficiently long period, and other problems, make it very difficult to produce reliable income-elasticity of demand coefficients by this method.

They are sometimes derived from current income and consumption data obtained from sample household surveys of consumer income, and expenditures on various foods. The data derived from a sample survey are used to calculate income-elasticity co-efficients on the assumption, which cannot be proved of course, that if income levels increase, consumers at low-income levels will alter their consumption patterns to conform to that of consumers at higher income levels, as revealed in the consumer expenditure survey.

A good sample survey covers consumer expenditures for food products at different income levels, and provides data on the consumption of individual foods, and total consumption of foodstuffs, at different income levels in a fixed period. If the sample is well-prepared, it will be representative of the whole population in a country and distinguish among families of different sizes (with or without children), since the consumption patterns of families of different sizes differ, especially at upper income levels. In large countries with considerable regional differences in diets, the sample survey must be large enough to take these, as well as rural and urban, differences into account. If there are seasonal variations in consumption, surveys must be made at different seasons to take note of such variations, too. And since tastes for food change, especially at upper income levels, sample surveys should be taken annually. They rarely are, however, and may be out-of-date when the data obtained from them are used as a basis for making projections.

Often, the use of household survey data is restricted because they are collected on the basis of outdated theoretical frameworks, without a clear notion of the use to which the data would be put. Many surveys in less-developed countries do not include information on current income and the data provided are frequently unsuitable for use in

commodity projections. In most, cruder methods of estimating demand elasticities have often been used.
    Since a major use of this concept is to help determine the volume of production required for each kind of food, it is desirable to compute income-elasticity of demand coefficients on the basis of the quantity of each commodity consumed rather than expenditures for it. An income-elasticity of demand coefficient based on expenditures is second-best because it may include increasing costs of processing or other services associated with the food, as well as changes in the quantity of the food consumed. If the elasticities are calculated for different classes of foods, e.g., cereals, the expenditure elasticity conceals shifts in consumption from one cereal to another (e.g., from less expensive millet to more expensive wheat).
    There may be significant differences between elasticities computed on the basis of quantities consumed as opposed to those based on expenditures for a food or group of foods. For example, if the cost of processing or market services, or both, increases sufficiently, expenditures for the individual food or group of foods concerned may rise while the quantities consumed may fall. In these circumstances, the expenditures elasticity would show up as positive while the quantity elasticity may be negative.
    Nevertheless, in practice, income-elasticity of demand coefficients are often computed on the basis of expenditures for food rather than on the quantity consumed, because it is easier to do it that way. The expenditures are then converted into physical quantities by the use of coefficients which relate prices to quantities. Despite the limitation of this method, it can provide reasonably good approximations of the physical amounts of food consumed in poor countries because there, in contrast to high-income countries, increased expenditures for food are presumed to be made largely for unprocessed farm produce with a minimum of additional costs for other marketing services. In fact, however, this is more likely to be true in rural than in urban areas.
    Where consumer expenditures are for foods which include appreciable costs for processing, transport or other services, the cost of these "value added" services must be eliminated to determine the final demand for the commodity as produced on the farm. For example, expenditures for bread must be adjusted by an appropriate factor to

determine the cost of the wheat used to make the bread. It then becomes possible to convert the cost of the wheat into physical quantities.

Where reliable data on income elasticities are not available for a country, income elasticities of demand of other nations have sometimes been substituted on the assumption that tastes for food at different income levels are likely to be similar from one country to another. While this assumption is a dubious one for specific foods, especially in the short-run, studies indicate that for broad classes of foods, and for long periods, income-elasticity of demand coefficients are surprisingly similar among countries.

Often, these coefficients are calculated by pooling time-series and cross-section data. Thus, where partial time-series data are available, they may be combined with data obtained from a sample survey of consumer expenditures, or each set of data may be projected separately and compared. The results are analyzed and the most plausible projections are selected. Similarly, data from a country survey may be combined with material obtained from other countries; and, in yet other countries, time series are combined with international comparisons. In short, what is actually done to obtain income-elasticity of demand coefficients must be determined by the data available in a country and by the skill of its planners

D. Domestic demand for agricultural raw materials. Projections of demand for agricultural raw materials must take account of programmes of industrial development wherever these are available. But where such information is unobtainable, as is true of many low-income countries (and there is an absence of other reliable information to guide agricultural planners), the methods employed to project domestic demand for agricultural raw materials are usually like those used for processed foods.

For some agricultural raw materials, however, there may be special problems. The variables involved may be different from those which affect the demand for processed foods. The demand for wood pulp, for example, used in the manufacture of newsprint and writing paper depends primarily on the degree of literacy in a country rather than on population or income; while the demand for wood used as fuel depends heavily on climate.

Furthermore, some agricultural raw materials, including wood, rubber, jute, and textile fibres, have several end-uses, which is likely to complicate the task of projecting demand for them. It requires, among other things, an assessment of the projected demand for each of the major end-uses, and the calculation of a conversion factor for each end-use to translate the final demand for the end-use product into the intermediate demand for the raw material.

Projection of demand for major end-use products usually requires special investigations to obtain data on income elasticity of demand plus other factors affecting the demand for each product, as well as information on population growth and per capita incomes. These investigations must also assess the possibilities of substitution of other commodities for the raw material concerned (e.g., synthetic for natural rubber), the likely impact which technological progress may make to reduce the input of the raw material, as well as the influence which a change in relative prices may have on the demand for the raw material and the end-product.

However desirable they may be, such studies require an intimate knowledge of each end-use product. This has often proved to be beyond the capacity of agricultural planners in developing countries. In practice, therefore, simpler methods of projecting demand for agricultural raw materials have been used, based on an extrapolation of historical consumption of the raw material related to expected increases in income, perhaps with one or two additional variables which are considered important in the country concerned.

E. Foreign demand for agricultural commodities. Methods of projecting exports often differ according to the nature of the commodity, and the provisions under which it is exported. Where exports of a commodity are determined by international agreement, the agreement becomes the basis for the projections. Agricultural exports are sometimes estimated as a residual after subtracting projected domestic demand from projected production. But since this approach ignores world demand, it is not to be recommended, especially where the share of agricultural exports in the gross national product is large. It is preferable to project exports of each major commodity independently of domestic production and demand, and balance exports with production and demand afterwards. If a commodity has a predominant export market, a two-step procedure is followed. First, a projection is made of total demand for the commodity in the major importing country. Second, this quantity is multiplied by the exporting country's share as derived from historical data. If a commodity is exported to many countries, none of which accounts for a preponderant quantity of the total import volume, the exportable quantity may be derived by fitting a trend line to time series data and extrapolated into the future. But it is not sufficient to estimate future exports solely by the extrapolation of past export trends, because this does not take into account the factors which determine foreign demand.

Projection of the export prospects for each major agricultural commodity should be made in two stages. The first requires an analysis of the likely world demand for the commodity which takes account of likely changes in consumption in importing countries, the production outlook in major exporting and importing countries (including the possibility that importing countries will increase their production of the commodity), the effect of synthetic and other substitutes, and possible input-reductions of the commodity in processing or manufacture as a result of technological progress. Protectionist and trade preference policies of importing countries, unified agricultural and other policies of common markets, (e.g., the European Economic Community), inter-national commodity agreements, as well as the effect on foreign demand brought about by likely shifts in relative prices of agricultural commodities, must also be evaluated. While some less developed countries have the commodity specialists required to follow world market trends for specific agricultural commodities, most countries must rely on forecasts of world demand and supply of each commodity prepared by international agencies like the FAO, the OECD, UNCTAD or the World Bank.

Within the framework of these forecasts, agricultural planners must, in the second stage, make an informed judgment of the likely share of the world market which their country is likely to obtain, taking into account recent trends in the country's share of the market. In projecting demand for a country's traditional agricultural exports, an analysis must be made of the past trend and direction of each major commodity exported as a guide for judging its prospects in the future. This requires, for each major country likely to import the commodity, an analysis of the factors determining access to, and the probable size of, the market,

including: the importing country's economic
prospects, trends in its population and per capita
income growth, likely changes in the income elasticity of demand for the imported commodity, competition likely to be encountered from substitutes, as
well as likely costs of production and transportation to markets as compared to those of competitor
countries. The analysis must also take account of
special factors affecting each commodity, including
bilateral trade agreements between the exporting and
importing countries.

Careful attention should also be given to
possibilities of increasing exports through reduct-
ions in costs, improvements in quality or better
handling and marketing procedures. It should also
be determined whether it is possible to expand
seasonal or uncertain export markets into year-
round or more stable and reliable markets.

Export demand projections must go beyond mere
extrapolation of past exports of traditional products to established markets, within the framework
of global commodity forecasts prepared by international agencies. Efforts must be made to stimulate exports of non-traditional commodities. This
almost invariably means that research must precede
production. The experience of countries which have
had great success in promoting non-traditional agricultural exports shows that the process by which
they are increased usually begins with careful investigation and analysis of potential markets, to
determine the extent and nature of existing or
latent demand for agricultural commodities in
foreign markets. This is followed by the establishment of producing and marketing systems which insure
that the right varieties of the selected commodities
are produced, sorted, packed and shipped and that
quality and costs are controlled to meet the standards of the foreign markets.

For a country whose volume of exports of a
particular commodity is too small to greatly affect
world supplies and prices, little consideration
needs to be given to the possible effect of an
increase in its exports on world prices. But for
countries which are major suppliers of a commodity
on the world market, a possible increase in exports
requires evaluation. For these countries, studies
should also be made on the possible short- and long-
term impact of increased exports on world market
prices, as well as the possibility of reducing costs
as a result of increased production of the commodity
to meet higher export demand.

90

Figure 7-5   COMPONENTS OF DEMAND FOR AGRICULTURAL COMMODITIES

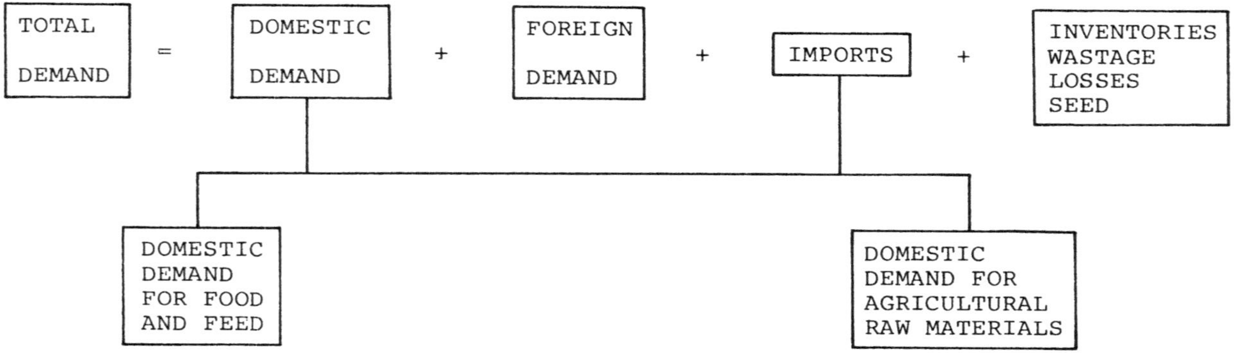

F. Conclusions. Figure 7-5 shows the various components which go to make up demand (consumption of,
or expenditures) for agricultural commodities. As
the figure indicates, the sum of domestic and export
demand of an agricultural commodity for human consumption and industrial use is less than the total
requirements for the commodity. The total of
domestic and export demand must be adjusted to allow
for the maintenance of working stocks or inventories
which are likely to be held by private traders and
government, wastage, losses in processing, feeding
of livestock, and for seed. Few poor countries have
realiable estimates of the quantities required for
each of these purposes. Allowance is then made for
these factors by a pro-rata percentage adjustment
which is equal to the total change projected in
demand for domestic human consumption, industrial
use and exports.
    In countries with more reliable statistical
data and a supply of trained technicians, it is
possible to use advanced techniques with several
equations to construct demand projections. It has
also been possible to carry out sophisticated projections of demand in some less-developed countries
with the aid of foreign technical assistance. But,
for most, there is little alternative to the use of
the simplest projection methods, utilizing linear
equations of two or three variables.

2. Projections of Output and Supply
A. The effect of price on output and supply. Besides affecting demand, price changes influence
production, and supply. They affect output and
supply indirectly by encouraging or discouraging the
introduction of inputs and farming practices which
make a direct contribution to output and productivity. Farmers generally have considerable latitude to substitute production of one commodity for
another. Where conditions permit, therefore, a
change in the price of one commodity relative to
others will usually stimulate farmers to adjust
output positively in response to the change in relative prices. The response may take the form of
changes in acreage under that commodity, as well as
changes in the amount of inputs employed in its production.
    However, farmers' responses to price changes
are sometimes inhibited by the conditions under
which they operate. This is true, for example, when
heavy overhead investments are useable only to produce one commodity. Thus, farmers find it harder to

respond to price changes when they grow tree crops
rather than annual crops, at least in the short run.
They also have fewer choices for changing crops on
rain-fed than on irrigated lands. And in subsistence farming areas, where marketable food surpluses
are generally marginal, farmers' choices for producing food crops may be almost independent of
relative price levels and changes. Because farmers'
responses to price changes are influenced by many
factors, some of which may have a stronger influence
than the price factor, it is difficult to predict
the extent and timing of output changes induced by
a specific price change.

This is so even when farmers are free to make
choices about what they produce. In part it is
because output is affected by uncontrollable, and
often unpredictable, external factors such as crop
diseases and weather (especially on unirrigated
lands); in part, because output often depends on
decisions of many small- and medium-sized producers
who use varying inputs and technologies; and, in
part, because the level of production is determined
not only by inputs and technology, but by institutional and human factors whose effects can only be
assessed imprecisely.

Apart from the inherent difficulty of predicting the future level of prices, these factors make
it hard to forecast the impact of specific price
changes on output and market supply. Another problem is that of estimating the time lag between a
change in price and farmers' adjustment to it.
Uncertainties about time lags are also a problem for
estimating the impact of new technology. For all
these reasons, projections of output and supply are
technically much more difficult to make than those
of demand.

B. Projecting output. Output projections involve
forecasting the area planted to a crop and the
average yield per unit of land. In Latin America
and Africa, expansion of cropped area has been more
important than increases in yield in the growth of
output. Although much unused cultivable land remains in Latin America and Africa, much of it can be
brought into production only by improvements in
tenure arrangements and agrarian reform in the
broadest sense, i.e., by the introduction of price
and tax policies, and government services which
stimulate agricultural growth. Because these
changes are likely to be slow in coming, an increasing proportion of future growth in output will

92

probably come as increased yields from lands
already in cultivation rather than from expansion of
cropped areas, as is already the situation in most
of Asia.

The area planted in a particular crop depends
mostly on farmers' price expectations, but average
yield per unit of land depends on many factors.
These include the quality of the inputs employed,
technological change, lags between the availability
of inputs and their use by farmers, shifts in relative prices of agricultural commodities, government
policies, institutional factors, and changes in
farmers' attitudes and behaviour. The effect of
each of these factors on output is difficult to
isolate and measure. Moreover, while it is possible
to estimate, with reasonable accuracy, increases in
long-term yields following improvements in cropping
practices and planting of improved varieties, it is
more difficult to forecast annual yield because many
factors which affect annual yields like weather and
disease, are beyond farmers' control. Because of
the problems involved, projection of average yields
is technically much more difficult than projection
of area planted. It is therefore better to make
these projections separately.

(a) Projecting area planted. Because of the direct
connection between cropped area and output, the
first task in projecting production is to estimate
the amount of cropped area during the plan period.
This may be done by preparing land utilization
sheets, along the lines indicated in Table 7-1 which
give for each region, and by summation, for the
country as a whole, the uses which have been made
for available lands in recent years and a first
approximation of the uses to be made of them during
the period of a forthcoming agricultural plan.

Since the projection of future land use requires knowledge of past and present trends, the
greater the number of years immediately preceding
the year in which the plan is scheduled to start (t),
for which data are available, the better. If regional land utilization sheets are prepared for
about 8 or 10 years before the year in which the
plan is scheduled to start and are then consolidated
into land utilization sheets for the whole country,
a solid basis exists for estimating future regional
and national land use patterns, taking due account
of differences in land quality and the suitability
of land for the various crops to be grown. The data
may show that a recent year is sufficiently

Table 7-1   First Approximation of Land Utilization
for the (Named) Region in (Years Listed)
(Acres, hectares or other Units)

Land Use	Base Period			Plan Years		
	t-1	t-2...	t-n	t	t+1	t+2... t+n
1. Total land use						
2. Forests						
3. Land under tree crops						
4. Permanent grazing and pasture lands						
5. Other land not available for cultivation						
6. Arable land						
7. Net area sown						
(a) irrigated						
(b) unirrigated						
8. Gross area sown (which takes account of multiple cropping)						
(a) irrigated						
(b) unirrigated						

representative of past production to be used as a
base period for projections, but it is more likely
that annual fluctuations in output need to be
smoothed out by the use of averages for several
years, usually three to five. A multi-annual base
period is especially desirable when there is a lack
of information for more than a very few recent
years.

More than one projection should be made. The
first projection could be a simple extrapolation of
past trends based on existing land-use programmes
and practices, on the assumption that no measures
will be taken to alter the existing trend. Other
projections might be based on the different assumptions about likely, feasible or desirable measures
which would alter the trend in one way of another.
In every case, projections would assume constant
prices. The projections would also have to be adjusted if further expansion of any land use is
likely to be restricted by lack of suitable land.
At a later stage in the planning process, when targets are set, adjustments will have to be made to
take account of likely price changes, and policies
and measures adopted to achieve development objectives and targets.

After completion of the land utilization

sheets, with their first approximation of the land
use pattern during the plan years, the second step
is to prepare area, yield and production sheets,
with projections of the way land would best be
allocated to major crops to meet demand, production
potential or other development objectives, on the
assumption that prices remain constant. The crops
for which estimates are made may be classified in
whatever way assists the analysis and the setting of
targets. For example, crops may be divided into
foods and raw materials; for domestic consumption
and export; or annual and tree crops. These divisions may be subdivided again into crops grown,
e.g., on plantations and other lands; with mechani-
zed and manual cultivation; or on irrigated and
unirrigated lands.

Table 7-2 is a sample area, yield, and production sheet, classified for illustrative purposes
by annual and tree crops, with a further subdivision
of annual crops into those produced on irrigated and
unirrigated lands. For each region, the table shows
the irrigated and non-irrigated areas allocated to
each major annual crop and the areas allocated to
each major tree crop as well as yield and production, for the past years which represent the base
period and for each year of the proposed agricultural plan period.

Table 7-2   Area Allocated, Yields and Production
for Major Crops in the (Named)Region
in (Years Listed)

| | Base Period | | | Plan Years | | |
| | | | | 1 | 2 | 3 | 4...n |
	Area	Yield	Production	Area	Yield	Production
Annual Crops						
Wheat						
irrigated						
non-irrigated						
Cotton						
irrigated						
non-irrigated						
Tree Crops						
Coffee						
Palm Oil						

As with land utilization, the longer the period immediately proceding the plan period for which relevant data are available, the firmer the foundation for making projections of the areas to be allocated to each crop, as well as yields and production, during the plan period. In extrapolating past trends, the main factors accounting for the trends should be identified, and adjustments should be made for factors which make deviations from past trends probable, even if the availability of land is no limitation to further expansion.

Since the amount of additional arable land is usually limited, output of a given crop obtainable on all land likely to be available for that crop during the plan period may be below the level of expected demand, if base-period yields remained unchanged. To assess the feasibility of raising the output of a crop to the level of expected demand, it is useful to estimate the extent to which yields would have to be increased to equate estimated output and demand during any year in the plan period. How this estimate may be made is shown in Table 7-3.

Table 7-3   Yield Required for Output to Equal Estimated Demand for Year One of the Plan

Base Period			Year One		
(1)	(2)	(3)	(4)	(5)	(6)
			Projected demand at	Estimated available	4/5 Yield
Crop	Production	Area	Yield	farm level	area	target
A	1000	100	10	1320	110	12

In the hypothetical example shown in Table 7-3, an average of 1000 units of crop A was produced during the base period (column 1) on 100 units of land (column 2) to provide an average yield of 10 units (column 3). The demand projected for crop A at the farm level in year one of the plan period is estimated to be 1320 (column 4), while the estimated area available for crop A in year one (as determined by projections like those described for Figure 7) is 110 units of land (column 5). Division of the projected demand for year one (column 4) by the estimated available land for crop A (column 5), gives the yield required to bring output to the level of estimated demand in year one (column 6).

Similar estimates for each major crop, on irrigated and non-irrigated lands, should be made separately for every year of the plan period. It then becomes possible to calculate an average yield target for equating the proposed average production of each crop with the estimated average demand during the plan period.

(b) Projecting inputs. Increased yields depend, among other things, on the availability of labour and other inputs, such as improved seeds, fertilizers, insecticides, agricultural machinery and water. It is, therefore, important to take stock of the main inputs available in the base period and project their prospective supply over the period of the plan. Because of data problems, projection of labour supply and demand, especially on a regional basis, is generally more difficult than projection of other inputs, but as these projections can be used in any attempt to rationalise the use of labour and improving its efficiency, an effort should be made to prepare these projections. Even in areas which normally have a labour surplus, seasonal shortages may arise during periods of peak demand, e.g., at sowing and harvesting times. For this reason, projections should be made for peak demand periods as well as for the overall supply and demand in each year of the proposed plan period. To this end, labour-utilization sheets as illustrated in Table 7-4 may be compiled. The labour-utilization sheet is based on man-years, which requires that woman and child labour be converted into man-year equivalents.

For all major inputs, knowledge of likely availabilities and demand during the plan period is essential for proper planning of their use. It is thus important that estimates be made of the use of other major inputs, like seed, fertilizers, insecticides, tools and machinery during the base period, and that the demand for each be projected for the plan period. If prospective supplies of inputs promise to be lower than needed to raise crop yields to required levels, ways will have to be found to increase supplies, where this is possible, either by expanding domestic production or by imports. In the case of labour, it may be necessary to change the cropping pattern to conform to the available labour, alter the factor proportions between labour and other inputs, bring about a shift in the regional distribution of labour, or take other action to bring supply and demand into equilibrium. Each of

Table 7-4   Labour-Utilization Sheet
(thousand man/years)

Regional Supply and Demand	Base Year(s)	Plan Years
		1 2 3 4 ...n
Region 1		
Labour Force		
Supply		
Demand		
Difference		
Wheat		
Rice		
Cotton		
Region II		
Labour Force		
Supply		
Demand		
Difference		
Wheat		
Sugar Cane		
Region III		
Supply		
Demand		
Corn		
Cotton		

these alternative courses of action need to be evaluated carefully.

(c) Contribution of inputs to output. After the supply of each major input for the base period, and for each year of the plan period, has been esti-nated, it becomes possible to estimate their contri-bution to output. Since the combination of inputs varies among crops, as well as among regions for the same crop, it is desirable to prepare for each crop separate estimates of the effect of varying combi-nations of technology in different regions or sub-regions. Table 7-5 illustrates how this may be done. When the subregional tables are combined, regional and national estimates may be obtained of the contribution of major inputs to output.

Table 7-5   Contribution of Listed Inputs to
the Output of Commodity (Named)

	Base	Plan Years			
A. Area (named) in acreage, hectares or other	Period	1	2	3	4 ...n

    1.0 <u>Irrigated land</u>
    1.1 with improved seeds
    1.2 with improved seeds and
          fertilizer
    1.3 with improved seeds, fer-
          tilizer and pesticides
    1.4 with improved seeds, fer-
          tilizer, pesticides and
          other input(s)

    2.0 <u>Unirrigated land</u>
    2.1 with improved seeds
    2.2 with improved seeds and
          fertilizers
    2.3 with improved seeds, fer
          tilizers and pesticides
    2.4 with improved seeds, fer-
          tilizers, pesticides and
          other input(s)

B. Yield (lbs per acre, kgs. per hectare, etc)

    3.0 <u>Irrigated land</u>
    3.1 with improved seeds
    3.2 with improved seeds and
          fertilizers
    3.3 with improved seeds, fer-
          tilizers and pesticides
    3.4 with improved seeds, fer-
          tilizers, pesticides and
          other input(s)

    4.0 <u>Unirrigated land</u>
    4.1 with improved seeds
    4.2 with improved seeds and
          fertilizers
    4.3 with improved seeds, fer-
          tilizers and pesticides
    4.4 with improved seeds, fer-
          tilizers, pesticides and
          other input(s)

Table 7-5 (continued)

C. Production (1,000 tons, etc.)	Base Period	Plan Years 1	2	3	4 ...n
5.0 Irrigated land					
5.1 with improved seeds					
5.2 with improved seeds and fertilizers					
5.3 with improved seeds, fertilizers and pesticides					
5.4 with improved seeds, fertilizers, pesticides and other input(s)					
6.0 Unirrigated land					
6.1 with improved seeds					
6.2 with improved seeds and fertilizers					
6.3 with improved seeds, fertilizers and pesticides					
6.4 with improved seeds, fertilizers, pesticides and other input(s)					
TOTAL PRODUCTION (5.0 + 6.0)					

(d) Output. Agricultural output may be projected by (1) extrapolating past trends, (2) relating output to expected changes in GNP, (3) from estimates derived from international comparative studies, (4) judgments of experienced exports, or (5) by relating output to inputs. Each of these methods has serious shortcomings.

When attempts are made to predict output by the use of simple linear projections based on past trends, there is an implicit assumption that the factors which determined the area and (or) the yield of a crop in the past will continue to operate with the same intensity and timing in the future. But there can be no assurance of this. Similarly, attempts to predict agricultural output by relating it (by regression) to GNP or its components (where the latter variables are obtained from an aggregate projection) assume a stable relationship between sector and aggregate output which cannot be justified on logical grounds. But demand and supply interrelationships between agricultural output and GNP are much too complex to be stated in terms of fixed relationships.

It is sometimes recommended that a country which is handicapped by inadequate planning data seek out a second country with good statistics which is similar in character, pattern of farming and general line of economic development. If one can be found, it is considered legitimate to use the relationships in that country to project output and other variables in the first country. This may appear to be a plausible approach, but it is hard to see how one can be sure that reliable estimates of output for a country may be obtained in this way.

The projection of output by combining estimates produced by technical, administrative or other experts familiar with the agricultural sector also has serious deficiencies since it necessarily introduces subjective factors which may or may not add up to good projections. Experts from different disciplines may have only a partial view of the agricultural sector and may, in addition, use amateurish methods to predict output.

Attempts to project production on the basis of inputs applied, as already discussed, also raise problems. Among these is the fact that in addition to the quantities of inputs used, crop yields also depend on the quality of inputs, the level of technology, and the way resources are combined and managed. The productive quality of land can vary widely, even within short distances; the extent to which capital goods are employed can greatly affect output; and the appropriate organization and management of complementary strategic resources can product interactions with dramatic effects on production. These factors are frequently difficult if not impossible to quantify. Nonetheless, attempts are frequently made to express relationships quantatively between inputs and output through one of the four following means: (1) a production function, (2) an input-output matrix or table, (3) linear programming, or (4) "yardsticks".

The ideal way of assessing the contribution which inputs make to output is with a production function, either simple or complex. In agriculture, returns to inputs typically tend to increase more than proportionately at first, then to level out and finally, to decline more than proportionately. However, the statistical, technical and economic data required to construct a production function which accurately describes output in terms of increasing, constant and decreasing returns is rarely available in developing countries. Even when accurate data are available from carefully controlled conditions on experimental farms, the results may not be applicable on ordinary farms, even in the same area. Moreover, although many variables are usually associated with changes in output, it is very difficult to construct an appropriate production function which includes more than a very few relevant variables. As a result, most production functions formulated in developing countries cannot explain past changes in output over time on the basis of the inputs applied.

Since a production function that cannot satisfactorily explain past output can hardly be used to project future changes, production functions have not been used widely in developing countries, except for functions applicable to a few research, plantation-type or model farms which are rarely representative of conditions prevailing on most farms.

An input-output table is also difficult to prepare and employ effectively. To be useful for projecting production, an input-output table must be disaggregated sufficiently to show major commodities or subgroups of commodities separately. To the extent that the table combines these commodities into groups so that it is no longer possible to identify them separately, the input-output table has reduced value for projecting the output of each major commodity. However, the scarcity of data in developing countries, especially for inputs, often makes it too difficult to construct an input-output table which is sufficiently disaggregated to be of much use for forecasting production of each major commodity. Even if data are available to prepare a sufficiently disaggregated input-output table, it is not likely to be applicable to different regions in a country because of the frequently considerable regional variance in types of farms and farming conditions.

Moreover, the usefulness of an input-output table is limited where there is only a small degree of inter-sectoral interdependence in an economy. The lack of sectoral interdependence is typical of peasant agriculture because it may not use many inputs from other sectors and much of the output goes directly into final consumption in producers' households.

Input-output tables have other important limitations. A major shortcoming is their use of fixed coefficients, a use which implies a linear relationship between input and output. In fact, however, most agricultural relationships are subject to diminishing returns, a non-linear relationship.

The use of fixed coefficients makes an input-output table a static model of production, in which the elasticity of inputs is constant over time, when the very nature of the development process is dynamic, i.e., one in which the elasticity of inputs varies over time. It varies because price and income elasticities of demand, technical processes, capital and labour productivity, substitutions of one input for another, etc., are likely to change as development proceeds. These actions usually generate changes in input requirements and coefficients. Moreover, since changes are likely to differ from one region to another, coefficients prepared for a nation or for a specific region are likely to be inaccurate in varying degrees from region to region

A cardinal feature of the input-output table is the assumption of constant prices. But this is an unrealistic assumption for planning purposes since development usually changes relative prices of products in each sector. It is not easy to make adjustments for these price changes and the resultant changes in the composition of inputs and outputs.

Since an input-output table refers to a particular year in the past, it is applicable to future years only on the assumption that the input-output coefficients in the table will prevail in the future. But this may be an invalid assumption. Weather, for instance, (the impact of which is inseparable from other determinants of output), may differ in the future from the past, with profound effects on input-output relationships. Technical progress may also make a difference to these relationships. It is possible to adjust coefficients in an input-output table on the basis of assumptions concerning the impact of technical progress. But there is no scientifically reliable way of doing so. It can therefore be a disadvantage in developing countries where the objective often is to change past ratios of capital, labour, and other inputs to land, to make output projections on the basis of input-output tables (or production functions, for that matter), which are necessarily tied to the past.

In this respect, linear or nonlinear programming techniques have an advantage, since they permit the systematic exploration of alternative assumptions concerning the effect of inputs on output. This approach allows projections to be made on the basis of changes considered desirable, within specified constraints, in the proportion of resources used,

the mix of commodities to be produced, the proportional contributions to different regions to output,
or other structural relationships. However, linear
programming is a refined mathematical technique
which depends heavily on the accuracy of the data
used; and although the data requirements for linear
programming models are usually more modest than for
input-output tables and production functions based
on time series, they are still great, even where
only two variables are involved. Where, in fact,
only two variables are employed, the problems which
linear programming can solve are restricted; and
where more than two variables are used, linear programming usually requires computer facilities.
Moreover, good results from linear programming depends on realistic assumptions, and it cannot always
be expected that such assumptions will be made.

Nevertheless, there is little question that
linear programming can be helpful, where the required data, sound assumptions and computer
facilities are available, in determining how scarce
resources should be allocated to yield the highest
income, or in determining what combination of inputs
will provide the highest output at lowest cost. In
the developed countries, as well as in a few developing countries with the required resources, these
potential benefits have stimulated the use of linear
programming. But the lack of data, computer facilities and other resources in most poor countries have
encouraged the use of less formal techniques than
linear programming despite their yield of less than
optimal solutions to projection problems.

A fourth way of expressing the relationship
between inputs and output is by means of "yardsticks" or response coefficients. These are essentially ratios which estimate required inputs or
predict specific crop yields for a given resource
input; and are norms calculated from field data
which provide estimates of the likely contribution
of specific inputs to specific crops. If the yardsticks are derived from a sufficiently large number
of trials for individual crops at the farm level
under average conditions (not experimental farms
where conditions are likely to vary substantially
from those on most farms), in different ecological
regions and subregions, with due account of differences in soil, etc., their application to specific
farms should be more realistic than coefficients
obtained from an input-output table or a production
function.

Although the yardstick as a concept is easy

enough to understand, it is often difficult to
apply. One limitation of the yardstick is that it
is likely to vary from one ecological area to
another; a second is that technological change may
make it necessary to revise yardsticks frequently; a
third applies to yardsticks expressed (as they often
are) in value instead of physical terms during
periods of changing prices; a fourth is that yardsticks imply constant returns to additional inputs,
in defiance of the principles of diminishing or increasing returns; and a fifth limitation arises from
the need for "composite yardsticks", which are
difficult to calculate, rather than yardsticks
which measure the effect on output of one input in
isolation, since several inputs are usually used
together.

Yet, despite these limitations and although
yardsticks provide much less information than production functions, input-output tables or linear and
non-linear programming, they are to be recommended
for developing countries, especially in the earlier
planning stages, since they are simpler to apply
than any other device.

It should be clear from the preceding account
that there is no way of projecting agricultural output without allowing for wide margins of error. The
actual methods used to forecast production must depend on conditions prevailing in the country concerned. Despite its deficiencies, extrapolation of
past trends is a widely used technique, in India
among other countries. FAO counsels the use of
yardsticks as the best available means to project
output on the basis of inputs in poorer countries.
Whatever the means employed, however, there is
always the need to use the best available judgement
to adjust the results obtained.

It is also useful, and a common practice, for
planners to carry out quantitative analysis built
around several scenarios. Typically, three
scenarios are chosen - a trend scenario, based on an
extrapolation of past trends in production, an optimistic scenario based on substantially improved
agricultural performance and a medium-growth scenario based on the hypothesis of more modest growth
rates in both agriculture and the overall economy.
These scenarios relate to demand projections, too,
reflecting different assumptions about population
growth and rates of economic development (and per
caput income).
(d) Projecting supply. The projection problem is
complicated further because for the preparation of

an agricultural plan the ultimate requirements are usually not estimates of future production so much as future supply; and, unfortunately, estimates of future supply are surrounded by even greater uncertainties than those of future production. For any period, the supply of a commodity is the algebraic sum of production plus imports, minus exports, plus additions to or subtractions from stock carried over from preceding periods. Thus, in addition to estimation of production, supply projections require the estimation of future foreign trade movements and domestic changes of stocks. In the short run, estimation of future production and foreign trade may be feasible, but estimation of future changes of stocks is always a hazardous undertaking because of uncertainties about the factors which influence the expectations of holders of stocks. The task of estimating supply in the long run is likely to be even more troublesome because of the difficulties of predicting technological changes, shifts in prices of agricultural inputs and outputs, the speed with which farmers will react to the promise of more profitable production than in the past, as well as long-term movements of foreign trade and stocks.

Attempts to predict supply response have been made by various methods, including budget analyses of model-type farms, linear programming, and analyses of time series data. In addition, the construction of agricultural supply models has become a common econometric exercise among scholars who seek to determine appropriate quantitative relationships to provide reliable estimates of changes in output associated with changes in inputs and prices.

Because the supply of agricultural commodities depends on output to a considerable extent, special attempts have been made to derive commodity supply elasticities and supply functions from production functions. Supply functions are mainly concerned with the way the output of a commodity is likely to vary with price in a specified technological and economic environment. But the results obtained thus far, from supply functions based on production functions, have not proved to be empirically reliable. Aside from the fact that it is exceedingly difficult to construct appropriate production functions, and to obtain production and supply data, it has proved impossible thus far to identify ex ante the inputs which will actually be employed by farmers.

Official input targets are sometimes used to project output, but there are likely to be great

differences between input targets and imputs
actually available as well between inputs available
and those actually applied by farmers. Yet it is
the inputs actually applied, not input targets or
total available inputs, which determine the yields
realized.

Unless and until it becomes possible to predict
with reasonable certainty such factors as relative
prices of commodities; production costs; availability of inputs and funds for their acquisition by
farmers; the lag between the availability of inputs
and the means to acquire them, on the one hand, and
producers' use of the inputs, on the other; as well
as technological change and the impact of policy and
institutional factors in raising productivity per
unit of input; a supply function derived from a production function can only be expected to serve as
one among several guidelines in the estimation of
supply.

The considerations which have thus far reduced
the usefulness of production functions for estimating future supply are also generally applicable to
attempts to project supply on the basis of input-
output matrices and linear programming. Although
research to devise reliable econometric techniques
for projecting production and supply is going forward, until now the determinants of output, and the
inputs which farmers actually employ in production,
have proved to be too elusive to enclose in an
econometric function.

In the absence of acceptable econometric means
for making direct estimates of market supply and indirect estimates of supply with production functions,
input-output tables or linear programming, simpler
empirical techniques have usually been employed in
less-developed countries for these purposes. These
usually relate supply to variables like acreage,
output or incomes. Since output is generally considered to be the best of these points of reference,
most projections employ average sales-to-output
ratios of different crops, estimated from surveys,
to project market supply. However, the use of constant sales-to-output ratios is likely to produce
inaccurate projections of marketed surpluses.
Furthermore, estimates of supply obtained from
sales-to-output ratios are subject to even wider
margins of error because the output estimates on
which they are based are themselves frequently only
rough approximations.

3. Reconciling Demand and Supply

When projections of demand for a commodity have been made independently of those of supply, it is necessary to balance the two. FAO recommends that this be done by the construction of a "balance sheet" for each major commodity, which shows the volume and value of the commodity (either in aggregate or per capita terms) likely to be available and the use to which it is to be put in a given year. A commodity balance sheet is generally expressed in the following form:

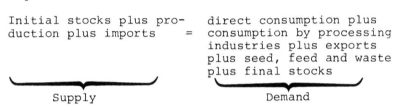

Initial stocks plus production plus imports $=$ direct consumption plus consumption by processing industries plus exports plus seed, feed and waste plus final stocks

Supply   Demand

The left side of the equation represents the availability or supply of the commodity, and the right side the uses or demand for it.

If prepared as indicated, balance sheets will contain the information needed to identify deficit and surplus commodities and to make adjustments required to equate supply and demand. If demand exceeds supply, one or more of the following adjustments is required: (a) the area in the crop concerned must be increased, either by transfer of land from other crops or by additional investment in land reclamation and (or) irrigation; (b) the rate of yield from land must be raised by intensified use of inputs; (c) demand must be reduced by appropriate price and (or) other policies; (d) imports must be increased to cover the deficit; or (e) stocks must be reduced. However, if supply exceeds demand, one or more of the following adjustments is required: (a) the area in the crop concerned must be reduced by transfer of the cropped land to other uses; or by reduced investment in land reclamation and (or) irrigation; (b) yields must be lowered by reduced use of inputs; (c) demand must be increased by appropriate price and (or) other policies; (d) exports must be increased, or (e) stocks must be increased.

As this listing makes very clear, the determination of the relative shares of total supplies to be met from domestic production and imports, or the allocation of resources between agricultural production for domestic consumption and for exports involves the making of choices. Since the same land, labour and financial resources may be used to produce alternative crops, decisions on the best balance between production and imports, production for domestic consumption or export, or the regional location of production require consideration of the cost-benefit relationships involved. It if is considered desirable that the choice made should result in the best use of available resources in accordance with the principle of comparative advantage, appraisals of costs and benefits in this context should be made. If foreign exchange, skilled labour or other scarce resources are constraints, this will have to be considered in estimating costs; or if employment, foreign exchange earnings or savings are considered important, the benefits to be expected from programmes in these fields will have to be taken account of, too. Indirect as well as direct costs and benefits must also be considered.

It is no easy matter to make the right choices among all possible alternatives. In practice, however, many factors tend to simplify the comparative cost-benefit exercise because the possibilities for increasing production of a commodity during the period of an agricultural plan are usually restricted. For example, the extent to which irrigation works can be completed during the period of a medium-term plan are limited by the capacity of the construction industry; the availability of extension workers is limited by the time required for recruitment and training; and the pace at which farmers adopt new production techniques is governed by traditional, institutional and sociological factors. Because of such factors, there are likely to be only a few practicable alternatives from which to choose.

Moreover, choices involving the allocation of resources and the determination of the shares of total demand to be met from domestic production and imports cannot be made without reference to national conditions and objectives. Where total imports, both non-agricultural and agricultural, exceed total exports, it may be necessary to revise agricultural production goals and resource allocations. For this reason as well as for others, it is essential that the cost-benefit relationships for all practicable alternatives be explored during the period of the stocktaking and diagnostic survey to allow planners the maximum flexibility in setting targets during the planning process.

While commodity balance sheets are attractive media for equating supply with demand, they have disadvantages. The data required for their con-

struction are often hard to obtain, and probably the
most difficult problem is to estimate subsistence
supplies - those produced by farm and other rural
households for their own consumption, or for local
barter. The construction of commodity balance
sheets is also a time-consuming affair. Moreover,
commodity sheets may be unnecessary for crops in
which little change in supply is required to meet
demand, or vice versa. The preparation of commodity
balance sheets may also be unnecessary where shortfalls in some crops are compensated for by surpluses
in others. These considerations help to account for
the fact that the commodity balance sheet approach
has taken hold in few developing countries thus far.

Chapter 8

SETTING TARGETS AND ALLOCATING RESOURCES

Summary
    Clearly defined objectives are a feature of
good planning. When these are quantified in
specific terms, backed up by policies, investments and other proposed actions, they become
targets. As social and political factors play
a crucial role in target selection, politicians
have the final say in this matter. Planners
have the task of explaining what is involved in
choosing the various targets. Target setting
is a difficult art. Set too high, targets may
become very discouraging or even meaningless,
and too low a waste of resources and output.
Targets are sometimes confused with projections
but they are quite different. Care is needed
in deciding upon the number of targets.
Generally the fewer the better and they should
be flexible enough to take account of changed
circumstances. Moving from projections to
targets involves a process of iteration, or
successive approximation, in an attempt to
harmonise demand, supply and resources. Several
methods are available to deal with this problem.
Basically, they all involve some attempt, however feeble, to allocate the nation's resources
to best advantage. It is not an exact calculation because reliable data on social costs and
returns in the agricultural sector are generally inadequate. Even so, and even in the poorest of countries, this effort should be worthwhile. Targets should always try to take
account of regional and local differences,
although excessive disaggregation can be self-
defeating. Target setting should be a two-
way process - with planning from the bottom
upwards and from the top downwards. But

sector input and output targets need not be the
totals of all regions or localities. National
objectives have priority and some adjustment
may be required in local and regional target
setting. It is imperative that those responsible for achieving production targets have a
voice in setting them.

Clearly defined objectives are essential to good
planning. If the objectives are unclear, even, as
sometimes happens, contradictory, they provide poor
guidelines for planners, with the likely result that
the planning process will produce a document chart-
ing an uncertain course.
    Even when an objective is clearly defined, it
is not always easy to determine from the plan
whether there are enough resources available for the
objective to be fully or even partially achieved. If
an agricultural plan aims to increase production,
for example, reduce rural unemployment or raise the
incomes of poor farmers, the question is not so much
what is generally meant, but what specific changes
are expected e.g., a 15% rise in wheat production
within 4 years, or a 10% cut in rural unemployment
in say 3 years. To meet this question requires the
setting of specific targets. They provide for the
viability of the objectives to be tested against the
availability of resources, the precise earmarking of
resources for achieving objectives, and, lastly, the
establishment of suitable criteria to measure the
success of the plan.
    Quantification of objectives in the form of
targets has importance for planning beyond these
advantages, it requires that those who set the targets choose from among available alternatives, the
direction, scope, relative priorities and size of
the development effort. This is ultimately a
political responsibility because, as with the
setting of objectives, it involves political, social
as well as economic choices. Consequently, targets
must be set by political authorities rather than by
planners. Nor may the political authorities cede
this obligation to the planners. For only if the
political authorities accept responsibility for
selecting targets, which set the levels of the development effort, is there any reason to hope that
they will accept responsibility for adopting the
strategies, policies and measures required to attain
plan targets.
    There are those who believe that planners
should try "to sell" their ideas to the political

leadership. But even they are likely to concede
that plans must be approved by politicians before
being implemented, and the political acceptability
of a plan is ... a prerequisite of any practical
programme. Planners almost always have their preferences and cannot be expected to stifle them in
pursuit of value-free planning. When these are
based on sound technical grounds, they have every
right to a hearing. But when they reflect their
social and political views, it is hard to see how
they, as planners, can claim special rights. Planners must accept the reality that the social and
political factors in the planning process are pre-
rogatives of the political leadership.

However, although planners must defer to
political authorities in setting targets, they do
have an important role to play. Thus planners can
provide political authorities with useful information about the economic consequences of setting
targets at various levels. Different targets
usually require different policies, investments and
other actions, and planners should present political
authorities with a series of alternatives, based on
projections or other estimates of current and future
situations, which allow the political authorities to
weigh the advantages and disadvantages of each
alternative. Only by careful consideration of the
cost and other implications of each target, is it
possible to make a rational choice among them.

Targets are thus a way of getting specific about
"who gets what" in the development process, and this
unavoidably affects people differently. The political authorities are likely to know what they consider desirable, but the planners should have the
technical knowledge to tell them whether what the
political authorities consider desirable is also
feasible. Targets selected should thus attempt to
balance the desirable with the possible. In the
end, therefore, planners must have a say in the
setting of targets if plans are to be capable of
being put into practice.

1. Targets vs. Projections

Success in reaching a target may mean, of course,
that the target was set too low in relation to what
might have been achieved with a more dynamic policy
... but experience indicates that what is considered
a "desirable" target is more likely to be higher,
not lower, than what is possible. This is most
likely for production targets, as understated targets are usually for inputs, e.g. fertilizer. It

sometimes happens that understated input targets and overstated production targets exist side by side. The outcome is not difficult to foresee, even if the input targets are fulfilled. Unrealistically high targets are sometimes justified on the ground that they are needed to inspire greater levels of effort. They may also be set for political motives. The difficulty is that when a target is set unrealistically high, it may have the opposite effect. Indeed, if a target is set so high as to be obviously impossible to attain, it runs the risk of being ignored. It fails then either to inspire high levels of effort or to guide planners in their proper work.

In the longer run, ridiculously high targets raise the possibility that success will not be recognised when it has, in fact, been achieved. If a reasonable production target calls for an average increase of, say, 3 percent per year, but the target is fixed at 5 percent, achievement of the 3 percent increase appears to be a failure rather than a success. One consequence then might be that in seeking successes to emulate and build upon, planners would pass over as failure what was actually success.

Despite the clear disadvantage of unduly high targets, they are common in development plans. While increases in agricultural production of 4 to 5 percent annually are widely considered to be very respectable, many developing countries set much higher targets.

There is nothing inherently wrong in setting agricultural targets at levels substantially higher than in the past, provided appropriate steps are taken to ensure the effort needed to achieve the targets. But few of those concerned seem to be adequately aware of the effort required to achieve targets included in agricultural plans. An example of realistic planning, however, is given in Table 8-1, comparing targets and actual results in Kenya's agriculture between 1966 and 1978, with a useful division between monetary and non-monetary production.

When governments, or planners, fail to provide for adequate measures, services or other means, required to achieve targets, it is in effect relegating the targets to the level of projections. No measures or special means need be employed in dealing with a projection, since it is merely an estimate of what will happen under given assumptions about the behaviour of producers, businessmen,

Table 8-1   Growth Rates in Kenya Agriculture, Actual and Planned, 1966-1978

per cent

Sector	1st Five-Year Plan 1966-1970		2nd Five-Year Plan 1970-1974		3rd Five-Year Plan 1974-1978		4th Five-Year Plan	
	Target	Actual	Target	Actual	Target	Actual	Target 1976-1983	Target 1978-1983(b)
Monetary Production	6.7	4.2	6.0	5.2	6.7	4.8(a)	6.9	6.3
Non-monetary Production	3.2	4.7	3.5	2.4	3.8	2.6(a)	3.0	3.0
Total (c)	4.8	4.5	4.5	3.7	5.2	3.7(a)	5.0	4.7

FOOTNOTES:
(a) Preliminary estimates from the Central Bureau of Statistics, based on information for 1974-1977.
(b) The plan period started at the beginning of 1979 which is in the middle of the crop and finan-
    cial year 1978-79. In this table, and throughout the plan the plan period is noted as 1979-83
    but covers the year 1978-79 to 1982-83.
(c) The total growth rate is the weighted average of the actual or projected growth rates of the
    monetary and non-monetary sectors. During the period of the 4th Plan, monetary production will
    comprise slightly more than half (51 percent) of the total production and non-monetary slightly
    less than half (49 percent). As the monetary sector is growing at a faster rate than the non-
    monetary sector, the monetary sector will have an increasing share of total production.
Source: Development Plan for the Period 1979 to 1983, Part 1, Republic of Kenya. Nairobi 1979.p.213

consumers, governments or combinations of these,
within a given economic, social and political
framework, and time horizon. And while a projection
may be converted into a target by adopting appropriate policies and other means to ensure its realisation, what is called a target is, in fact, no more
than a projection if palpably inadequate provision
is made for its fulfilment. There is only one
possible exception to this rule: long-term (perspective), as distinguished from medium- and short-term
plan targets (like objectives) may be used as indicators of future trends than as operational
devices. Nevertheless, even for long-term targets,
it is desirable to indicate what supporting means
will be required to achieve them.

Although planners are supposed in theory to
carefully distinguish between projection and targets
in practice they often do not. The test of a target
is whether adequate means are provided for its
attainment. To the extent that the means are inadequate for this purpose, the "target" is really no
more than a projection.

The need to provide appropriate means for
achieving targets is all the more important where,
as in market economy countries, plan targets are
only guidelines, or indicative, of government in-
tentions rather than orders whose violation may
invoke legal or other sanctions. In the classic
version of the Soviet planning model, there was no
need to stress that targets were more than projections, since the system of balances employed in the
planning process was a conscious attempt to ensure
that a sufficient amount of needed inputs would be
made available to achieve output targets.

It is fair to say that output targets in the
Soviet planning system generally meet the test of a
target enunciated in the preceding paragraph to the
extent that planners are successful in balancing
inputs and outputs (Yet, Soviet agricultural planning has had very mixed results in practice.).

In the planning regimes of the market economy
countries, however, command production targets,
supported by commanded supplies of inputs which
planners have estimated to be necessary to attain
production targets, are virtually unknown. In these
countries, therefore, governments need to make
special efforts to provide that inputs are made
available at appropriate times and in amounts, combinations and locations calculated to attain plan
targets. Experience has shown that it is crucial,
of course, to be reasonably sure that the physical

means and organizations required are available.

2. The Kind and Number of Targets

Planning specialists have different views about the kind and number of targets which should be included in an agricultural plan. Those at one extreme contend that the plan must contain specific targets for each of the activities designed to affect agricultural output, while others hold that for market economies which participate in international trade (and hence can import agricultural commodities they do not produce domestically), agricultural productivity targets are more useful than output targets. Other specialists have other views. Thus, Arthur Lewis states flatly that "most of the targets for commodity output are not to be taken seriously; what matters is the level of total investment and output..."

However, if the targets included in agricultural plans are any indication, most planners prefer to set targets for many, if not all, efforts designed to influence agricultural output.

Production targets have been set in virtually every plan in various degrees of aggregation. Thus, while many countries have set targets for the output of individual crops, some have them for groups of crops e.g. cereals, vegetables or fruits, for subsectors such as field crops, animal products, forest products or fish, or for the entire agricultural sector. Targets have been set in physical terms; in value, usually in constant prices; or as production indexes (sometimes subdivided into subindexes for domestic consumption and export).

Not all the targets in a plan are likely to be of equal importance. Thus, a target for the construction of a number of farm buildings during a given period is less important than a target for increasing production of a major crop, and could be dispensed with. Every plan is likely to include targets which are not essential to the plan's implementation. Since the greater the number of targets, the greater the difficulty of fulfilling them, the more desirable it is to reduce the number of targets to a minimum. Even the U.S.S.R., which used to consider it necessary to set production targets for many individual commodities, now sets far fewer.

One way of reducing the number of targets is to combine several targets into one. A combined target is usually easier to achieve than separate targets for each component because one component can be substituted for another; for example, the output target for grain may be reached despite a shortfall in rice production because the wheat and millet targets are over-fulfilled. Aggregate targets are useful as measures of overall progress, but they provide limited guidance to producers as to the emphasis to be given to individual commodities.

The greater the number of targets, the greater the need for information; and the information gap can be more than statistical. Ambitious farm mechanisation targets set in some national plans, for example, may have little real basis for achievement, in the light of limited experience with the upkeep and repair of farm machinery.

There is a widespread tendency for planners, who sometimes believe they can foresee the future, and administrators, who may wish to control it, to engage in the practice of "targetry", even when it makes little sense to set targets for activities over which a government can have little control. Thus, while it is reasonable for political authorities to set a target for a major increase in irrigation which will receive the investment funds required from the government, it makes no sense for the government to set a target for minor irrigation which requires decisions by many farmers about digging wells and canals, when the decisions are to be encouraged by nothing more than the exhortations of extension workers.

In summary, therefore, it is desirable to limit the number of targets to the minimum to fulfil plan objectives; to aggregate the targets as much as possible, given the need for targets to provide guidance to producers; and to avoid setting targets for activities which the government cannot influence or control.

Since most planners do not seem ready to rely solely on targets for productivity increases or for improving technology, production targets are needed. Because climate, plant diseases, pests and other relatively uncontrollable factors are likely to cause great variations in output from year to year, which cannot be foreseen, it may be better to fix production targets for the last year of a plan period rather than for each year. Production targets for the terminal year of a plan also provide the time needed to adopt measures required to change trends. However, fluctuations in output are sometimes so great that even a target for the terminal year of a plan period may not be effective. It may thus be best to use either an average annual output target or an aggregative target for a plan period.

Events occurring after the start of a plan period may soon make it obvious that targets have been set too high or too low; or targets may have to be set tentatively because of uncertainties which cannot be resolved at the time a plan is prepared. In either case, targets may have to be revised after the start of the plan period. In agriculture, more than in any other sector, targets must be flexible and subject to revision to take account of changed resources and other circumstances. It is important that the trend of production conforms to longer-term rather than to annual targets.

Input targets are often useful. But they should be used with discretion since they are not by themselves a satisfactory measure of development; they may overstate progress because they are usually stated on a gross rather than a net basis e.g. including new irrigation canals dug while ignoring those which are falling into decay, and input-output relationships on which they are based may be faulty. Nevertheless, use of input targets may be justified because increased outputs may require the planned provision of certain inputs. Moreover, where they are used, a shortfall in input targets can provide an indication of why output targets were not achieved, or whether estimated input-output relationships were accurate.

3. From Projections to Targets

A. Methods of setting targets. It is possible, and indeed common, for planners to obtain agricultural targets simply by setting output targets equal to the estimated increase in demand for agricultural commodities over a plan period; and input targets equal to the estimated inputs required to achieve the output targets. Aside from the circular reasoning (since demand often depends on output), this approach implies that output is a function of inputs solely, rather than a complex amalgam of technological change, institutional factors, climate and producer motivation, interacting with the inputs.

This approach also implies that the planning problem in developing countries is to raise output to the level of demand. But this is not necessarily correct. It is true that if a country has a chronic food deficit which has to be met by imports, it should give priority to expanding food production and reducing imports. However, if a country is self-sufficient in food production, it might give priority to increasing exports or the output of nutritionally superior foods.

If the major weakness is on the supply side, targets are likely to differ from those when they are on the demand side. Or if priority is given to increased production for domestic consumption, agricultural targets may differ from those set when the priority is to increase production for exports. And if the objective is to increase rural incomes, targets probably will not be the same as when the primary objective is to increase agricultural output.

Yet, regardless of the targets to be set for a plan period, estimates must be made of demand for domestic consumption and exports; as well as for supply from current production, imports and stocks accumulated from previous years. In addition, estimates must be made of the extent of financial and real resources, especially those in short supply, that are available for use as inputs. Together, these elements are essential ingredients for the setting of targets and all are inter-dependent.

Because of the closeness of their relationship, it is possible to begin the target-setting process with the resource, supply or demand estimates. While planners might differ about which of the three to start with, all would agree that supply and demand must eventually be equated, within the limits of available resources. This equilibrium is not easy to achieve because inconsistencies often show up among the supply, demand and resource estimates. When this occurs, the method by which they are made mutually consistent must be repeated as often as necessary, with changed assumptions and considerable backward and forward adjustments until, after as many exercises as necessary in iteration, and successive approximation, final targets are evolved. So frequently is the process of iteration and successive approximation employed that it has been called the essence of target setting. The need to harmonize demand, supply and resources implies that regardless of which of these estimates are made the starting point of target setting, the first targets derived from the sequence adopted are likely to be tentative and subject to considerable adjustment. Indeed, the choice of one or another estimate is only the beginning of target-setting.

There are countries which have started the target-setting exercise by allocating available resources to different subsectors, branches or crops in the agricultural sector. This approach is used where demand is not thought to be as limiting a factor as resources. In some countries, target-

setting starts with a review of projected supply
which is justified on the ground that past agricultural production provides the best basis for determining whether future growth targets are realistic.
This approach is also supported, despite its
inadequacies, because statistics on past production
are likely to be more readily available than demand
information.

But in most countries, the process by which
tentative targets are set begins with demand because
it is considered that the best way of increasing
welfare is to adjust available resources and supply,
to the greatest extent possible, to meet demand requirements. In this approach, the process begins
with calculations of market demand, followed by
estimation of resources and production capacities in
whatever sequence seems best.

In calculating demand, it is important to
include food supplies (including provisions for
nutritional improvement) as well as reserve stocks,
requirements of raw materials for domestic industry
and expected exports. More than one set of projections of domestic demand may have to be made
before even a first approximation of the likely
level of demand can be estimated for the plan
period. The eventual result will be a set of data
of the kind given in Table 8-2 which illustrates the
targets set in Kenya for food, industrial and export
crops, and livestock products, in the period 1976-83.

B. <u>Allocating resources</u>. Once demand has been tentatively estimated, the problem is then one of selecting, among feasible alternatives, a pattern of
resource use designed to exploit to the maximum the
production possibilities of the available resources
to meet demand, within the limits of plan's objectives. While the primary objective is generally to
increase the value of production as much as possible,
another area may have priority. If, for example,
the objective is to increase the level of farmers'
incomes, resources must be allocated in ways consistent with this in mind. Whatever the prime
objective, resources should be used in such a way as
to maximise the value of output, after adequate provision has been made to achieve that objective.

To obtain the greatest possible value of production within the limits set by development
objectives, available resources must in theory be
allocated to provide equal marginal productivity
to each resource in each use. The question of what
quantity of resources should be allocated to each

Table 8-2   Total Value of Production of Agricultural Commodities
in Kenya, Actual and Targets, 1976-83

(K£'000 in 1976 Prices)

	1976 Actual	1978 Estimate	1983 Target	AVERAGE ANNUAL RATES OF GROWTH	
				1976-83 Per Cent	1978-83 Per Cent
Food Crops:					
Maize	94,486	101,188	120,224	3.5	3.5
Wheat	11,248	11,429	12,030	1.0	1.0
Rice (paddy)	2,670	3,217	4,449	7.6	6.7
Sorghum, millets, etc	14,196	15,372	19,614	4.7	5.0
Pulses	22,946	24,994	32,340	5.0	5.5
Potatoes	20,400	22,200	27,400	4.3	5.5
Other Starchy Roots	11,900	12,776	15,241	3.6	4.3
Fruits & Vegetables	8,346	9,399	14,469	8.2	3.6
Bananas & plantains	11,600	12,650	16,550	5.2	9.0
					5.5
TOTAL	197,792	213,225	262,317	4.1	4.3
Industrial Crops:					
Oil seeds and nuts	3,354	3,659	5,286	6.7	7.6
Sugar-cane	8,678	8,925	17,850	10.9	14.9
Seed cotton	1,669	1,773	3,546	11.4	14.9
Tobacco	237	444	1,096	24.5	19.8
Barley	2,644	2,805	6,042	12.5	16.6
TOTAL	16,582	17,606	33,820	10.7	14.0

Export Crops:					
Coffee	98,792	117,315	138,309	4.9	3.4
Tea	32,763	45,975	57,601	8.4	4.6
Sisal	3,856	3,739	4,674	2.8	4.6
Pineapples	1,314	1,823	3,562	15.3	14.3
Pyrethrum	4,347	4,347	7,763	8.6	12.3
Cashew-nuts	1,159	1,546	2,318	10.4	8.5
Wattle	515	515	552	1.0	1.0
TOTAL	142,746	175,260	214,779	6.0	4.2
Livestock Products:					
Milk (dairy products)	60,900	67,515	86,100	5.1	5.0
Beef cattle	34,198	33,223	39,770	2.2	3.7
Sheep and goats	17,050	17,574	21,509	3.4	4.1
Pigs	1,048	1,114	1,441	4.7	5.3
Poultry meat	8,890	9,843	12,383	4.9	4.7
Eggs	7,350	8,050	10,500	5.2	5.5
TOTAL	129,436	137,319	171,703	4.1	4.6
	486,556	543,410	682,619	5.0	4.7

Source: _Ibid_ p.215

sector, is inseparable from the returns which these resources can obtain from the different uses to which they can be put within each sector. For agriculture, this means that the resources it can claim solely on economic grounds depends on the extent to which the returns from these resources are lower, for the sector as a whole, than can be obtained from other sectors.

However, it is frequently difficult to obtain reliable data on social costs and returns in the agricultural sector. Agricultural development is largely a process of creating and building institutions, and investing in such things as research, extension, credit and marketing systems, for all of which it is often very hard to estimate the marginal costs and returns. Farmers, too, are guided by market prices which are often so distorted that the prices do not reflect accurately the true social cost of inputs or the social value of outputs. Unless "accounting" or "shadow" prices can be calculated which reflect the true social values, resources are likely to be wasted by allocation to uses of low productivity. At best, the calculation of accounting or shadow prices in agriculture is no easy matter and, at worst, it is extremely difficult.

These considerations have made it impracticable for most countries, rich and poor, to apply the principle of equal marginal productivity to each resource in each use. In practice, allocations to agriculture are often made on the basis of collective value judgements.

Yet, the severe limitation of resources in most poor countries is a sufficiently compelling reason to impose upon themselves the discipline of economic analysis to help make choices among alternatives for achieving development objectives. It is true, of course, that the techniques of economic analysis must often rely on ratios, coefficients and other data of less than desirable reliability, and that in the end there must always be a large element of judgement in the allocation of resources among different uses. The allocation of resources among crops, institutions and regions is usually more than a technical matter, since political and social as well as personal and sectional considerations are bound to enter the process. But far from obviating the need for economic analysis, these considerations make it all the more compelling that political authorities recognise the extent of the real price paid when they select economic alternatives - which

are less than the best available. In considering
alternatives, their comparative economic costs must
be examined. For one commodity, it may be more economic to meet imbalances between supply and demand
by imports and to pay for them with surpluses of
other commodities in which the country enjoys comparative advantage; for another commodity, it may be
more sensible to expand domestic production.

Commodities for which foreign demand exists
need to be evaluated to identify those whose export
is to be promoted. Commodities selected for this
purpose may vary depending on the primary development objective. If this is to increase national
output and income, most frequently the case, then
calculations should be made of the likely real profitability to the nation of each potential export
commodity so that they may be ranked in order of
preference.

If the primary aim is say to raise the level of
incomes of the poorer farmers, or to increase employment in rural areas, commodities which would
contribute to the achievement of this "non-growth"
objective should be identified first. Those which
contribute most to social profitability and foreign
exchange earnings should be selected in order to ensure the most efficient allocation of scarce resources.

Since capital and foreign exchange are scarce
resources which limit development in most poor
countries, final selection of commodities for export
promotion should be made on the basis of the commodities' ability to provide the highest possible
social rates of return on capital investment, and
earn the largest net amount of foreign exchange for
each unit of real domestic resource cost. This
implies that where foreign inputs (e.g. machinery or
fertilizers) are used, their cost must be deducted
from the foreign exchange to be realised from the
export price on earnings for each commodity. (See
Table 8-3). If the exchange rate is undervalued or
overvalued, or if a change in the exchange rate is
foreseen during the period of a forthcoming plan,
this must be taken into account in making the
following tests. The first test is to ensure that
capital yields a rate of return which is as high as
possible while satisfying social objectives, or in
other words, which yields a rate of return which is
above the minimum required to satisfy social objectives. A convenient way of applying this test is to
compare the real internal rates of return for all
potential export commodities which have been

Table 8-3

Estimated Impact of the Agricultural Plan on
the Balance of Payments, Kenya, 1976 – 1983

(KE'000 1976 Prices)

	1976 Actual	1978 Estimate	1983 Target	AVERAGE Annual Rates of Growth, Per Cent	
				1976-83	1978-83
Agricultural exports	191,000	226,500	277,400	5.5	4.1
Import substitution	48,811	53,453	99,285	10.7	13.2
SUB-TOTAL	239,811	279,953	376,685	6.7	6.1
Foreign exchange content of inputs	19,817	22,686	31,945	7.1	7.1
Net contribution to balance of payments	219,994	257,267	344,740	6.6	6.0

Source: Ibid p. 218

identified as capable of satisfying social objectives. The second test should be applied to ensure
that commodities selected for export promotion have
domestic resource costs at the prevailing shadow exchange rate which are lower than those of other commodities; or that such commodities should give
promise of earning more foreign exchange per unit of
cost than other commodities. Conversely, for agricultural commodities imported, those which should be
selected for domestic production should give promise
of saving the greatest amount of foreign exchange,
per unit of cost. Meeting this test ensures specia-
lisation in commodities which are consistent with
the principle of comparative advantage. It also
guarantees consumers in the exporting country prices
competitive with international prices, thereby contributing to the maximisation of their welfare.

In general, however, foreign exchange should be
given greater weight than the rate of return on investment because use of the foreign exchange test
precludes the possibility that a country, in pursuit
of a high rate of return, might unwittingly be led
to promote commodity exports in which it does not
have a comparative advantage. Since failure to pay
sufficient attention to the foreign exchange test
could lead to inefficient allocation of internal
resources, it must be considered the basic criterion
to be applied to commodities for export. Thus, if
the domestic cost of foreign exchange in terms of
e.g. a U.S. dollar earned exceeds the shadow rate of
exchange for a commodity, it should not be selected
for export production even if its rate of return on
investment is relatively high, unless there are
over-whelming non-economic considerations involved.
Exchange-rate policy may well largely determine
whether adequate incentives are available for agricultural production. There is still a tendency in
many developing countries, particularly in Africa,
to let real official exchange rates become over-
valued because of higher inflation at home than
abroad. Governments tend in these circumstances, to
rely more heavily on import restrictions rather than
on devaluation to conserve foreign exchange. Import
restrictions are likely to handicap agriculture,
however, particularly in its export trade, as high-
cost domestically produced inputs reduce its com-
petitiveness in world markets. Careful analysis of
trade and exchange-rate policy should thus have an
important place in any review of ways to improve the
efficiency of resource use in agriculture.

Where economic analysis is explicitly used in

the allocation of resources, whatever the shortcomings of the data and techniques, there is at
least recognition of the need for economic impar-
tiality in decisions involving the distribution of
scarce resources. And while it is true that impar-
tiality may have limitations at times, and that
judgment based on experience must always have the
last word, attempts to quantify costs and benefits
of available alternatives can add useful information
to help political authorities make rational decisions about the allocation of resources.

While different methods - simple and complex -
may be used to determine the resource allocation
pattern for agriculture, they should have in common
the capacity to allow comparison of the gains obtainable from one use of a given quantity of resources, with those from alternative uses of the same
resources. This is an essential condition for allocation along economically rational lines. But the
choice of a rational pattern of allocation goes far
beyond economic criteria. The setting of a target
almost invariably involves assumptions about policies, projects or programmes which differ from the
assumptions which apply to another target. While
technically, it is easy enough to introduce into
each of several output projections the policy, project or programme assumptions for achieving the target selected, thereby providing a "package" of items
for each target, it is frequently not done. For
reasons which do not withstand much scrutiny, some
assume that policy considerations, as well as the
allocation of resources, should follow rather than be
an integral part of the process of setting targets.

This cannot be desirable because each target
requires measures specifically designed to ensure
its realisation. Moreover, if there should be a
social or political limit to the degree to which a
particular policy or programme can be applied, it is
essential that this be known before final targets
are set. Otherwise, as happens frequently, targets
have little chance of being realised.

As stated earlier, in addition to the need to
relate targets and policies, it is also important to
relate output targets to physical inputs such as
fertilizers, pesticides, improved seeds and irrigation water. While the total volume, or value, of
inputs going into a country's agricultural sector is
often broadly known (see Table 8-4 as an example of
planned use of agricultural inputs, in Kenya, in
1976-83) the appropriate allocation to individual
crops is usually based on estimates from local know-

ledge. Many attempts have been made to estimate the
production equivalent of a particular crop attribu-
table to additional physical inputs. To the extent
that these estimates have proved reliable, they have
furnished useful yardsticks for allocating resources
to specific crops, regions, localities and farms
which specialise in these crops.

Table 8-4   Planned Use of Agricultural
             Inputs in Kenya, 1976-83

(K£'000 in 1976 Prices)

	1976 Actual	1978 Estimate	1983 Target	Annual Increase Per Cent	
				1976-83	1978-83
Fertilizer	9,664	11,481	17,666	9.0	9.0
Fuel and power	7,049	7,920	10,599	6.0	6.0
Bags	3,466	3,821	4,877	5.0	5.0
Feeds	5,441	6,113	8,181	6.0	6.0
Seeds	2,796	3,261	4,792	8.0	8.0
Chemicals	4,277	4,715	6,018	5.0	5.0
Livestock drugs	2,669	2,999	4,013	6.0	6.0
Services	5,344	6,005	8,035	6.0	6.0
Other	2,280	2,514	3,208	5.0	5.0
TOTAL	42,986	48,829	67,389	6.7	6.7

Source: Ibid p. 216

The use of the "input-output" or yardstick
approach calls for both the determination of the
most profitable combination of inputs, and identification of the most promising production units. The
inputs estimated to produce given outputs may then
be included in a series of budgets for regions,
localities and farms. Each budget is in fact an
estimate of costs and returns of what might happen
if a certain course of action were taken. By reference to these budgets, resources may be allocated
down to the farm level. This technique of "resource
budgeting" is particularly useful where one or more
resources are in very short supply. An important
part of planning is to ensure that adequate supplies
of scarce resources reach appropriate regions,
localities and producing units at the right time.
This may involve planning for the provision of
foreign exchange if inputs must be imported, or, if

necessary, public investment in transport and ware-
house facilities if these are required to distribute
and market the inputs efficiently.

In allocating resources, planners must try to
find out what production possibilities do in fact
exist. The planners' task is to allocate resources
known to be available and not, as is too often the
case, merely to estimate the quantity of resources
which would be required to meet a previously-fixed
target. When a target has been set with knowledge
that the resources required to realise it are not
available, the allocation exercise has little
practical value. While it is permissible, and even
desirable, to set preliminary e.g. demand-oriented
targets before allocating resources, the targets
have to be modified if subsequent study indicates
that the preliminary targets cannot be reached with
available resources.

When preliminary targets have been set, planners must check for compatability. They must
balance the target for overall agricultural consumption with the sum of production to be obtained
from various crops; they must also equate the provisions made for overall inputs and investments in
the agricultural sector with the sum of the inputs
and investments allocated to achieve production targets for each agricultural commodity; and they must
balance the global value target of agricultural
exports for the various products. Depending on the
development objectives, planners may also have to
check upon other targets. For example, if nutritional objectives are part of a plan, the value of
the diet obtainable from the planned production for
domestic consumption (in terms of calories, proteins
vitamins, etc.) has to be compared with the nutritional target set in the plan.

Comparisons of these balances will often reveal
incompatibilities which will necessitate revision of
some or all targets. But the task or harmonizing
the targets is much more than an arithmetical exercise, since to bring the balances into equilibrium
with each other may require changes in policies,
programmes and projects. This in turn, may introduce problems which will influence the setting of
final targets. Lastly, the targets for the sector
as a whole must be made consistent with the regional,
subregional and local agricultural targets. This
raises special problems.

4. <u>Regional and Local Targets</u>
An agricultural plan should ideally have a high

degree of specificity to take account of variations
in conditions and requirements among regions and
localities. This implies that each geographic unit
must have targets related to its condition. These
are required not only because each area is unique,
but also because of the inherent interdependence of
inputs in determining outputs. If input and output
targets in a national agricultural plan are specified only as aggregates, the interdependence of inputs may be overlooked. Thus the yield from irrigated water supplied in one place, fertilizer in a
second, and improved seed in a third will almost
certainly be lower than the same quantities of all
three inputs applied to the same acreage.

Because of the complementarity of inputs, targets for inputs and performance should be given in
the plan for each of the smallest feasible geographical units which will, however, vary in size
from country to country. Where, as in India, state
governments are responsible for implementing agricultural programmes, at least targets at the state
level are necessary. Within India's states, targets
have been divided into local targets for districts,
communities and villages. However, experience indicates that there is a productive limit to the
degree of disaggregation. It is a valuable incentive to have regions and localities establish and
try to realise their own production targets within a
state or national plan. If, however, the local targets must be phased, coordinated or aggregated into
a state or national plan, the effort involved may be
greater than it is worth.

For this reason, and also to avoid too circum-
scribed an approach, it is undesirable to set
separate targets below the level of the largest geographic area where agricultural conditions are
relatively homogeneous. For example, where a district includes several villages with essentially
similar supply, sale and other marketing conditions,
it is unnecessary to have targets for each village
if targets are set for the district.

It is not easy for central planners to set targets for the various regions and localities within a
country. Where farming systems are relatively homogeneous over most, or over sizeable areas of a
country, it is possible to select a few kinds of
farms as representative of the farms in the area concerned, and set targets for locality or region by
multiplying the targets for the representative farms
by the number of such farms in the area.

However, for most countries, the diversity of

farming systems makes it impossible to find a few "average" farms which can be considered as representative for substantial geographical areas. Moreover, apparent similarities among regions may be misleading. Thus, two regions with the same amount of production may still differ substantially in economic performance. For example, if there are important differences in the distribution of wealth in the two regions, their propensities to use labour or land-intensive methods, or to save, invest or use capital may differ. If the distribution of income in one region conforms to the normal or bell-shaped curve, the "average" farmer could be considered to be a representative producer for the region. But if the distribution of income in the other region were heavily-skewed, the "average" farmer (whether the mean, the median or the mode) would not be a representative producer because most of the output would not have been produced by average farmers, but by the few farmers who were wealthier than the average. And, of course, the "average" farmer in one region would differ from the "average" farmer in the other. Small wonder, then that there is increasing distrust of the concept of an average or representative farm for setting targets.

An agricultural plan with targets for an entire country based on an "average" situation in an "average" region, with similar targets, number of kinds of projects, work patterns or allocations of funds for every region and subregion, may prove unsuitable or inapplicable for particular areas in most countries. This approach to sector planning, aside from producing unrealistic targets and other errors of commission, may also lead to serious errors of omission.·

Indeed, there is a question whether it is even possible to get realistic regional and local targets by setting national targets and disaggregating them, without first determining for each region and locality the precise conditions which cultivators face, and their capacities to utilize inputs and increase production. It is not surprising, therefore, that where agricultural planning is based on the disaggregation of national targets, without adequate account taken of regional or local conditions and attitudes, that great differences may occur between expectation and achievement.

The failure of targets formulated at the centre to take adequate account of regional and local conditions had led to the suggestion that production targets be set from the village upwards instead of from headquarters downwards.

Clearly, however, a nation's targets for agriculture must be more than the sum of local or regional targets. If regional or local targets are set without regard to the general framework provided by national development objectives or resources, they may be inconsistent with national objectives; just as sector targets set without regard for regional and local conditions may be inconsistent with regional and local capabilities or aspirations.

Target setting for agriculture must, therefore, be seen as a two-way process involving planning from the bottom upwards as well as from the top downwards. To achieve this requires an upward and downward iterative process, through which by successive approximations, regional, local and sector targets are harmonised. Only by such mutual interaction can sector targets be set which are sufficiently realistic to meet both national aspirations and the needs of each region and locality. Limitations of combining the 'top-down' and 'bottom-up' approaches to planning are related to the time it involves (extensive consultation is time-consuming) and the spatial distribution of planning expertise, which is often very scarce at the local level.

But harmonisation does not mean that sector input and output targets must be totals of the input and output targets of all regions or localities. Where national objectives require that national targets be set for some commodities, it may be necessary to set targets for these commodities in regions and localities where they can be, or are, produced; but where national targets have not been set for commodities, there normally is no need for regional or local targets, except insofar as these areas may wish to set them for their own purposes.

Regional and local targets which take account of the conditions, capacities and aspirations in the areas concerned, can be set by the centre after consultations with regional and local authorities. In principle, this is done in a series of steps of which the following is illustrative:

(1) The central planners set national production targets which are desirable from the national point of view.

(2) These targets are broken down by major agricultural areas in consultation with agricultural planners from the various areas.

(3) The planners from each area indicate the production targets which farmers in the area can be

expected to achieve, and the socio-economic conditions which must be established to enable and
motivate the farmers to realise the targets.

(4)   These targets for the various agricultural
areas are aggregated to yield an estimate of national agricultural production from the point of view of
the various areas in the country.

(5)   If the production targets of the various
areas deviate widely from the nationally desirable
production targets, a 'feedback' procedure is
applied to bring about a reconciliation of national
and area targets by readjusting national and/or area
targets and, if necessary, farm production budgets
and plans. This may also involve certain adjustments in the environmental conditions in the various
farming areas and in national economic and agricultural policies.

(6)   After discussions between the planners at
the national and regional and/or local levels, final
national, regional and local targets are fixed.

Some countries, including India, and Sri Lanka, have
made an attempt at such two-way planning. But
others have gone further to achieve adequate interaction. Among the market economy countries, Israel
has probably had the greatest success in this
respect. But in most such countries, there has been
failure both to recognise that the feed-back process
is essential for setting viable targets and achieving them; and to understand that target-setting
requires active cooperation between local planners
and farmers, as well as among planners at all levels
from the local farming areas up to the national
planning agency and back down to the local level.

Among the socialised countries, the U.S.S.R.,
and China have followed most closely the process of
planning "from the bottom up and from the top down".
The procedure followed in China is particularly
illuminating. The process begins in every commune
after each mid-year with a review of the previous
year's performance and the proposed targets for the
next year. The commune's proposed targets, which
largely reflect its own needs and priorities, and
what it considers to be the best use of available
manpower and financial resources, are sent to the
county in which it is located. After discussions
between representatives of the county and the
communes, the county passes on to the province in
which it is located the county's targets for production and inputs (e.g. fertilizer and machinery).
The province then submits the targets to the Central

Planning Commission. At the annual meeting between provincial and Planning Commission representatives, the adequacy of the targets for all major crops is reviewed. Attempts are made to have provinces with deficits in grains, sugar, cotton, vegetable oils, etc., increase production targets, and adjustments are made in the targets. The adjusted provincial targets are then disaggregated and transmitted to the counties and communes and a second round of meetings are held between provincial and county representatives, and county and communal representatives before the targets are made firm.

It may seem obvious that those responsible for achieving production targets should have a voice in setting them. However, the lack of adequate consultation is so common that the point needs stressing. Not only are farmers who help set their own targets likely to be more committed to their realisation, but these targets may well turn out, if conditions are made favourable, to be higher than those set by outsiders, since producers are almost always better acquainted than others with their own capabilities and limitations. Whether the targets are higher or lower than those set by outsiders, they are likely to be more realistic.

The ideal arrangement is for central authorities to abstain from modifying regional and local targets whenever possible. Since this is likely to be difficult or impossible in most instances, however, the ruling principle is that direction and control from above should be reduced to the minimum required to harmonise regional, local and farm targets with national objectives.

Chapter 9

THE CHOICE OF STRATEGIES

Summary
Policy making is the heart of planning but the
choice of suitable policies can be a complex
matter. A frame of reference is needed and
this is what a development strategy should provide. Often, however, there is a total absence
of a policy framework as well as confusion
between objectives, strategies and policies.
Different types of strategies are discussed:
concentration versus dispersal of particular
resources, short- versus long-term, emphasis on
small farmers, import substitution, export expansion, diversification. Various constraints
limit the choice of strategies and there is a
need for systematic analysis to arrive at a
compromise between typically conflicting
economic and social aims, and to secure effective use of the scarcest resources. A vital
step is to recognise what the major constraints
are. They will normally change as a country
develops. There are different constraints at
national, sector, local and farm levels at any
given time. The best way of dealing with this
"restricting" problem is to choose a strategy
or strategies least bound by constraints. Take
full advantage of relatively abundant resources
and use most carefully the scarcest. If development proceeds according to plan, strategies
will gradually change to adjust to a new resource situation. Whatever strategy is adopted
its full implications should be carefully
thought out in relation to expected changes in
e.g. output, inputs, incomes and their distribution and other social consequences.

1. Why a Strategy is Needed

A variety of policies may be needed to achieve an objective, a target, or both. The range of potentially useful policies is wide, covering fields as diverse as manpower, land resources, investment, prices, taxation, research, and nutrition. Policies adopted may require activities to be carried out in a variety of ways, perhaps differently in various regions of a country, or even for different farmers in the same region. Some policies can stand alone such as one for improving laws, others are complementary and have to be used together for the best results; still others are mutually exclusive. Some are slow acting, others have an almost immediate effect. Some policies differ in their demands on scarce resources and vary in their capacity to utilize the more abundant ones. Some have a direct impact on production, while others exert their effect indirectly by changing the environment in which farmers make their investment and production decisions.

Policy-making is difficult because of the complexities involved. Nevertheless it is the heart of planning, more central to it than any other element, because success or failure in planning largely depends on the choice of policies adopted. To be effective, policy-making requires the identification of relevant and potentially desirable policies and, then, selection from these policies of those which are best for the purpose.

2. What a Strategy is

To facilitate identification of relevant policy alternatives, and the choice of those likely to be most effective, requires a frame of reference. This is what a development strategy provides. By laying out the broad approach, or general direction, to be taken to achieve a specific objective or target, a strategy allows planners to choose from a variety of potentially useable policies, projects, programmes and other measures, those which are best suited to that approach, and to relate them to each other in an integrated network.

More than that, a strategy is a convenient means (because it is intermediate between an objective and the policies required to achieve it) for testing whether all the policies, programmes, etc. needed to realise an objective are being or can be adopted. For example, if a high yielding varieties

(HYV) strategy is adopted, it provides a convenient
reference point against which to check the variety
of policies, etc., needed to ensure that adequate
amounts of fertilizer, pesticides, water, credit,
technical information and other inputs are made
available to farmers at the right time and place.
A well-considered strategy could reveal that, because of farmers' attitudes, policies for application
of government funds and the use of a wide array of
incentives could not achieve, say, increased production, in the absence of structural reforms. A
carefully chosen strategy can also help to identify
constraints, i.e. a shortage of managerial and
technical personnel, and lack of land clearing capacity, which have to be dealt with before an objective can be achieved.
     A strategy can also be considered as a means
of selecting elements, or factors, on which to
concentrate in developing the agricultural sector.
These elements involve choices among different
technologies, spatial arrangements, time horizons,
production mixes and human groupings, as well as the
emphasis and sequence to be given to each element in
achieving a given objective or target.
     A development strategy for agriculture may thus
be seen as a framework for a consistent set of
policies, measures and activities, within defined
constraints, which together constitute an organized
thrust toward fulfilling a particular objective or
target. However, the adoption of a strategy to
achieve a given objective or target does not imply
that everything outside the strategy will be ignored
- only that the strategy will be emphasised. Thus,
adoption of a two-fold strategy for multiple cropping and increased yield rates for rice production
does not mean that e.g. the production of jute,
tobacco, sugarcane, cotton and other crops would get
no attention, but that the production of rice would
get the greatest attention.

3. Theory vs. Practice
At least, that is the theory. In practice, one frequently finds policies in effect without reference
to a clearly defined development strategy, in
national as well as in agricultural planning. In
fact, the total absence of a policy frame is the
most conspicuous feature of several 'planned' economies. One can only speculate that if this is true
for countries well-endowed with planners, how much
more it is likely to be so in the many countries
less well-endowed.

138

Many poor countries, in practice, pay scant attention to the development strategies required to achieve their agricultural objectives. Some countries even have a shotgun approach, with policies headed in different, sometimes opposite, directions.

Part of the problem may be that many agricultural plans fail to distinguish between objectives, strategies and policies. This has already been mentioned earlier. The point worth noting here is that when an objective is taken to be the same as a strategy, the need for a unifying framework for the policies is likely to be overlooked; and when a policy is taken as a strategy, it is likely to be too narrowly defined to provide that unifying framework.

A well defined strategy allows resources to be combined in specific ways to achieve an objective or target. Clear definition is important because different strategies use resources in different ways, e.g. the way they are used will be different with a high yielding varieties (HYV) strategy, which relies on a discrete technological jump, than with one which relies on a gradual improvement and intensification in the use of traditional inputs.

4. Types of Strategies

A. Concentration vs. dispersion of resources. While different strategies may be used to achieve the same objective, a given objective often requires a particular kind of strategy. Experience shows that if, for instance, the objective is greater equality in the distribution of income, a strategy involving agrarian reform produces better results than one which concentrates on new agricultural services. This is because farmers respond better to attempts to improve agricultural productivity when they have an adequate stake in the land they work. In contrast, if the objective is a rapid increase in agricultural output without regard to improved income distribution or promotion of employment, a HYV strategy is likely to be more effective than a gradualist strategy. There are several reasons for this. First, the HYV strategy can be implemented quickly and with small expenditures of time and money for development since, after local testing of HYV seed, it can be imported for distribution to farmers; then, the HYV strategy allows two, three or even four crops per year to be grown on the same land when water is adequate; and third, it permits resources to be concentrated among farmer groups with the greatest propensity to adopt innovations,

who are usually found in a few regions with high
production potentialities. For example, in India,
the HYV strategy was designed to ration scarce inputs on a selected and restricted regional basis
where soil, climate and irrigation conditions were
favourable for intensive use of inputs to maximise
output, at greatest profit and least risk. This
approach was justified on the grounds that the high
yielding varieties of wheat required a new technology with an entirely different set of husbandry
practices than other seeds. Thus, if farmers were
to realise the genetic potential of the seeds, they
might need to increase the plant population, change
the time of planting or the depth of seeding. They
also had to irrigate more frequently than with other
seed, and with more precision; use fertilizer in
large quantities; and weed carefully to prevent
waste of fertilizer on weeds. Not all farmers in
the country were equally able to carry out HYV
strategy at that time. In contrast, the gradualist
strategy spreads resources over wide areas to
assure that increased output is accompanied by an
adequate return for most farmers, without reference
to their innovative response.

The record in India, Mexico and elsewhere indicates that concentration of resources may be an
acceptable strategy where increases in output are
readily obtainable, if the objective is to increase
production as quickly as possible. But the price
for rapid increases in output may be high. For
example, the HYV strategy may require a change in
the scale of agriculture with attendant displace-
ment of farm tenants and workers which can lead to
a conflict between increased output and social
justice. This happened in India. In addition, subsidies for inputs and price supports in connection
with India's HYV strategy for agriculture led farmers to reduce the production of pulses, an important
source of protein. The same thing happened elsewhere in the Far East. This is likely to have a
serious effect on poor consumers who rely on pulses
as a source of cheap protein. In Mexico, the concentration of resources on the larger, commercial
farmers included substantial economic incentives
for increasing production which greatly increased
the public costs of carrying out the HYV strategy.
Moreover, a study of the results obtained in the
agricultural sector revealed that large farmers were
less efficient in the use of capital than small
farmers. It is interesting to compare the Mexican
strategy with that of Israel, Japan, Republic of

Korea, and China (Taiwan), all of which adopted a strategy for increasing the production of export crops which stressed labour and skill-intensive products. The strategies of all four countries (other than Mexico) coordinated major investments for raising the general educational level of rural people with subsequent creation of productive employment opportunities in rural areas.

Because of the possibly high social costs of a strategy which concentrates resources, there is something to be said for a strategy of gradualism. Experience demonstrates that the gradualist approach may be the most stable and reliable way to develop agriculture in poor countries, although it may not be the quickest. Indeed, the less urgent the need for short-term increases in output, the greater the benefits of a strategy which calls for combining limited amounts of capital with increased use of surplus labour, to gradually improve production methods on as large a proportion of the farmers as possible. The gradualist approach has shown not only that it can increase output, but provides more employment and a more equitable distribution of incomes than a strategy based on concentration of resources. In contrast, where resources have largely gone to the larger farmers, mechanisation of agriculture may be promoted, accentuating the problems of employment and the maldistribution of rural incomes.

B.   Short-term vs. long-term strategies. Some strategies require a longer time to carry out than others. It is, therefore, desirable to determine how long a given strategy will take to produce results. If they are wanted soon, it is important to avoid a strategy which relies on major reforms in technology, administration or organisation. Long lead times are typical in agriculture, and careful evaluation of potential strategies is essential to separate those with short- or long-term effects.

Long- and short-term strategies may conflict with each other. For instance, expansion of irrigation by flooding may be a sensible strategy for increasing output during the period of a five-year plan. From a longer point of view, however, the cost of land lost because of the resulting salinization may make it preferable to forego the short-run benefits of the flooding strategy and adopt a longer-run strategy of drainage and desalinization, as has been done in Pakistan.

Similarly, the choice between the concentration

141

of resources and the gradualist strategies raises
the question of whether the diversion of large
quantities of resources to a specific area of crop,
as in an HYV programme is worth the expenditure in
people and money, if it yields a lower rate of
social return than the gradualist strategy, over a
long period of time. This does not mean that the
gradualist strategy always has the edge. A gradualist strategy may involve long-term research on
traditional crops and such projects as drainage,
irrigation, flood control, land development, settlement, plant and animal breeding, improvement of
marketing and agrarian institutions all of which
have a long gestation period. In these circumstances, it is understandable why some governments feel
impelled to emphasise concentration of resources
strategies, like an HYV programme, with their
promise of quick increases in output. It is a
difficult question of priorities.

In practice, most countries attempt to achieve
a balance with their strategies, to meet immediate
as well as longer-term objectives. For example, in
its First Five-Year Plan (1973-78), Bangladesh
adopted two broad strategies to achieve objectives
of self-sufficiency in foodgrains, and reduced unemployment and under-employment: first, by an
increase in cropped area through multiple cropping,
made possible by low-cost, labour intensive irrigation projects, and second, by the introduction of
high yielding varieties of seeds in irrigated areas.
The longer-term strategy involved expansion of the
area under irrigation during the Plan period
according to a fixed time table, while the short-
term strategy involved the concentration of physical
inputs, credit and technical information to existing
irrigated areas.

C. Resource cencentration for small farmers. The
question of resource concentration has also arisen
in dealing with the problem of small-holder development. Here, two principal strategies have emerged.
The first concentrates on a cash crop of high
potential as a focal point for rural development.
The Kenya small-holder tea project is an example.
It provided credit, extension services, tea-process-
ing factories and access roads for small-holders in
tea-growing areas. This cash crop strategy has the
advantage of spreading the benefits of development
widely among small farmers, but has limited scope
where market prospects, climate or soil conditions
are not particularly favourable.

The second strategy concentrates on small-
holders in a geographic area which has both high
potential and a manageable size. While seeking to
increase agricultural productivity among small
farmers in a selected area, it may also include such
activities as soil conservation, improvement of
local marketing facilities, provision of agricultural inputs, road construction and social services. A
variant of this strategy calls for the selection of
a village or other sub-regional area in each of a
series of regions as a model for the introduction of
a package of improved production inputs and techniques. This strategy was employed in India's
Intensive Agricultural Development Programme during
the Third Plan period.

D. Other strategies. Import Substitution. A basic
feature of agricultural planning in most developing
countries is the priority given to attaining self-
sufficiency in certain key commodities, as a means
of becoming more self-reliant generally and to cut
down on imports. This strategy may involve not only
increased domestic production, i.e. import substitution, but also changes in dietary habits.

Traditional Exports. Some countries have thought it
best to try to increase agricultural output with a
strategy for promoting such traditional exports as
bananas, coffee, cocoa, sugar, tea or rubber. This
strategy has sometimes included policies for increasing income through more efficient marketing
arrangements, or agreements between importing and
exporting countries designed to get a better balance
between supply and demand. Export promotion of
agricultural products generally involves commercial
and capital-intensive activities, and requires a
certain degree of sophistication about standards,
packing, handling, etc., and a minimum scale of
operations. Lacking these, an export promotion
strategy must take into account that it is generally
applicable only to advanced farmers and that other
farmers are likely to be excluded unless they can
work through cooperatives or marketing boards. If
this is not possible, an export promotion strategy
may not be appropriate if improved income distribution is a major objective.

Agricultural diversification. Some countries which
are dependent on one or two export crops for a large
proportion of their export earnings, have sought
greater security through a strategy of agricultural

143

diversification. During its Second Five-Year Plan, for example, Thailand achieved success with this strategy in lowering its dependence on rice. Corn and sugarcane became major crops, while cassava root and various kinds of beans also increased their shares in agricultural output at the expense of the traditional rice.

Brazil is another interesting example of diversification in response to changing priorities in planning. In addition to producing food for the domestic market, as well as crops for export (such as cocoa, coffee and soyabeans), the country's agriculture has in recent years been supposed to help cut the oil-import bill. The Brazilians aim to do this by growing sugar cane to be made into alcohol and wood for charcoal used in industry, and by replacing 16 percent of diesel fuel with vegetable oil.

The first essential in pursuing all these agricultural aims is more land. Brazilian farmers have more than doubled the area they cultivate, from 20m. hectares in 1970 to 45.5m. hectares in 1981. To secure all the nation's agricultural targets - in food, exports and fuel - this increase would have to be doubled to a rate of 5m. hectares a year.

However, the strategy appropriate to one country may not be suitable for another. In large countries, strategy can be aimed at satisfying domestic demand, especially when an equitable pattern of development generates a mass market, while in small countries the best plan is usually export orientated.

E. Who selects agricultural strategies. This discussion of strategies should make clear that their choice, like that of a development objective, involves decisions about which groups are likely to benefit from them and which are not. A strategy, like the HYV approach, may be "neutral" in theory with regard to farming scale or location, in the sense that even a small-holder located anywhere can apply the package of inputs required to obtain profitable returns. But, in practice, neutrality breaks down quickly because the control of irrigation water by larger (and wealthier) farmers and their better access to credit, inputs and officials make it much easier for them than for poorer farmers to apply a strategy like an HYV programme and to benefit from it. The selection of a strategy is more than a technical matter. Almost invariably, some groups of farmers - usually the larger or

wealthier ones - have tended to benefit more from
development efforts than others. Although a
strategy has technical content and implications
which planners and other technicians are qualified
to deal with, the political and social aspects of a
strategy are even more important. Consequently, it
is the political leadership, assisted by planners
and other technicians, which has the ultimate obligation and responsibility for selecting the strategy
to be followed.

5. Constraints on the Choice of a Strategy
A. Need for a systematic analysis. Since ideals of
social equity and economic efficiency often conflict, strategy for the agricultural sector must aim
not only at an acceptable compromise between conflicting social and economic aims, but also seek to
obtain efficient use of the scarcest resources.
There is a need here for a systematic analysis.
    A good analysis requires the collection and
consideration of as much information as possible
about the costs, benefits, advantages and disadvantages of each alternative, as well as a determination of the relative abundance and scarcity of
major resources. For example, an analysis which a
World Bank team made for Sri Lanka identified
foreign exchange and investment capital and, to a
lesser extent, managerial skills as relatively
scarce resources; and unskilled and educated manpower as relatively abundant resources, with
considerable unutilized potential in natural resources. The information required will depend on
how big an effort is to be made in agriculture and
on the objectives to be achieved.
    While the benefits and advantages of a possible
strategy are generally easy to assess, its full
costs and disadvantages are frequently less apparent.
One reason is that the nature of the constraints for
a given strategy may vary greatly from one country
to another. Another is that it is necessary to
adjust a strategy to the special situation in a
country before all the costs and disadvantages can
be determined. Planners frequently fail to recognise that substantial differences in constraints
from country to country make it essential to identify constraints in specific environments rather than
to look for a strategy that will be suitable in a
wide range of conditions. Zaire provides a good
example of why specificity is essential. Because
the overall man/land ratio is extremely low in
Zaire, a cursory review might make it seem

desirable to increase agricultural production by
expanding cultivated areas. But more careful study
by a World Bank mission made it clear that labour
constraints militate against this. Nor did mechanisation offer an easy way around this difficulty,
because uncertainties exist about soil qualities and
the possible impact of mechanisation on them. Moreover, land tenure arrangements and the attitudes of
the people preclude large resettlement activities,
at least in the short-run. This left raising
current crop yields as the most promising way of
increasing total output, especially since yields
were below earlier levels. The World Bank mission's
examination of the possibilities inherent in this
approach, revealed that production could be increased quickly in this way. Once adopted, the measures
and policies to be part of the strategy became
apparent. The key element for raising yields was
seen to be the need to restore the quality of planting materials. This called for policies, and a
concerted programme, to encourage the production,
multiplication and distribution of improved seeds.
Other policies and measures which could have
relatively fast results were also recommended.

B. Resource constraints

    (i) Recognition. Recognition of resource con-
straints influencing the choice of an agricultural
strategy may spell the difference between success
and failure in achieving targets and objectives.
    One of these is imposed by the natural con-
ditions in a country. Climate, endemic disease
and the scarcity of water are examples of natural
conditions which set limits on agricultural strategies. Planners in India must take cognisance of
the monsoons, just as those in Tanzania must take
account of sleeping sickness borne by the tse-tse
fly; and countries where water is scarce must devise
strategies which make the most of available supplies, as for example, in Saudi Arabia and Israel,
where there is the need to allocate scarce water to
high value crops.
    In Kenya, identification of the importance of
a labour constraint led to the restriction of tea
plantings to less than one acre per holding through
strict control of seedling distribution. This
restriction prevented farmers from planting more
seedlings than they could care for properly.
    However, a word of caution: resource con-
straints of today may not be those of tomorrow.

Planners must look ahead and try to estimate which resources are likely to increase and which to decrease.

(ii) The stage of development. A second constraint is a country's stage of development. Clearly, at the early stages of development a country should not normally select a strategy which, like mechanisation, requires skills, foreign exchange and other resources which it lacks; any more than a country in an advanced stage should adopt a strategy which emphasises labour-intensive techniques. Nor should a strategy be selected which is otherwise inappropriate to the actual situation in a country. If land fragmentation is a serious problem, for example, adoption of large-scale mechanisation would be ill-advised unless adequate steps could be taken to consolidate holdings or otherwise permit efficient use of mechanised equipment.

(iii) Institutional, attitudinal and organisational constraints. A nation's social, political and economic institutions and beliefs is a third determinant of strategies. At the international level, they are likely to embody a country's attitudes towards the role of foreign trade, aid, and private investment, the importance of international regional cooperation, desirability of attaining economic independence, etc. At the national level, they will reflect public attitude toward the roles of the private and public sectors, regional development, family planning, unemployment (and, therefore, among other things, the choice of technology for public investment projects), the pattern of income distribution, levels of consumption, retention of traditional ways and forms, institutional reform and so forth.

How underlying attitudes and assumptions influence the choice of strategies is clearly seen in China and India, among other countries. Chinese leaders held the view that agriculture was backward mainly because of China's feudalistic institutional framework. The Chinese approach to agricultural development was, therefore, based on the assumption that existing "feudalistic production relations" had to be replaced by collective farming before agricultural productivity could be increased.

In contrast, India assumed that it could gradually improve existing backward production relations, and when this attempt failed adopted a strategy which sidestepped them. Immediately after

147

independence, India approached agricultural development with the three-fold assumption that: the technology required for agricultural development was
available; farmers were wedded to backward production techniques because of ignorance and illiteracy
which made them suspicious of innovations, and
impeded their acceptance of new and profitable techniques; and landlords (zamindaris), moneylenders and
merchants exacerbated farmers' inadequacies by
exploiting them. The Indian strategy for remedying
these conditions took the form, respectively, of:
extension service systems to inform farmers about
new production techniques; literacy programmes to
increase the level of education and social welfare
programmes to gain the confidence of cultivators;
and land reform programmes which sought to abolish
the "zamindari" system, the provision of alternative
sources of credit to free cultivators from the money
lenders, and regulation and provision of alternative
means of marketing agricultural commodities to protect farmers from exploitation by traders.

however, when it proved to be too difficult to
reform the existing agrarian structure in India, and
it became clear that the spreading of available resources thinly over the entire country would not
lead quickly to desired increases in agricultural
production, a new strategy was adopted which concentrated development efforts in areas of assured
irrigation. The introduction of the Intensive
Agricultural District Programme in 1960-61 in three
districts marked the first phase of the new strategy.
The Programme was later extended to an additional
thirteen districts. A modified version of the
strategy, the Intensive Agricultural Area Programme,
was extended to more districts between 1964-65. The
strategy, which involved the use of high yielding
varieties of seed, reached a more advanced stage
from 1964 onwards with the introduction of high
yielding varieties of wheat and rice.

Some constraints are self-imposed, like a
government's attitude toward the private sector or
its price policy for foodstuffs for urban workers,
which may actually discourage production. Some are
not, but occasionally the line between the two is
thin. For example, foreign exchange constraints on
the choice of a strategy are usually independent of
a country's social, political and economic attitudes.
However, if a country avoids certain kinds of
foreign aid as a matter or principle, the foreign
exchange constraint is at least partly self-imposed.

Planners may sometimes wish they had the power

148

to change a government's self-imposed constraints. They may not always be able to do this. But for planning purposes, they should determine the extent to which they must accept, as given, existing attitudinal and institutional constraints on the choice of strategies, and the extent to which the constraints are subject to revision. Only a good understanding of the political leadership's thinking can make it possible for planners to help select an appropriate strategy.

In many developing countries, the state of the public administration is a serious constraint on agricultural development. Failure to recognise this fact has led to the adoption of strategies which make demands on public administration that are greater than it can support. Frequently a government administration is called upon to carry out more projects, or to intervene more frequently, than it can manage effectively.

(iv) Constraints at varying levels. In choosing a strategy it is important to distinguish between constraints at the national, sector and farm levels. Lack of investment resources may be a constraint at the level of the agricultural sector but not at the national level, where a government has decided to concentrate available resources on industrial rather than agricultural development. And just as constraints may differ between the national and sectoral levels, they may differ between those at either of these levels and at the farm level. Thus, where the availability of fertilizer may not appear as a constraint at the sector level, unreliable deliveries at the farm level may prove to be a serious problem, and while skilled manpower may be a limiting factor at the national level, producers may have all the knowledge required to farm better than they do, if only deliveries of fertilizers could be improved. Since the constraints faced by farmers are the ones which actually retard development at any given time, assumptions must fit the difficulties which farmers actually face, if effective strategies are to be selected. Too often, they turn out to be answers to the wrong questions because they are based on assumptions which are applicable to constraints at national or sectoral levels, instead of those at the farm level. A strategy must be designed to ensure that the farmer sees the actions taken under it, as contributing to the solution of his problems and the achievement of his objectives.

149

Sometimes, a single strategy will not be enough. This is true, for example, where improvement of both commercial and traditional farming is attempted. Since the problems and constraints of commercial differ from those of traditional agriculture, two strategies, or two distinct components within an overall strategy, have to be identified; one dealing with commercial agriculture; the other with the usually more pervasive and thorny issues of traditional agriculture.

In some countries, a single strategy may not be possible for other reasons, e.g. in a country with diverse ecological, climatological or economic regions. In Brazil, for example, great regional diversity and a tradition of regional automony in matters of development make the formulation and execution of unified agricultural strategy impracticable. Turkey has two distinctly different regions - the highland plateau and the coastal zone-each of which requires a development strategy different from the other. This is also true of the dry zone and coconut-lands regions in Sri Lanka. Peru has three zones which required separate strategies. Frequently, differences in development strategies arise from economic differences among regions of a country. Thus, economically backward regions in southern Mexico and Italy, and in northeastern Brazil, require development strategies of their own which differ from those of other agricultural parts of these countries; and the same may be true for a region which is more advanced agriculturally than others, e.g. the Punjab in India.

(v) Dealing with constraints. The best agricultural strategy is one which is least bound by constraints. Thus, in a country with a foreign exchange constraint, a strategy which makes maximum use of domestic resources, like labour is better than one like mechanisation, which requires costly imports. Implicit in strategy selections is the requirement that the greatest use be made of a country's abundant resources. Where land is plentiful, as in Brazil, a good strategy would make the fullest use of land. In countries with great rural unemployment and under-employment, as in Bangladesh, a good strategy would make the fullest possible use of surplus labour by means of labour-intensive projects, programmes and production techniques. Where land is in short supply relative to labour, a good strategy also calls for a labour-using strategy. Land-scarce but labour-plentiful Japan, China and

the Republic of Korea have all developed successful
strategies based on labour-intensive agriculture and
small-scale, labour-intensive rural industry. As
labour has become scarcer in Japan, the degree of
labour-intensity has been reduced as it will eventually in China and Korea. And where capital is
plentiful relative to labour, as in the oil-rich
countries, a capital-using strategy which conserves
scarce labour is desirable. Location can also be
treated as a resource. For example, Panama's development strategy treats its geographic position as
an advantage and builds a set of appropriate
policies and actions on it.

While constraints impose limitations on the
choice of strategy, they can be dealt with either by
sidestepping them or by devising a strategy with
elements which fit the constraints. Thus, when India
formulated its HYV strategy, it sought among other
things to sidestep the constraints imposed by its
traditional farmers. Sri Lanka shows how an agricultural strategy can be adapted to a specific situation. The conservatism of farmers, which restricted rice production in that country was a constraint
against a HYV strategy. In these circumstances, an
intermediate strategy was devised which involved the
promotion of two local improved rice varieties.
These gave significantly better results than other
local varieties, but did not require as much investment, water, water control and discipline as did the
HYV's. The local improved varieties were also
suitable for small farmers; something not always
true of the HYV's because of their more stringent
financial, educational and labour requirements.
Moreover, the adoption of the intermediate strategy
provided hope that it would help train farmers
sufficiently to permit the later adoption of more
advanced technologies, such as the HYV approach required.

6. Implications of a Strategy

Before selecting a strategy its possible repercus-
sions should be explored with care. Sometimes, it
may easily be seen that a certain strategy will not
achieve its objective. For example, a strategy
which emphasises sophisticated and capital-intensive
production techniques is unlikely to raise the incomes of poor farmers. Sometimes, even if it is
clear that a strategy will succeed, there may be
side effects which need to be considered. The
Mexican experience is especially revealing. The HYV
strategy there was aimed at large farmers. It

allowed large producers, who were beneficiaries of
subsidies, relief granted from taxation, and other
economic incentives, as well as the good prices they
received for their crops, to do so well financially
that they were slow to adopt efficient production
techniques. In contrast, small private and _ejido_
farmers produced wheat and other crops more economically than the large commercial farmers in the
irrigated areas by combining small amounts of scarce
and expensive capital inputs with abundant cheap
labour. However, they were largely neglected or by-
passed by the new strategy. Since the Mexican
strategy also made worse the existing income inequalities between the large commercial landowners
and the small farmers in the private sector and the
ejiditarios (farmers on cooperative farms), the
social cost of the Mexican strategy was much greater
than was necessary. If speed was important the HYV
strategy aimed at large farmers might have been
justified despite its high cost. However, if the
"best way" of increasing output was interpreted to
mean increased production at low cost, the strategy
adopted might have been directed toward the small,
private and _ejido_ farmers.

The process by which a strategy is selected
from among available alternatives should, therefore,
include careful consideration of its possible negative effects. From the examples cited throughout
this chapter, it is clear that some negative effects
might have been foreseen, and provided for with con-
tingency measures, if a systematic analysis of the
strategy had been made prior to its adoption.

The HYV strategy is a good example. An HYV
strategy usually has implications for regional and
personal income distribution. Since an HYV strategy
must usually be confined to areas with adequate
water and water control, it may lead to considerable
increases in income inequalities among regions of a
country. It may also lead to increased income inequalities among farmers.

The problems raised by HYV strategies have been
dubbed "second generation" problems. This is misleading since it implies that the problems were
unpredictable or unavoidable. Actually, most of the
so-called "second generation" problems were likely
to have been predictable had the implications of the
HYV strategies been considered with the care they
deserved. Certainly, in India, planners were aware
of some of the negative implications of the HYV
strategy before it was adopted, although they made
little effort to assess their impact. In any event,

it is prudent to assess the full implications of a strategy, negative as well as positive, prior to its adoption.

Finally, it is vital that those who will be closely affected by a strategy are kept fully informed about its nature and implications. Too often the one certain quality of a strategy is its lack of clarity, and even if this is not a problem, it often does not draw forth the necessary response because of failure to keep farmers and local officials fully informed about it.

Chapter 10

POLICY AND POLICY INSTRUMENTS

Summary
    Key policy decisions involve what is to be
    attempted and how objectives are to be
    achieved. In any given country, policy makers
    will come up against constraints. It is their
    job to identify and, if possible, overcome
    them. As this chapter shows, there is likely
    to be a range of options open to them, from
    direct measures to increase farm output and
    productivity to less direct such as price and
    tax incentives, institutional changes (parti-
    cularly land reform), credit and marketing
    improvements, etc. They will have to develop
    policies, also, which tackle very awkward
    inter-related problems of un- and under-
    employment in rural areas, mechanisation and
    the use of appropriate technology. The various
    types of measures used in agricultural develop-
    ment make different demands on resources. The
    most scarce are likely to be foreign currency
    and skilled personnel, particularly admini-
    strators and managers. Care is therefore
    needed to put together the right bundle of
    measures to take full account of which re-
    sources are abundant (often unskilled labour)
    and which scarce. Time needed for the various
    measures to show results must be weighed care-
    fully. Too often, slow-maturing projects and
    measures take the lion's share of resources at
    the expense of current, and possible future,
    improvements. A time-sequence of policies
    needs to be established early, together with
    priorities for the different measures - as part
    of the continuous process of policy planning.
    The common tendency to choose complex all-
    embracing solutions must generally be resisted.

Decision-making can be assisted, by pilot projects, trial programmes, by tackling part of a problem and by decentralisation. The final question may well concern which comes first and which later, rather than what to leave out.

There are two broad types of policy matters to be concerned with. First, there are priorities among regions, subsectors and objectives. Strategy helps here by laying down the broad outline or framework to show where the sector is to go. This is only guidance, however, when it comes to working on policy issues like incentive structures, reform of marketing and input supply, employment technology and investment criteria. Priorities must be worked out in detail to establish the criteria by which decisions can be made in the day-to-day implementation of the plan. Investment policy, for instance, should set the discount rates at which funds are made available for different private and semi-public activities. Natural resource policy may have to allocate water, for instance, between rural-agricultural and urban or industrial uses.

The second type of policy problem involves the choice of instruments for achieving objectives. Price supports, taxes, marketing boards, credit, tenure systems, extension services, and provision of inputs are all means for carrying out policies. They cover activities directly undertaken by the government as well as those designed to influence the private and semi-public sectors.

Establishment of priorities, and selection of ways to carry out objectives, are related aspects of the policy setting process. Different policy instruments may also be connected. For example, price policy may be ineffective at reaching largely subsistence farmers. Hence, it will be necessary to establish land tenure, marketing and extension policies to bring these farmers more fully into the market economy if price policies are to reach them. But suppose farmers would respond to price changes but cannot get the inputs they need to expand production. In this case, price policies must be joined with other policies to ensure that necessary inputs are available to the farmers. If they are available, it may also be necessary to provide credit and extension services.

The problem the policy-maker faces thus has three parts. First, he must identify the specific constraints that are hindering movement towards the objective, second he must determine whether the policy instruments available can remove or reduce the constraint. If these are inadequate, then a third step must be taken: institutional reform of which the most significant are generally land tenure and marketing.

In practice, there is usually no easy way to determine whether a policy will work without trying it. Even if successful, it may only reach a small proportion of the farmers, usually the larger and more commercial ones. The effects of institutional constraints, in particular, are only roughly known. Experience with policy variations is fairly limited and new policy instruments will often, therefore, have to be adopted on a trial and error basis, preferably in pilot schemes.

1. Inputs

A. Package programmes. On the face of it, when a Government intervenes in agriculture to raise output and productivity, the most logical approach is to put together a 'package' of physical inputs and policies to bring about this desirable result. A typical package may include better marketing, steadily improving technology, local availability of needed supplies and equipment, production incentives and improved transportation facilities. In practice, the difficulty arises that for the package to have maximum impact all its ingredients must be available in the right quantities, at the right time and in the right place. Frequently, however, such policies fail because of difficulty in putting together the most appropriate package, or, if it is a suitable package, to ensure that its particular inputs are, in practice, available together. Fertilizer, improved seeds and pesticides, for example, key elements in most package programmes, may be in short supply, or badly distributed.

One way of coping with this problem is to concentrate the packages in a few areas of a country or on a limited number of farmers, usually the better-off.

Package programmes have often not worked out as well as their sponsors had hoped. Output has not risen as much as expected and adoption of new practices has lagged. The most frequent complaint is that the technology they are built around is inadequate. In India, for instance, it was reported that the technical package there was not profitable enough.

There is some reason to doubt that this is the real problem. Because packages are made up of several elements it is often difficult to determine where the difficulty lies. Studies in Africa were not able to distinguish whether low profitability or high risk discouraged farmers from using technical packages. Other reasons for failures are also possible. Many farmers simply do not want more fertilizer, improved seed or other innovations.

The technical package is sometimes a problem, however. In Ghana a maize package required a change in planting time and the people felt the new maize was not as suitable for consumption. The 'improved' practices included growing maize alone rather than inter-planted with other crops. This might have reduced overall farm income. The project failed to generate much interest in this package. In many places new technical packages have been inadequate because they ignored the additional labour required. Problems with technical packages are much worse when they are rigidly applied, as happened in Indonesia. Local government had no authority to adapt the packages to local conditions. As a result, yields were not up to the farmers' expectation and the farmers became resentful and many defaulted on credit obligations.

Technical packages often require a number of changes in the farmer's mode of operation at one time. This makes the package highly risky from the farmer's point of view. The only way to eliminate this risk is to offer the farmer a guarantee if he adopts the package. This is what is done in contract farming and production for some producers' associations. In most cases, however, there is no guarantee so the farmer must learn a lot about a number of new things quickly if he is to understand the new technology, and accurately estimate the risks involved. Not surprisingly this is often too large a task, so the farmer either rejects the package, adopts only part of it, or adopts it on only part of his land. For instance, farmers almost always use less than the recommended amount of fertilizer. Even many large farmers in Java in Indonesia diversified their rice crop among high yielding, local and national varieties. Farmers at Puebla in Mexico experimented with new practices and often adopted them a little at a time. If farmers typically adopt new technologies a little at a time, it suggests that the package approach may be heading in the wrong direction. A sequential approach based on a step at a time may be more appropriate.

This does not mean that packages are always a failure. The packages associated with dwarf varieties of wheat and rice have been highly successful in raising output in some parts of the world. But even this may turn out to be a mixed blessing. These packages include large amounts of fertilizer at a time when the price of fertilizer has risen drastically. The cost of importing fertilizer is a serious burden in many countries.

Thus, although farmers do need all the 'essential' ingredients of a package it is often very difficult to determine what these essentials are. The result is that many packages have failed because of inherent weaknesses e.g. an inadequate technology. Since this has been true so frequently and the same problems have led to the failure of many extension programmes, package programmes are not a good idea unless they have had complete field testing, and are significantly and consistently adopted by farmers in these tests.

B. Testing individual programmes. The major altertive to introducing measures in packages is to introduce them one at a time and this is the approach used by many developing countries. In most countries the first step was public works for transportation and water. Next came the provision of inputs and measures to improve technology, primarily extension services. Only then have marketing reforms or policies to improve incentives been tried, e.g., price policy and land reform.

There is a certain rationality in taking these steps in this order. Since governments often do not know how serious the parts of a problem are, it makes sense to begin with the broadest, easiest and least controversial measures and work up to the narrower, harder and more risky measures. Transportation is an easy first step as it benefits all industries, the government and the military and fits in with ideas of nationalism. Provision of inputs and extension are more specifically agricultural but not usually controversial.

When a country considers changes in tax, price, tariff, import, and other policies, which have broad income distributional implications, the problems become more complex. What is given to one group, e.g., higher incomes for farmers due to higher prices, is taken from another group, e.g., urban consumers who must pay more for food. Finally, there are the institutional reform issues which mean fairly major changes for significant groups. Land and marketing reform and the formation of farmer associations and co-operatives may raise major political and social questions. Hence it is not surprising that institutional reforms are the policy changes which have been put off the longest except where extraordinary circumstances such as revolution, e.g., in Bolivia, China, Cuba or Peru, or threats of revolution or conquest from abroad, e.g. China (Taiwan), Japan, have generated the commitment necessary to undertake such reforms.

In practice, there have always been reasons for hope that easier measures would work. At each stage some farmers responded to the improvements, increased output, adopted new techniques and became more commercialized in production. As policy improved and more of the essential items became available, more farmers took advantage of this situation. They were, however, usually middle- and large-scale farmers. Generally, the smaller the farmer, the less likely that he has been drawn into commercial production or that his output has expanded beyond what more use of land and labour could provide.

One of the reasons that larger farmers succeed in adopting new methods and increasing output is that they can obtain their own essentials. They can afford to entertain an extension worker or to go to town to pick up inputs or deliver produce. This may be totally beyond the small farmer who is ignored by extension workers and faces much higher costs of transportation. In addition, when the delivery mechanisms for services, especially those providing inputs, break down, the larger farmer has a greater capacity to overcome such breakdowns. He can get first choice of what little is available or bypass breakdowns by going further afield for services.

C. The choice of inputs. Physical and policy inputs are essential for all farmers. The question is whether and how these inputs will reach particular groups of farmers. The package programme approach has the right idea: supply everything that is needed. It is just that in practice the correct package has eluded polcymakers. Essential measures have been omitted. But this is also true of adding one policy at a time. There has been a tendency for governments to never get to the harder issues; again essential measures have been omitted.

Thus the key to success is not the use of a technical package or a step-at-a-time approach. The key to success is including the measures that are essential in particular circumstances. In virtually all cases these measures have included the provision of physical inputs either through co-operatives,

farmers' associations, processors or the private
sector. Beyond this there has been no substitute to
finding out from the farmers what they need. In
many countries what the farmers say they need is
land.
   Finally, one vital element in any group of inputs is flexibility in application. One of the
defects that has led to the failure of package programmes is rigid application. This is not only
contrary to the way farmers learn to adopt new
practices but often leads to a poor fit of the
package to local conditions. Both packages and programmes must be tested and adapted in field trials -
but also on the farmer's land.

2. Incentives
Price, tax and other policies are closely related to
input supply since it is the prices of inputs almost
as much as their availability which determines their
use. Prices and taxes on output, land and income
also affect incentives. The combination of input
and output prices, taxes, etc., must be such that
the farmer finds it is in his interest to adopt new
technologies and expand output. Nowhere has development or expanded output come about when farmers
have not found the increased effort and investment
worth the effort involved.
   The farmer's decision is also influenced by incentives on the consumption side, what he wants or
needs income for: the availability of consumer goods
and services, like health and education services for
himself and his family, and the direct taxes he must
pay. The incentive to the farmer is not the amount
of money he makes but the goods and services this
money will buy. Money is an intermediate objective.
Thus it could be that a farmer's unwillingness to
increase production is due to a low valuation of the
things he can buy. This in turn may result from the
limited selection of things to buy.
   Many observers have noted that there is a wide
range of consumer goods available in stores in rural
areas in China, much more so than in countries with
a less dynamic rural sector like India. This may be
due to more equal income distribution in China
which provides an increased consumer market. The
hypothesis that these goods also have an incentive
effect, however, cannot be excluded. In Japan a
land tax paid in cash helped commercialize agriculture and forced farmers to increase production.
Medical care and education for children also have
this effect. A lack of consumer goods is commonly

reported to have discouraged agricultural production. In many countries, the consumption side of incentives has been largely neglected.

A. <u>Yields and input subsidies</u>. Yields have a significant place in any incentive system because the greater the physical return, the lower the price can be and still give the farmer the same income. The greatest incentive effect is created when both prices and yields are favourable. The combination of higher yields, subsidies for inputs and price supports led to the adoption of new technologies, e.g. tube well and pump irrigation and high yielding varieties in Bangladesh, India, Pakistan and elsewhere, and striking increases in output to larger scale farmers. This combination was also a main cause of increased cotton production in Tanzania.

It would obviously be desirable, however, if yield increases were sufficient so that farmers kept increasing output without higher prices. This would allow increased farm income without imposing a burden on consumers. This happened in Mexico, for instance, where crop prices declined nearly one percent a year from 1940 to 1962 at the same time that quantity and variety of food increased. Developed countries generally seem to have reached a point where improved technology is habitually adopted and output increases regardless of relatively minor declines in price or acreage. Japan and China (Taiwan) have also reached this state. Thus, technological improvements are the preferred method of increasing farm income if the conditions for the systematic development and adoption of such changes can be created. Significantly more productive inputs may be especially helpful when farmers are just beginning to adopt new technologies.

The profitability of a new technology also depends on the prices of necessary inputs. Thus, if inputs are not significantly more productive than traditional methods but input costs are high, and any input cost may seem high and risky to a farmer who has not used purchased inputs before, then it is unlikely that farmers will feel it desirable to purchase such inputs. This problem can be overcome by either increasing input productivity or lowering input price (in addition to raising output prices discussed above). Because the productivity of inputs is generally fixed in the short run, many countries adopt input subsidies as a way of encouraging farmer use of inputs. Fertilizer is subsidized frequently. In some cases, such subsidies are

161

necessary to compensate for the price raising
effects of import duties, protection of local producers and high marketing costs.

One advantage of input subsidies is that they
are paid only to those who use the inputs. Price
supports go to all producers who sell in the market.
A disadvantage is that low prices for inputs may
discourage private producers from entering the input supply trade as happened in India, Indonesia and
Nigeria. The latter problem could be handled in the
way the subsidies are provided as in Bangladesh
where the government introduced reforms in fertilizer distribution arrangements which shifts functions
from government agencies to private traders.

B. Output price policy. Of all the incentive
policies, output price adjustments are most common.
Frequently, governments hold down prices to provide
cheaper food for urban consumers who are more
politically active. In other cases export duties,
marketing board surpluses and exchange policies
reduce farmer prices. Compulsory procurement at set
prices also reduce farmer incentives. Farm output
generally falls. The discouraging effect of these
policies is especially clear when the policy is
changed to one promoting greater output when significant increases often occur.

The price policy situation is not quite this
simple, however. Almost universally, it is found
that farmers respond to shifts in relative prices,
especially when the crop involved is a small part of
the total crop area. Attempts to increase the output of all crops by raising all agricultural prices,
however, are not as successful. In India, for
instance, in one period, prices increased much more
rapidly than output, even though the use of inputs
such as high yielding variety seed, fertilizer and
water also increased. Even in developed countries,
the response to total supply of all crops to higher
prices is low.

In addition, there may be considerable variation among regions, crops, scales of farming and
individual farmers in price responsiveness, which is
increased by the existence of strong commercial
markets and the availability of inputs. Price
changes may do little to help the small farmers who
need help the most, since benefits from higher
prices depend on marketed not total output.

Three other possible uses of price policy have
been proposed. First, higher prices can increase
returns to market sales and thus, over a period of

162

time, draw subsistence farmers into the market.
Unfortunately, the output of larger producers tends
to increase rapidly so this becomes a costly way to
commercialize small farmers. Second, price stabilization can reduce risks to producers, encouraging
the use of new technologies and purchased inputs,
and stabilize prices for consumers. In Pakistan,
for instance, the imports of PL 480 grain facilitated by the shift of many farmers to cash crops
because it stabilized the price of food crops. In
Brazil, farmers began growing sugar cane but re-
verted to cereals due to price instability. Third,
price policy can be used to redistribute income
between urban and rural areas. This will not,
however, solve the redistribution problem within the
agricultural sector. The two countries which have
been most concerned about income distribution in
rural areas, Israel and China, used price, or terms
of trade policy to shift income towards rural areas
but they have had to provide other means to equalize
income distribution within rural areas.

In summary, output prices must be high enough
to pay the farmer for his imputs and give him a
return for the extra effort and risk involved in the
use of any technology. The output price high enough
to do this will depend on the prices and productivity of inputs and technologies.

Also, price policy alone can be highly effective in helping shift production from one crop to
another. However, raising prices will not be of as
much help in raising gross agricultural output once
prices are high enough to pay the farmer's costs.

C. Methods of adjusting prices. A major problem of
any price policy, for inputs or outputs, whether up
or down, is that someone has to pay the cost. For
example, food prices are often kept low because
forcing urban consumers to pay the full costs of
adequate production is considered too risky politically. As a result, shortages develop which lead to
increased imports. In the past, when PL 480 grain
was plentiful and could be paid for in local
currencies, this was a low cost way to make up food
deficits in many countries. Increased shortages
have drastically raised the costs of such policies.
As a result, higher food prices are the rule in much
of the world.

Where cheap methods of bearing costs are not
available, coercion is often tried. Many countries
have tried compulsory grain procurement and rationing as solutions to the problem of grain costs. This,

however, often causes declines in grain output. It also places a tremendous burden on the administrative capacity of these countries. Black markets arise, governments fail to achieve procurement targets and imports are increased. Many governments lack the control and understanding of trade necessary to enforce compulsory procurement programmes.

There are several ways to reduce administrative and other costs of price policies. First, the greater the costs will be, the farther the price the government is trying to establish is from a price that would match supply with demand. For this reason it may be desirable to let the market establish a price level and then to stabilize prices in that vicinity rather than to try to push prices up or down. Price stabilization has become one of the more popular price policies in developing countries.

Similarly, if input subsidies are used it is preferable that they are kept as low as possible. As farmers become accustomed to their use and farm productivity rises, these subsidies should be reduced unless they are to compensate for duties or other price raising actions elsewhere in the economy. When artificially low prices for inputs are maintained for long periods, they lead to over use of such inputs and neglect of alternative methods. For instance, the free provision of irrigation water in Sri Lanka allowed very inefficient and wasteful use of this resource. In Pakistan, plant protection activities were provided free of charge. This did spread pesticide technology throughout much of Pakistan but it was a very costly way to use the limited technical personnel.

Second, it may be desirable to support only a few prices as this greatly reduces administrative costs. This policy has frequently been followed but it tends to lower production of other crops as it increases the production of price-supported crops. This makes sense only if the price-supported crops use a more productive technology so that production gains are greater in the supported commodities than the losses in other commodities. Even then there are limits to such a strategy. In the Philippines, for instance, price supports for rice led to an oversupply and a fall in prices for rice. The same thing happened elsewhere. Generally, it will be necessary to provide for diversification to cash crops once price support and other measures have generated a significant increase in basic food grains.

Price stabilization is best achieved by government buying, selling and storage operations for domestic crops and by financial averaging for exports (financing averaging is the creation of a reserve in years when exports bring high prices that can be paid out to bolster domestic prices when international prices are low). Such operations are not costly if they average out gains and losses over time. There will, however, be capital costs in providing the storage necessary for buffer stocks.

For the farmer, a major element in price instability may be the difference between farm-gate harvest-time prices and prices a few months later, or prices received if he could sell in a competitive market. Hence one of the least costly ways of increasing returns to the farmer is to increase his ability to store grain at low cost or to sell in competitive markets. When Brazil instituted a system which permitted the producer to hold more easily part of his production beyond harvest time, an estimated 20 to 30 percent of rice stocks in major producing areas were still in producers' hands five months after the harvest.

If incentive programmes are to be successful they must provide the farmer with a combination of input prices, increased yields and output prices which together make it worthwhile for him to increase his output. Taxes, duties, tariffs, exchange rates, marketing board surpluses, and subsidies all enter as factors in either input or output prices and so should be considered only when their effects on agricultural development are being kept in mind.

Clearly, the preferred way to promote agricultural development is through improved technology. Where this is not feasible, or where specific crops need to be developed, price increases or input subsidies will help. The lowest cost price programme, however, will be one of price stabilization around the trend of balanced supply and demand. Price increases will not generally help small farmers, sharecroppers and tenants as much as large farmers. Hence there are institutional barriers. A price increase may only present a windfall to merchants or landlords. A subsidy on inputs is of no use if input distribution systems cannot deliver the goods. Institutional reforms such as improved marketing, co-operatives and land tenure reforms will be needed. Countries that achieve high agricultural growth rates tend to be those that have a minimum level of government incentives together with effective institutional arrangements.

3. Credit

A. The need for credit. There is considerable
agreement that increased farmer credit is a vital
need in developing countries and many have introduced credit programmes. Credit is particularly
necessary to finance increased use of new inputs and
thus to increase production and incomes.

Farmers receive considerable credit in most
countries from informal sources like relatives,
friends and moneylenders. In fact, even in countries like India, where moneylenders are inevitably
pictured as extortionate, private lenders are able
to compete successfully with public credit due to
more flexible and streamlined loan procedures and
competitive financial terms. Often governments make
the situation worse by tying credit to the use of
inputs or other entanglements that discourage farmers from using it. This is especially serious when
credit is tied to the use of inputs that are late in
arriving.

Although farmers frequently report a need for
credit, it is clearly not a need in the same sense
that physical inputs like fertilizer or seed are. It
is easy to mistake lack of credit for the real
problems. In India, for instance, farmers bought
pumps, often with non-government loans, but the real
constraint was lack of promised electrification that
would permit the pumps to pay for themselves.

Empirical studies have often found that credit
has not been a constraint on the use of new inputs,
especially in Africa. In Nigeria and Ghana, for
instance, it was found that traditional sources of
credit could finance higher rates of growth than
were being achieved although not the maximum growth
possible. Many more farmers in Malawi bought inputs
with cash when credit was not available, than when
it was. Credit is often unnecessary for modern inputs because these are self-financing. When inputs
are worth the effort, they pay for themselves in a
single season, including indigenous credit costs,
or they can be adopted in small doses so the farmer
can develop the necessary capital in a few seasons.

Most investment in agriculture can be undertaken with labour if tenure conditions and prices
make this worthwhile. If tenure and prices are inadequate, then credit is unlikely to be sufficient
to generate changes in output. For the poorest
farmers, their greatest need is more income rather
than credit. This does not mean credit has no role
to play in agricultural development. Short-term
credit may speed up development processes that are

already going on for other reasons. Credit may be
especially helpful to the poorer farmers who have
the least capacity for self-financing. Credit may
be more important following a land reform or other
major institutional reform as such reforms disrupt
traditional credit systems and make credit more
necessary.

Small farmers have special needs for consumer
as well as production credit. In some cases, farmers do not distinguish between production and consumption credit. In South East Asia over one half
of all borrowing by farm households goes to finance
consumption. As a result of his need for cash, the
small farmer is often forced to sell to larger
farmers part of the inputs he receives through loans
in-kind. In Tanzania this situation was aggravated
in a tobacco growing programme because farmers were
unable to grow maize for their own consumption needs.

Unfortunately, the small farmer's demand for
consumer credit is often ignored by official credit
programmes. Such programmes often explicitly
exclude consumption credit, e.g. by providing loans
in the form of production inputs rather than cash.
Official production credit often requires repayment
at harvest thus depriving the farmer of gains from
delayed selling. To prevent the use of production
credit for consumption, many credit programmes
require the farmer, with the aid of an extension
agent, to prepare a farm plan which is supervised to
see that the farm plan is implemented. Supervision
may also be a part of in-kind lending. In some
cases, credit is used to require farmers to grow
particular crops and to market through approved
channels.

There is frequently a need for medium- and
long-term credit to purchase cattle, or equipment,
or to make building or land improvements. Small
farmers may require longer-term credit to pay off
obligations to moneylenders and thus free themselves
to invest in and improve their farms. Longer term
credit may be required to finance market development
and storage. Since marketing expands much more
rapidly than output as production increases, it may
have a special need for credit. This type of credit
may be required by co-operatives, farmer associations and small food processors. Artisans, small
merchants, boatmen, etc. who live in rural areas
may also have needs for medium- and long-term
credit. Longer term credit becomes especially important when equity and rural development become
government objectives as it is precisely these types

of small farmer and rural production, and service
activities, that will form the basis for more equitable growth and rural development. Most government
sponsored rural credit programmes, however, specifically exclude all but short-term production
credit. Where longer term programmes are approved
they are often not funded.

Thus the first step in developing any credit
programme is to determine whether farmers really
need credit, then if they do to find out which farmers need it, for what purpose and for how long?
With this information, credit programmes can be designed that are truly responsive to the problems
farmers face.

B. <u>Collateral, subsidies and repayment rates</u>. In
many countries small farmers are excluded from
credit schemes because of collateral or down payment
requirements that they cannot meet. Even when there
are no such problems, there is often a presumption
that small farmers are unreliable, so they are
excluded simply because screening committees do not
trust or like them. Where such factors cannot be
shown to be operating, small farmers receive a dis-
proportionately small part of total loans.

The collateral problem for small farmers is
made worse by another common feature of credit programmes, especially those supposedly aimed at this
group. Often they are subsidized as an aid to small
farmers, or as an inducement to adopt the technology
package of which the credit is a part. This subsidy
has two unfortunate affects. It reduces the amount
of funds that can be loaned and it increases the demand for loans, often for less productive purposes.
The drain on loanable funds is further increased
when the administrative costs of lending are high,
as they are when dealing with large numbers of small
loans, or when complex loan provisions and production plans make supervision expensive. The result
is that credit must be rationed by some means other
than interest rates among the available consumers.
The usual tendency is for the amount of security,
i.e. collateral, to become a rationing criterion.
Thus low interest rates tend to indirectly exclude
small farmers from getting credit by raising collateral requirements and reducing the funds available.
Large farmers not only benefit from the cheap credit
but often re-lend the money to small farmers at
higher rates. Thus the subsidy goes to the traditional moneylenders rather than to the small farmers.
Not only is subsidized credit frequently

damaging to small farmers, it is usually unnecessary. The most successful credit programmes for small farmers tend to be those that charge the full cost of funds and credit administration, especially on short-term loans, which means, however, that administrative costs must be kept low.

Discrimination against small farmers persists even though empirical studies of loan repayments show that small farmers have better repayment rates than large farmers. Exceptions to this practice occur where small farmers have begun to regard loans as an income supplement, which they need not repay, or where crop failures prevent repayment.

C. Loan administration. A great deal can be done to increase the use of credit by small farmers while maintaining high repayment rates. It must be made clear that the loans are not grants, and that farmers must repay them. This does not mean telling the farmers what they already know. Rather, it is necessary to take action against defaulters as rapidly as possible. Some defaults may be deliberate. Larger farmers or moneylenders may try to destroy the credit programme to regain their control of rural lending. A second type of wilful default results from farmers waiting to see if the lender is, in fact, serious about repayment. They are testing the political will of the government. Both types of defaulter must be discovered and dealt with early if their example is to be kept from spreading.

Credit for small farmers must actually be for what the farmer needs. This means that loans must be granted for consumption as well as, or even before, it is granted for production. When credit is tied to technical packages, the packages must actually be what the farmer needs.

Loan conditions such as collateral or down payments must be eliminated or modified, at least until the farmers get the necessary resources. The evidence suggests that lack of collateral need not lead to unacceptable default rates. Paradoxically, granting consumer loans seems to improve repayment on both consumer and producer loans. In Mexico, farmers receiving consumer credit had ten to twenty percent better repayment rates on their production loans than farmers who received only production loans. The Wolamo Agricultural Development Unit in Ethiopia also increased repayment rates by granting consumption credit in the crucial pre-harvest period.

Longer repayment periods have also been shown

to increase repayment rates. Where repayment dates are set at normal harvest time, default is automatic if the harvest is late.

In addition, since crops can often be held for higher prices later, there are strong incentives to delay repayment.

Another method of preventing defaults is not to tie loans to inadequate production packages. In Kenya, the greatest reason for failure to repay was that farmers failed to receive the output expected in the official drafted plans on which the loans were based. This was due to both over-estimates of what was possible and failure of the farmers to behave the way the technicians thought they should behave. In Japan, government policy to stabilize prices helped repayments on lending to cereal producers. The key to this point seems to be that the farmers' technology must generate the income necessary to pay the loan rather than that a particular type of technology be used. If traditional technologies are insufficient then a new technology must be provided. If a good technology is available even if traditional, this is a sufficient basis to secure a loan.

Joint responsibility for loan repayment has been a big help in encouraging repayment. The most popular and successful form of credit group at Puebla in Mexico was the solidarity group of only three to nine members. Thus, very simple organizations are possible. In Thailand, administration of lending was turned over so completely to local authorities in one area that group responsibility for loans was not enforced. Instead local lenders had considerable flexibility to use locally accepted methods to obtain loan repayments. These methods were effective.

For joint responsibility to work there must be an organisation of farmers, and this unit must genuinely be responsible in the sense that a committee representing the organisation has the task of assessing credit needs. The unit must have the power to enforce action against defaulters. Where land holdings are unequal and wilful defaulters a problem, farmers may try to get the government to eliminate joint responsibility. Instead, it might be preferable to treat early losses as a cost of learning to run the system. This would allow societies to expel wilful defaulters and thus develop acceptable payment rates. More complete farmer administration of loan programmes would also drastically reduce the administrative cost and tedious procedures of small farmer loans which not only discourage lenders from making such loans, but also antagonize borrowers.

For credit systems that insist on some form of collateral, it is always possible to lend money on the crop produced. This has been done in Kenya and India. If this is to work as an enforcement mechanism, however, there must be some way of controlling the sale of the farmer's crop. In Kenya loans were only granted to farmers who had marketed their crop through the co-operative for at least three years and this worked satisfactorily. In Ethiopia, Tanzania and Japan, the co-operatives or marketing boards were made the sole legal outlet for marketing. To control the problem of defaults due to conditions beyond the grower's control, there may need to be some system of crop insurance such as the one required by the Kenya lender mentioned above. Compulsory insurance was not, however, popular with borrowers at Puebla in Mexico. They felt it protected the lender rather than the farmer.

It is clear that credit can be safely made available even to small farmers. However, this works best when the farmer is allowed to define his credit needs and the farmers are responsible for the lending operations and repayment. Down payments for inputs and collateral do not increase repayment rates when granted under the above conditions and when the farm technology used is adequate to increase farm incomes. Down payments and collateral do, however, exclude the farmers who need credit the most from the programme. Credit will not reach small farmers unless a decision is made to direct credit towards them and unless other policy changes necessary to achieve this objective are made.

4. Marketing Policy

Marketing concerns the monetized exchange of goods and services. There is a market sector in all countries where there is exchange of goods and services for money. In some countries the markets are run by the government; in others, by private enterprises; in still others, by a combination of the two. Combinations may mean some markets are purely private or public, or it can mean a system of quasi-private institutions, like co-operatives, which are tied into marketing boards or public trading corporations.

Regardless of the form and ownership of markets, certain characteristics are common to all marketing systems. They must provide for the movement, storage, collection and distribution of goods. When goods are perishable, provision must be made for preservation or speedy processing and distribution. When goods are not sold to consumers in the same form as they are obtained from producers, marketing must see that these goods are routed to and from intermediate processors.

Sometimes marketing is an independent activity, e.g. small traders who buy direct from producers and sell direct to consumers. In many cases, however, marketing is integrated in some way. Producers or consumers may operate part or all of the marketing system. Marketing co-operatives are an example of such a system. The marketing system itself may be integrated but be independent of producers or consumers. Finally, there are many mixed cases, e.g. where marketing is independent but there are connections as with preferential credit arrangements or monopoly, between part of the marketing system and producers or consumers.

No matter who performs the marketing functions or how these functions are organized, each marketing operation -- transportation, storage, processing, information gathering and risk bearing -- has costs which must be paid. Thus the marketing system must either be designed to cover these costs or a system of subsidies must be created to provide for their payment. Farmers and government officials must recognize the existence and legitimacy of such costs.

A. The role of marketing in developing agriculture. Without markets, there will be no agricultural development, as barter has nowhere provided a basis of exchange sufficient to support a modern agriculture. But markets must do more than keep pace with increased agricultural production. In fact, marketing expands much more rapidly than either agricultural output or gross national output in most developing countries. It is easy to see why; in an agricultural economy where some proportion of output is produced by farmers for their own use, but this proportion declines as the farmers' incomes increase, the proportion marketed will increase faster than total output. For instance, a farmer may grow 100 bushels of corn of which 80 bushels are consumed by his family, 20 bushels sold. If he grows 120 bushels, he may sell 30 bushels and consume 90. Thus a 20 percent increase in production means a 50 percent increase in marketing. This decline in the proportion of subsistence production during development is the normal state of affairs in agriculture the world over.

The tendency for marketing to increase faster than agricultural output is re-enforced by other factors. As production rises, more purchased inputs are used and these represent an addition to the sum of marketed goods. As confidence in the market system grows, farmers may choose to specialize in cash crops resulting in increasing proportions of their output passing through markets. Finally, government policy may deliberately favour market participation by taxing land or farm production, and thus forcing farmers to increase marketing in order to pay taxes.

Markets are the means whereby prices, a key aspect of the incentive system, reach the farmer. Without expanding markets at reasonable prices, domestic or foreign, there will be no reason for farmers to expand production. Farmers expand production in order to get the income to buy consumer goods. This buying, in turn, increases demand in consumer goods industries and spurs their growth. All too often the multiple effects of marketing on agriculture are neglected by policymakers. As a result, incentives are low and inputs for farming are scarce, expensive, unavailable or late. In many cases, the best investments in agriculture may be in agricultural marketing rather than directly in increasing output. Marketing, however, is a difficult system to understand, plan for and improve. When a policymaker examines the agricultural marketing system in his country he usually sees inadequate storage, poor transportation, a lack of uniformity in weights and measures, no standards for grading produce, inadequate credit, an almost complete lack of processing, and no system of market information.

That all these problems exist does not imply that the government should attempt to solve all of them at once. For instance, uniformity of weights and measures and a system of grading are prerequisites for an effective system of market information for all but the most homogeneous of bulk commodities. Transportation improvement will usually precede the development of agricultural processing industries. A high yielding varieties strategy must be supported with input supplies. However, once farmers begin to adopt the new varieties on a wide scale, storage and transportation will become more critical as the increased output has to be stored and moved to market. Weights, measures and grading will be less critical because grains are relatively homogeneous and traditional marketing systems can handle the existing quality variations.

If the strategy involves diversification or export promotion, priorities will be different. For exports and perishable products, weights and grading are critical and marketing laws to establish standards for these crops may have to precede all other measures.

Timing is often more important for export crops and perishables than for other crops, so all stages in the marketing chain may have to be more exactly controlled than is necessary for bulk crops. This requirement for tight control for export crops and for perishable crops, like fresh vegetables and cut flowers, has led to the development of a systems approach to commodity marketing for such products. However, such an approach assumes that the marketing system can be entirely rebuilt if necessary. Although governments frequently act as if they want to completely rebuild marketing systems, e.g. when they take over trade in certain commodities, experience shows that this is rarely possible if the marketing system is to work well. In fact, the system often works better if trade is returned to private hands.

Governments should build on the marketing systems that already exist by deciding to which national objectives they want marketing to contribute and then concentrating on getting markets to make those contributions. This may mean that traditional markets will be improved in specific ways, or that new marketing systems will be developed but only for those crops that require it.

If sound improvements in existing marketing systems are to be made, a first step is to obtain some idea of what the existing marketing system is and how it works. Developing countries often lack such information and a market survey may be necessary. Particular emphasis should be put on how the marketing system affects the incentives faced by the farmer, as the impact on agricultural output is a major concern in making market improvements. In some cases, retail marketing will also be a significant concern. Demand studies are especially important when export crops are being considered.

B. Traditional marketing. In all developing countries there is some form of traditional marketing, usually in private hands, that is well established. In many countries these markets handle primarily the surplus production of mainly subsistence producers. This means that, on one hand, farmers are little affected by market prices or other market incentives since they produce little for the market. They simply sell surpluses there. On the other hand, farmers are likely to sell their produce immediately after harvest for less than they would receive if they could wait. The buyers, in turn, often have limited storage facilities since the average surpluses sold are small. As a result of the low overall storage capacity and high seasonal sales, price swings are often wide. This instability makes the farmer even less interested in producing for the market and less influenced by price incentives, as price fluctuation increases the risk of investing in increased output.

The conditions which make a farmer primarily a subsistence producer are largely beyond the control of the merchant. Land tenure may play a big role if it limits the returns to farmer efforts. Low prices for farmer output and low demand prevent farmers from seeking higher incomes by expanding production. The lack of consumer goods and services to buy make higher income less meaningful for the farmer. The lack of inputs and technologies that would provide adequate returns to the farmer also discourage market participation. All these things are beyond the control of the marketing system. No amount of market reform or government procurement will encourage increased farmer marketing unless these conditions are remedied.

There are some incentive defects which are clearly related to the market system, however. For instance, price fluctuations due to poor storage facilities. Poor inter-market integration is also a problem. Even where local markets are fairly well integrated with more central national markets, they may be largely uncoordinated with each other, leading to large price differences between regional or local markets.

This lack of lateral coordination is due to the pyramiding structure of markets. After a merchant buys and collects a product at one level, e.g. from the farmer, he moves it to the next higher level where it is sold to another merchant who similarly collects from lower levels and sells to higher levels. This structure continues up through several middlemen to processors, major cities or export markets. It is a structure which allows each middleman or woman to personally inspect the produce bought. In Ghana, for instance, there were three middlewomen between sorghum growers and a beer producer 60 miles away. In Ethiopia, there were an average of four to five middlemen between the farmer and retail sale or an assembly point for export in Addis Ababa. Such market structures orient the whole market system towards major collection points and tend to overlook inter-market differences within the economy.

The combination of market fragmentation and unstable prices has hurt many agricultural development projects. If the project leads to increased production there is an especially large drop in price. This is because of the low capacity of the local marketing system to handle large quantities and the isolation of each local market from other local markets. This problem has discouraged agricultural development, or led to the inclusion of marketing schemes in agricultural projects, all over the world.

C. Marketing reform. The role of demand and markets in expanded production is perhaps most clearly seen in the differences between the role of markets in the expansion of largely subsistence crops and of cash crops. Other than the recent cereal successes based on high yielding varieties, the major successes in agriculture have been reforms in the marketing of particular cash crops such as cotton, coffee, cocoa, tea, sugar, tobacco, groundnuts, rubber and palm products. Although a variety of types of production organization are responsible for these successes, everything from plantations to both highly supervised and relatively unsupervised small farmer production, there has been one common factor – the existence of highly organized marketing systems to supply a growing demand.

In many cases marketing organizations sought out willing farmers, trained and financed them. In Bogota, Colombia, for instance, the Carculla Company provided help to growers of perishable fruits and vegetables for its stores. Other stores then began developing their own suppliers. In Puerto Rico, a supermarket chain fostered a similar system for eggs. The development of processing facilities led to expanded marketing output in many cases, e.g. the establishment of sugar mills in Greece, Kenya, Sudan, Tanzania, Uganda, Pakistan, Iran and Chile led to the creation of a marketing system and expanded sugar production.

These marketing and processing facilities developed before agricultural output increased. This was because significant marketable surpluses were not produced until markets became available. But this meant that marketing facilities had to be

prepared to accept losses during the early years of
their operation. Thus it is not surprising that
marketing-and-processing-led agricultural development has been associated with high value cash crops;
it is these crops that justify the high initial investments involved. This also explains the frequent
participation of governments, foreign investors or
large companies in the development of such processing and marketing facilities. Such organizations
can afford these large investments, which can be reduced if the marketing project includes provision
for developing agricultural output along with processing and marketing facilities. A sugar mill in
India accomplished this by growing sugar cane on a
plantation basis until local growers became sufficiently interested so that the cane growing operations could be turned over to them.
Starting small and expanding may work where
economies of scale are not so significant as to
render a small operation unprofitable. This has
worked well in exporting out-of-season vegetables
and flowers from Central American countries to U.S.
markets, for instance. Similar opportunities have
been exploited in the Mediterranean region for sending fruits and vegetables to European countries.

D. Standards, grades and market information. One
important step in improving the marketing of most
agricultural products is providing standard weights
and measures. In India, farmers' preferences for
markets where standard weights and measures were used
drove non-complying markets out of business. Thus
the introduction of standard weights and measures
was self-enforcing in this case. To come about generally, however, there must be both a marketing law
to establish standard measures and information programmes to make farmers fully aware of how they can
use the law.
    Almost as important are standard grades for
produce. As markets develop it becomes important
that buyers are able to contract for commodities on
short notice and at long distances. Since these conditions mean that the buyer cannot personally inspect
the product, there must be standard grades reliably
used if such transactions are to be made. The alternative is to continue the traditional chain of
middlemen where each one can personally supervise
the quality of commodities bought and sold. Introduction of standard grades facilitates the development of production and the reduction of wastage.
Grading can drastically cut wastage as products which

are waste to an urban market may not be waste in a rural market or if culled from the marketing chain sooner. Even unacceptable products may become live-stock feed if separated soon enough.

The need for grading and measurement standards is increasingly being recognized and marketing laws are being passed. Benefits from grading have not, however, been universal. In Latin America, some grain buying was by grade but sales were not, so it was difficult to convince farmers that buying by grade was justified. Clearly the justification of grades and standards depends on their usefulness to the trade and hence their ability to generate higher returns to farmers for graded produce. Standards for bulk grains will be hard to justify until long distance trade develops and in significant volume.

As stated earlier, the primary purpose of grad-ing is to facilitate communications where personal inspection is not practical. But simply grading produce serves no purpose if information about prices and grades is not available to buyers and sellers. Grading helps marketing only if buyers are aware of what is offered and sellers are aware of what is wanted, i.e. where and when prices for particular grades are high and low. Grading makes the transmission of such information practical since produce can be described in terms of standard grades rather than by having each lot individually descri-bed by the seller. Not only do grades make improved information possible, but improved information forces producers to adopt the grading standards in order to sell their produce or get higher prices. Thus extension services should be prepared to pro-vide information to farmers on grading systems as this becomes more important.

Market information must be timely to be useful. Prices often change rapidly and produce may spoil. Buyers and sellers need information that is current up to the day and, in some cases, even time of day. Thus market information programmes must be establi-shed that will make farmers aware - if farmers are aware, you can be sure buyers will be - of what prices are currently being offered, or what the official prices are. Where transportation costs are a big factor in farmer prices, they also need to be well publicized so farmers can discount the central market prices that are officially quoted. In many countries high transportation costs and poor infor-mation mean that farmers must sell their crops for whatever price is offered when transport is avail-able. Poor information is also a major cause of price discrepancies between rural markets.

Another type of market information is also important: long term prices and price expectations. Information on future demand and prices is also necessary to officials conducting price stabilization operations. Such information should be as clear, accurate and precise as possible and available far enough in advance so that the farmer can use it in his planning.

In practice, marketing reform has been most successful when it has proceeded on a crop-by-crop basis. As a processor or international market develops, so do marketing facilities and organizations, standard weights, measures and grades and improved marketing information. The first step in planned market improvement for crops that cannot support their own marketing system would be standard weights and measures. This is a key step in increasing producer confidence, and hence output, and is the basis for later improvements in grading of produce and market information.

Attempts to improve marketing may well mean a fuller degree of competition between the different public and private agencies. Governments can often protect farmers more efficiently by making markets more competitive through better information, roads and marketing facilities than by acting as substitutes for traders. The indigenous trading system should often be more fully exploited even where the tradition of local entrepreneurship is weak. Its merit lies in its small-scale, decentralised and flexible structure.

5. Employment, Mechanization and Technology Policies

A. The problem of unemployment and under-employment

Unemployment and under-employment are serious problemt in developing countries. Where the seasonal nature of agriculture prevents unemployment from continuing throughout the year, under-employment is still a problem. In Mexico, the number of days worked by farm labourers declined between 1950 and 1960 from 190 to 100 days per year. Similar conditions exist in many other countries. Such under-employment is often coupled with labour shortages during harvest time. Rural-urban migration is also a problem. Urban areas attract rural workers but modern economic activities are relatively capital using, so urban employment grows slowly. Migration means moving the unemployment problem to the city and perhaps worsening rather than solving it.

Under- and un-employment are often caused by

increasing population. Even in countries where
over-population is not yet a problem, rapid population growth may contribute to the unemployment
problem by producing workers faster than jobs can
be created. Labour surpluses are also caused by
government policies which encourage labour-replacing
mechanization or lead to reduced demand for farm
output through low food prices or policies which
discourage exports.

If the unemployment problem is to be solved,
many of the new jobs necessary will have to be
created in agriculture and in rural society generally. Some developing countries have created
sufficient non-farm employment so that the absolute
number of workers in agriculture is declining. This,
however, is not typical. India is faced with increasing rural unemployment and no prospect of major
transfers of labour to non-agricultural employment.
In most of Asia, for example, agriculture will have
to provide more employment in coming decades.

B. <u>Mechanization and employment</u>. If a country is to
be successful in significantly reducing agricultural
under- and un-employment, reconsideration of its
policies affecting mechanization is likely to be
required. Although awareness of the employment problem is growing, as shown by the extent to which
employment goals are set in development plans,
changes in policies towards mechanization have been
much slower in coming. Where policy turned against
mechanization in South America, for example, it was
because of foreign exchange constraints rather than
a preference for labour-using technologies to provide employment. In Africa, some tractor schemes
failed because of rapid wear and corrosion coupled
with poor maintenance, poor operation and management
and inappropriateness for local soils, ecological
conditions and size of fields. In Spain, and in
other countries, mechanization was inhibited by farm
plot size and increased operating costs. Clearly,
if headway is to be made against unemployment,
serious thought must be given as to what types of
mechanization are desirable and under what conditions they will work best.

Currently, developing countries have many
policies that favour mechanization. Over-valued
exchange rates, inflation, subsidized credit, and
tariff and tax exemptions all tend to make mechanical equipment artificially cheap. There are also
subsidies on operating costs such as fuel, repair
centres and driver training. Crops which lend

themselves to mechanization enjoy special price or subsidy advantages.

Thus, farm mechanization which, of course, is encouraged by manufacturers and may be very profitable to them, is frequently also profitable to equipment users, but only because of the various subsidies. Such mechanization cannot, however, always be justified from a social viewpoint.

Sometimes mechanization policies are part of a consistent overall development scheme, e.g. in Republic of Korea. Often, however, the mechanization bias of policy seems to be a chance element or due to a mistaken notion that mechanization is the only way to modernize. For instance, in Latin America, although farm machinery is usually exempt from import tariffs and domestic production enjoys tax exemptions, spare parts are subject to heavy duties. Shortages of imported spare parts have immobilized many expensive imported tractors. Many mechanization schemes in Africa, promoted by governments trying to modernize agriculture rapidly, have turned out to be costly failures.

The result of the mechanization bias of policy has been widespread replacement of labour by equipment. This is particularly true in Latin America but also in other areas e.g. Turkey. In the Indian Punjab, for example, the man days per acre required for wheat on well-irrigated 10-acre farms rose from 33.4 to 42.5 with the introduction of high yielding varieties but fell to 18.1 man days per acre when tractors were used and only 12.1 man days per acre with both tractors and reapers.

Where mechanization has already developed to a significant extent and unemployment has risen, social unrest is likely to follow. Tenants are evicted and farm workers displaced by equipment. Profits from subsidized production on large farms lead large holders or outsiders to buy up small holdings as has happened in India, Pakistan and the Philippines. If wages rise, landlords may increase mechanization which will further worsen tensions with workers.

Some technology is not labour replacing, however. The use of powered pumps, for example, can have a major employment impact by allowing more intensive use of the land. To take advantage of the potential of water development, India reoriented its rural electrification priorities towards areas where underground water could be developed for irrigation. With commercial crops, the need for accurate grading, rapid response to orders, and shipping of products while fresh may make mechanical graders essential if producers are to keep their market.

Multiple cropping often demands rapid harvesting and threshing of one crop and soil preparation for planting the next crop, at the same time. In India, bullock and human power were not always able to cope with the demand for speed, especially on larger farms. As a result, mechanization was introduced in conjunction with high yielding varieties. Total labour demand rose by 14 percent even though tractors and electric pumps reduced the labour needed for traditional varieties by more than 50 percent. The shortage of bullock power was especially acute because bullocks were used for both threshing and tillage. Since the high yielding varieties raise both output and allow multiple cropping, threshing and cultivation needs go up sharply and concurrently. Time becomes even more critical when three or four crops are grown successively.

Rain and other weather conditions also increase the returns to rapid tillage. In Turkey, trials over twelve years showed that planting cereals in October rather than November increased output about 40 percent. In Zambia, delaying planting a week after the rains started reduced the yields of groundnuts and maize by 500 to 700 kilograms per hectare. In Kenya, maize planted to take advantage of early rains yielded about 50 percent more than maize planted 28 days later. Tractor use proved to be employment-creating in the Mvea irrigation scheme in Kenya. In Thailand, tractors can plough before the monsoon rains, a job that buffaloes are too weak to do, resulting in a net gain in labour use of 20 to 30 man days per hectare because rice can be transplanted, a labour-intensive activity, rather than broadcast.

These types of mechanization or technology are labour-using because they allow production of crops that greatly increase labour demand during non-peak periods. Increased labour use is especially likely when mechanization permits multiple cropping.

Mechanization, however, encourages multiple cropping only where land is scarce or irrigation, though needed, is limited to certain areas. Where good land is plentiful, tractor mechanization is much more likely to be labour- than land-saving. Even in irrigated areas, there may be no justification for tractors if multiple cropping is not putting a premium on harvest and planting speed, as for instance, in parts of Sri Lanka.

Furthermore, if output increasing mechanization

182

is to help all farmers, special provision must be
made for making it available to small farmers.
Intermediate degrees of mechanization should be
used. Tractor hire schemes can be established although in Nigeria and Tanzania these were costly and
inefficient. In some areas of Thailand, the government helped farmer groups to jointly purchase tractors. Governments must provide for equal access if
mechanization is not to lead to increasing rural
inequality.

Even if harvesting-planting speed is important
small scale locally made threshing machines to
mechanize harvesting may be preferable to using
tractors for planting. Improvements in ploughs and
introduction of harrows for bullocks can save planting time. In India, the moldboard plough and a
modern harrow reduced seedbed preparation time to
18 hours compared to 94 hours for the traditional
plough and plank method. Hand-operated seed drills
can speed planting, reduce wastage and make weeding
much easier, as has happened in Portugal. Where
tractors are necessary, two-wheeled rather than
larger four-wheeled can be used. In China (Taiwan),
these have reduced the labour in seedbed preparation
but increased total employment and farm income by
increasing the number of crops that can be grown.

On coffee estates in Kenya, use of herbicides
and mechanical applications of inputs has reduced
non-harvest labour while higher yields have increased harvest labour. The result is that a permanent labour force has been transformed into a
casual, seasonal labour force. Weeding can be a
labour-intensive activity because there is little
other need for labour when weeding should be done.
If mechanization of this task is encouraged, fairly
simple hand-operated weeders can be provided.

Mechanization may be labour-saving, labour-
using, or both, with a net employment effect that
depends on factors such as the degree of land and
water scarcity, the practicability of using high
yielding varieties or growing cash crops and other
factors. Regardless of whether increased employment
is a primary or secondary goal, it will be necessary
to look closely at the local circumstances and develop a mechanization programme suited to them.

C. Alternatives to mechanization. With few exceptions, traditional agriculture in developing countries has been carried out with labour-using technologies. At the same time, output per worker has
been low. Mechanization has helped increase output

per worker but frequently by decreasing the number of workers employed. Thus, in addition to adopting more selective mechanization policies, governments which intend to increase employment will also want to consider technologies which increase output while also increasing employment. As long as output increases more rapidly than employment, both productivity and employment will rise.

One way of increasing both is to foster the substitution of high value, more labour intensive crops or livestock for traditional food crops. In Kenya, for instance, increased employment has been one of the major benefits of the smallholder tea project. Tea is extremely labour intensive and difficult to mechanize. As a result, it has provided considerable employment for both the growers and for casual labour from the surrounding areas. Tea growing has also created considerable employment in tea factories, marketing and with tea-linked industries, e.g. transport, fuel supply and small-scale activities like production of bags and baskets. Cotton production in Mali attracted large numbers of seasonal workers and significantly decreased the number of young men who were leaving the villages to go to the capital. In Guinea and Liberia, the employment effect of expanding iron ore or bauxite exports was found to be negligible compared to expanding exports through smallholder production of export crops.

Another way of increasing both output and employment is to adopt more labour-intensive cultivation methods, i.e. biological improvements for food crops. Diversification can spread labour demand out over the year as well as increase employment. The largest possibility in this field lies with the high yielding varieties because they have shorter and more flexible growing seasons and allow for more than one crop a year on the same land. This means labour demand can expand with the intensity of cropping. In the Pakistani Punjab, roughly proportional expansion of labour use and cropping occurred. In Ludhiana, India, agricultural labour wages rose significantly and employment became available all year around due to the high yielding varieties that were used in the area.

The high yielding varieties increase employment in other ways. In the Philippines, for instance, the increase in labour requirements was estimated to be 30 to 50 percent due to the use of new rice varieties even without multiple cropping. This is because cultivation practices are more demanding for

184

high yielding than for traditional crop varieties. There is increased labour demand for tillage, application of fertilizer and pesticides, weeding, water control and harvesting, unless labour-saving mechanization reduces labour demand.

The potential for even greater increases in employment exists. In Japan, farmers use about 170 man days of labour to grow and harvest high yielding varieties of rice while Indian farmers use about 125 man days and 100 man days are use in the Philippines. In spite of this, output per man, and hence farm income, is higher in Japan than in developing countries and is higher for high yielding variety growers than for those of traditional varieties in all these countries.

In Japan, the use of new cultivation practices, improved varieties and fertilizer, coupled with pumps, better animal-drawn ploughs and harrows, weeders and pedal threshers have been the basis for a remarkable rise in yields.

Expanded and improved use of animal power is another alternative to mechanization. In much of Africa, the increased use of draft animals is one of the more promising ways of increasing the amount of power being applied to agricultural tasks. It can also expand labour use by extending the area under cultivation. Increased use of animal power can be more economical than expanded use of land, labour or tractors, although this has not always been the case. Animal power has the further advantages of economizing on expensive fuels and providing many useful products such as milk, manure and eventually meat and hides. Some of the potential of animal power lies in improving the technology of animal drawn equipment.

D. Non-farm employment. It is unrealistic to expect agriculture to solve all of the rural employment problem, however. Even with large scale land reform, as in Japan, where most farmers only work part-time on their holdings, it is rare that everyone gets enough land to be fully employed. If the employment problem is to be solved, other solutions are needed.

(i) Rural public works. One solution is labour-intensive public works to build infrastructure in rural areas. Simple projects can be adjusted to fit in between seasonal peaks in demand for agricultural labour thus avoiding a drop in farm output. This has the virtue of turning unused

185

labour into a national asset as in China and
Pakistan. India, Indonesia, Republic of Korea, and
other countries have also had such programmes. In
some cases rural works programmes have been supported by internationally supported "Food for Work"
programmes. Mostly, however, the country will have
to finance the programme itself which makes it
especially urgent that it is not just a welfare
measure but contributes significantly to growth in
output.

Public works programmes which create productive
infrastructure such as roads, canals and public
buildings, provide the basis for generating further
employment in agriculture, services and industry
once the programme itself is complete. This is
essential if such works are going to do more than
delay the unemployment problem rather than solve it.

If public works programmes are to be self-
financing to any significant extent, it is necessary
that they be undertaken in a context of rising agricultural productivity. The return to the public
works investment will be migh higher when followed
by rapid changes in technology and increased agricultural output and marketings than if agriculture
remains relatively stagnant. Thus, to get the full
benefit, rural public works must be coordinated with
input supply development and other rural services.

Since labour is the major cost in rural works,
it must be closely supervised. Basing wages on performance has worked in some cases. However, this
would be unfair to or even exclude some of the
people who need help the most where malnutrition is
a problem, or where many of the unemployed are
women, the sick, or the very young or old. Providing
a meal during the work day has been found to increase productivity a great deal on some projects.

(ii) Other sources of employment. Although
rural public works sometimes have a tendency to become permanent because of rising unemployment or
political pressures, they are not a permanent solution to employment problems. Even where programmes
are long-term they shift from area to area as the
most useful projects are completed and allocations
to particular areas vary from year to year. As more
marginal projects are undertaken, the programme becomes less self-supporting and more of a burden on
the rest of the economy. Only China seems to have
been able to escape these problems sufficiently to
maintain continuous public works programmes in
rural areas. Generally when there is insufficient

agricultural employment, there must be alternative sources of non-farm employment in addition to public works.

If the public works have been well designed, they will have laid the basis for much non-farm employment, as well as much farm employment. Roads will increase demand for transportation. Higher incomes will increase the need for commerce and construction. Much of the higher income will be spent on food which will increase the prosperity of farmers and increase their demand for labour. All these activities will spur the demand for others and create new opportunities for local people to start or expand businesses of all kinds. In many countries, a considerable amount of a farmer's time is already spent on non-farm economic activities such as crafts and trading. If rural income grows, these activities should also increase.

Processing of agricultural products, marketing and input supply are other ways of expanding employment. If mechanization is to be undertaken, further employment can be generated if the machines used can be locally made and repaired. Tractors will often be imported or produced in large capital-intensive factories. Tools and simple animal-drawn implements can be made by local artisans. Threshers can also be manufactured locally. Even simple pumps and diesel engines can be manufactured in local labour-intensive factories.

China has gone the farthest with rural industrialization policies by encouraging the development of fertilizer, cement and farm machinery factories in rural areas. Although quality is often inferior in such factories, it is quite adequate for rural uses and far superior to nothing at all. These factories generate considerable employment, although this is not their intended purpose, and save freight costs.

A great deal can also be done to generate industrial jobs in rural areas through systems of subcontracting of certain types of production to small scale rural industry, and locating industries in rural areas when economies of scale are not critical. Japan has developed enough such industries so that many farm people in rural areas have some non-agricultural job. The Republic of Korea is encouraging the growth of rural industry of a similar type. This may not prove as practical in countries where densities are less and distances greater, though it would still seem appropriate in the vicinity of larger urban centres.

Such small-scale activities will not develop, however, if government policies are not favourable. If increased agricultural income is drained out of rural areas by landlords, low prices for agricultural products, or other means, such activities will not come about. Initially, emphasis should be placed on making necessary policy and institutional changes. For instance, any significant growth in rural economic activity may require institutions which mobilize rural savings but keep them in rural areas. Governments must be prepared to foster such institutions. Initial projects should be small in scale with quick payoffs to generate the employment, skills and savings necessary for further activity. After this, emphasis should be placed on maintaining the momentum of rural-based development by simultaneous expansion of agricultural output and incomes, processing and input supply, and the whole complex of goods and services which go with rising income and the growth of rural towns.

E. Choice of technology. Although it is impossible, without examining the circumstances, to determine whether mechanization is desirable or how employment in agriculture might best be increased in conjunction with rising productivity, certain general principles do emerge.

Mechanization of farming will increase in all developing countries. However, the degree and pace will depend on the wisdom and policy of the governments concerned. When employment is a consideration, mechanization should be selective and begin with improvements of traditional labour and animal-powered activities where possible. In some cases more advanced mechanization may have to be promoted for particular crops or areas. Intermediate forms of technology, e.g. pedal threshers, will be highly beneficial in many cases. The particular type and degree of mechanization for a specific set of farm conditions can only be determined by careful regional, farm and crop need research and analysis.

Perhaps the biggest obstacle to such careful work is the prejudice that mechanization means large-scale farms and equipment, and that only mechanization is modern and therefore desirable. Events in Japan, China (Taiwan) and, on a smaller scale elsewhere, have shown this prejudice to be wrong. The true essence of modern technology is more chemical and biological than mechanical. The new technology is chemical fertilizers, pesticides and new disease-resistant and high yielding varieties.

If mechanization is to complement rather than displace labour in agricultural production, then present policies which subsidize the use of capital should be eliminated so that prices will more closely reflect actual costs in the country. Not only must direct contributions to capital costs, e.g. subsidies, artificially low interest rates and low fuel prices, be reduced or eliminated but indirect contributions like over-valued exchange rates must also be removed or adjusted. Where, for whatever reason, a subsidy measure cannot be corrected, e.g. changing an over-valued exchange rate may be politically impossible, it will be necessary to take counterbalancing measures, e.g. impose a tariff on the particular types of equipment. Policy changes of this type will conserve scarce capital, foreign exchange and fuel as well as preserve and provide employment.

When mechanization is going to be permitted or encouraged, it is necessary to take great care in selecting the type of innovations. Pumps for irrigation will almost always be employment as well as output-increasing. Commercial crops, high yielding varieties and multiple cropping are all dependent, in many environments, on increased water supply and control. In most other cases, only a careful analysis of the local situation will determine where mechanization will actually increase employment.

Finally, it has to be recognized that in some places, none of these measures will solve the unemployment problem or significantly help equalize income. In Latin America especially, the only effective way of providing full employment may well be land redistribution. This may be the only way to get a sufficient degree of labour use in agricultural and small scale industrial technology. Small scale farming is the most labour intensive method of agricultural organization.

6. Land Reform
A. Access to land and water. For the vast numbers of people living and working in the rural areas of the developing countries, the land is virtually their only productive asset apart from their own labour. Their rights to land and water are of fundamental importance in determining living conditions.

Gross inequality of the distribution of rights to land remain a fundamental problem, leading to a concentration of wealth at one end of the scale and rural squalor, waste and poverty at the other. Another factor, population pressure, has turned

millions of marginal farms into uneconomic units,
even for bare subsistence. Badly implemented land
reforms have led to the eviction of tenants and so-
called "voluntary surrenders" where shifts to entrepreneurship were more rewarding than usury and
rentier ownership, large owners have bought out the
small ones, pushed out the share-cropper and even
leased in from the marginal owner who had lacked the
means needed to benefit from new production methods.

In many countries, tenants (many of them small
and mostly sharecroppers) continue to form a significant proportion of the total number of cultivators,
despite the trend towards large commercial farms.
There has been a marked rise in the number of marginal and small farmers. Between 1960 and 1970, for
example, the proportion of farmers in Bangladesh
holding less than one hectare increased from 52 to
66 percent; and in India from 40 to 51 percent. In
Latin America, the growth in the number of mini-
fundia, and the consequent increase in poverty,
resulted in migration from rural areas to urban
slums. Even in parts of Africa, where customary
technical arrangements have afforded some protection
against these developments, changes in customary
tenure in favour of individual interests in land
have led to fundamental changes in the traditional
economic homogeneity, and enabled priviledged individuals to accumulate wealth and influence.

The inter-relationship between exploitative
land tenure systems and environmental degradation in
rural areas is becoming obvious in many countries.
Farmers who are deprived of access to fertile land,
which is monopolised by large landowners or by foreign companies, have no other resource but the
cultivation of marginal zones, contributing to
erosion, deforestation and soil exhaustion.

B. Major obstacles to land reform. Land reform in-
tends to bring about a more equitable distribution
of rights to land and water, as a start towards
increasing productivity of small farmers and meeting
the needs of the rural poor. It generally has some
part - often the major part - in agricultural development strategies. Experience has shown only too
well, however, that there are major obstacles to
land or agrarian reform. These should be borne in
mind when rural development strategies are being
considered.

There are three basic types of land tenure reform: (1) redistribution of private holdings, (2)
settlement of unoccupied lands and (3) regulation of

tenancy.

The first type of reform is the most difficult, calling for hard political decisions and popular support for their implementation. In many cases, redistribution of private lands has required constitutional amendments, action to close legal loopholes, and effective administration and often new financial and technical measures to implement the reform laws. Even where there are no constitutional obstacles, a serious problem is often the ambiguity in the intent and language of the legislation. In many cases these laws were not designed primarily to achieve equity and social justice. Effective administration calls for reliable records of ownership and tenancy, avoidance of delays between enacting and implementing legislation, the means of quick take-over of eligible land and its distribution to the new peasant proprietors. The experience of several countries suggests that all these administrative requirements can be met more effectively when the beneficiaries of the reform group together and are able to take part in the process. In a number of cases, attempts to redistribute rights of land and water have been impeded by lack of funds to pay for expropriated land and to cover the costs of administration. Some governments have overcome the financial difficulties by confiscating land and other assets, others have devised systems of compensation by state bonds or the repayment of costs by the recipients of expropriated land.

Settlement schemes of unoccupied lands have been handicapped by a scarcity of productive land and high administrative costs. An FAO-Unesco study of land quality in Latin America, for example, indicates that 90 percent of the soils in the Amazon region are low in fertility and too fragile to support settlements. Twenty percent of the continent is arid and cannot be farmed without irrigation. Other apparently available lands in the Andes are too mountainous. The study concludes that there are no sizeable unoccupied areas in Latin America which are suitable for farming, and consequently that land settlement does not represent a viable option for rural development in that region. In some African countries, complex and sophisticated settlement programmes were tried in the early 1960s but failed because the necessary administrative and technical skills were lacking. Less ambitious projects which involved only modest changes in the traditional agriculture and were appropriate to the abilities of the local people met with fewer diffi-

culties. Nomadic populations have presented
special problems for settlement projects in the Near
East and parts of Africa. Large-scale settlement
schemes on newly irrigated land have been carried
out in a number of countries including Egypt, Iran,
Iraq, Libya, Pakistan, Syria and Sudan. In the Far
East, only a few countries (e.g. Malaysia and Sri
Lanka) have sizeable unoccupied areas of land. They
have implemented major settlement programmes but met
a number of common difficulties in coordinating work
in the field, providing adequate work for the people
involved and developing efficient supporting
services. Costs have been high in relation to the
numbers taking part.

Regulation of tenancy, the third type of reform, has been important in countries with high
population densities, especially in the Far East
(e.g. Bangladesh, eastern parts of India and Nepal,
the Philippines) but there have been common difficulties, including the lack of accurate records of
tenancy, the inability of poor tenants to seek re-
dress in the courts, the absence of tenant organizations and the lack of participation by tenants in
the implementation of regulatory measures. Where
population pressures are great, and alternative non-
farm employment opportunities few, land values rise
to very high levels and make regulation of tenancy
extremely difficult. Under such conditions, fair
rents and scarcity of tenure are unlikely to be
achieved through open market negotiations between
landowners and tenants. In Africa, the emergence of
individual rights and increasing land speculation,
especially around the capitals and large urban centres, have attracted absentee landlords. In some
countries measures have therefore been taken to
limit ownership and to protect rights conferred
under customary tenures.

C. Land reform in a development strategy. For land
reform to be effective, it has to be accompanied or
followed by policies to provide inputs and services
to the reformed sector and to other rural areas.
Rural development strategies with strong emphasis on
agrarian reform demand considerable investment in
economic infrastructure, basic community services
including health care, production support services,
etc. The most serious constraints on investment
have been experienced in the poor countries in sub-
Saharan Africa and the Far East. A shift of investment in favour of rural areas is required in these
and other countries but is only likely to be effec-

tive in a context of generally increasing investment. Moreover, policies of governments have often
had conflicting aims and have lacked specific
directions, target dates and means of checking and
evaluating progress. A common weakness in almost
all developing countries is the acknowledged in-
adequacy and incompleteness of land reform programmes.

All the various factors outlined above, which
have a bearing on the success or failure of land
reform, should be taken into account when a development strategy is being revised or prepared afresh.
A key element in this assessment is, of course, the
special pattern of land tenure in the country concerned and farmers' preferences for a new system of
tenure. The people need to be given a type of land
tenure they are satisfied with and on which they
can learn new techniques and acquire new needs.
Tenure and type of organization can then be modified
gradually. As a matter of strategy, it may help to
separate major land ownership reforms from changes
in production organization.

7. <u>Characteristics of Different Types of Measures</u>
As a general guide to the choice of measures which
can be used in agricultural development, Table 10-1
summarises their main characteristics. A few
points may be noted. Not many agricultural measures
make heavy demands on the most scarce resource,
foreign exchange. Large-scale irrigation, fertilizer and mechanization programmes have the largest
demands in this respect. Skilled personnel is probably second only to foreign exchange in degree of
scarcity. Many kinds of projects make considerable
demands on this resource, particularly management,
but in some cases skilled personnel required may be
conveniently obtained from abroad. The need for
domestic funds is fairly considerable for most types
of projects, contrary to the general view. However,
for off-farm projects with a high labour content,
food aid may be an important substitute for domestic
wage funds.

A striking conclusion from Table 10-1 is that
most development projects in agriculture have high
administrative requirements in the form of organisational networks reaching far into rural areas. For
many projects, this network can be provided by
farmers' associations or cooperatives, and high
priority should be given to their establishment and
co-ordination.

From the preceding discussion, it should be

Table 10-1   Characteristics of Typical Agricultural
Development Measures and Projects

Measure or Project	Gestation Period	Non-farm investment requirement		
		Foreign Exchange	Domestic Capital	Labour
Irrigation				
- large scale	long	high	high	high
- small scale	short	low	medium	low
Development of new land				
- by government	long	medium	high	low
- by private farmers	short	low	low	-
Land settlement	long	medium	high	low
Soil conservation	long	low or nil	high	high
Feeder roads	short	low or nil	medium	high
Fertilizer supplies	short	high	medium	low
Breeding better crops or livestock	long	low	medium	low
Wider use best existing seeds	short	nil	low	low
Farm mechanization	short	high	high	low
Feeds for livestock	short	low	medium	low
Research and physical surveys	long	low	medium	low
Extension and training services	medium-short	low	medium	low
Higher agricultural education	long	medium	medium	low
Agrarian reforms	long	-	-	-
Improved marketing systems	short	low	medium	low
Credit institutions	medium	-	high	-
Farmer's association and cooperatives	long	-	medium	-
Stabilization of farm prices	short-medium	-	high	-

Production expenditure on farms		Current government expenditure requirement	Administrative requirement	
Monetary	Non-Monetary		Organizational Network	Skilled Personnel
low	high	low	medium	high (or foreign)
medium	high	low	medium	low
-	-	low	medium	medium (or foreign)
low	high	low	-	-
may be high	high	high	high	high
low	high	low	-	medium
-	-	medium-low	-	low
high	low	low(subsidies)	high (non-govt?)	low
-	-	medium	low	high
-	medium	medium	high (non-govt?)	low
high	-	low	" "	high(n-gov?)
medium	-	low(subsidies)	" "	low
-	-	medium	low	high (or foreign)
encouraged	encouraged	high	high	high
-	-	high	low	high (foreign)
encouraged	encouraged	compensation?	high initially	-
encouraged	encouraged	low	high (non-govt?)	medium (non-govt?)
encouraged	-	medium	high (non-govt?)	high(n.gov?)
encouraged	-	low	high (non-govt?)	medium (non-govt?)
encouraged	encouraged	medium	high	high

Source: Introduction to Agricultural Planning (Agricultural Planning Studies, No. 12) Rome, FAO, 1970, p.68.

195

clear that not all the measures listed in the table
are alternatives. Many are complementary to each
other and give their best results only when combined.

Governments often tend to concentrate too much
expenditure on agricultural measures which have long
gestation periods, not only causing the capital-
output ratio to be far too high in say the first
plan period, but also to require diversion of
foreign exchange for food imports. (If food or
financial aid is readily available, it may, however,
be possible to adopt such a long-term approach from
the beginning). Usually, shortages of foreign exchange and capital force governments to achieve a
better balance between immediate and longer-term
needs.

8. <u>Simplicity and Success</u>. "The success of development depends first and foremost on the extent to
which policy is designed to overcome not just one
obstacle, however important it may be - as for
example land reform - but rather to deal comprehen-
sively with the whole range of problems." Recommendations by the World Bank and other donor or
advisory institutions often urge such comprehensive
planning and coordination. Many others take the
same approach. Of the many policy actions possible,
many are recommended and few are regarded as unnecessary. How is the planner to decide which are
important? The rule seems to be: do everything so
you won't leave out anything vital. Unfortunately,
the planner and policy-maker do not have the time
or the resources to do everything. Choices must be
made and priorities established.

China (Taiwan) achieved a fine balance between
incentives for agricultural production and skimming
off rural savings for investment in other sectors
with a policy package including land reform, farm
organization, monopolistic supply and purchase of
farm inputs and outputs, price stablization and
other policies. With a different policy package,
Israel achieved both conservation of scarce water
and a large positive foreign exchange balance by
fostering the growth of high value crops for domestic use and for export. The early establishment of
a network of agricultural colleges and research
stations, coupled with great flexibility in revising
and correcting policies when experience showed them
to be inadequate, was the basis of early Japanese
agricultural development. The original agricultural
cooperative law of 1900, for example, was substan-

tially revised by later amendments to widen the
responsibilities of the cooperatives and to extend
their benefits to all farmers. The price stabilization law of 1920 was constantly being amended or
even replaced by new laws. In Bengal and Bihar in
India, local officials concentrated on raising
output and neglected the problems that would arise
when output increased. This was sensible since
these areas had a significant grain shortage.
Government priorities in these two states reflected
this concentration of effort. In other stages, e.g.
the Punjab, output had increased and transportation,
storage and marketing had become priority problems.

None of these countries had plotted out the
total policy package they ended up with. In all
these countries, policy changes are still being
made today. Policy planning is not a single activity completed once and for all, or even complete once
for each five-year plan. The test of application
to a local situation almost always turns up a wide
range of conflicts in any policy package when the
policies are formulated to apply to a wide variety
of circumstances. Policymaking is a permanent process of working out and adjusting means to changing
circumstances in order to achieve national objectives.

When the continuous nature of policy planning
is recognized, it is much easier to avoid the tendency to try to do too much at one time and to concentrate on a few key measures to get a definite
result. Thus, for instance, successful land reforms are generally those that take one step at a
time and separate change of ownership of land from
attempts to reorganize farms and farm methods.
Where production organization is mixed with land redistribution, the result is often output declines,
farmer unrest and the failure of organizational
changes.

In the discussions on various aspects of rural
development this theme of simplicity and relatively
small, specific steps has recurred a number of
times. In marketing there is a strong tendency for
governments to see a problem and then try to create
a new government marketing system to replace the
existing one. Experience shows that this has rarely
been successful even in countries like China. Many
countries which tried this approach have given it up
and restored part or all of the affected marketing
channels to private or semi-private hands. In
farmer organization and extension, governments
frequently tried to promote western type coopera-

tives or complex technologies. Often simpler forms
of organization and technology were more successful,
especially at introducing farmers to organizations
or new practices. Credit was also a field where
elaborate collateral, supervision and cooperative
forms were frequently tried but less successfully
than simpler procedures.

The Joint Commission for Rural Reconstruction
(JCRR) in China (Taiwan) was often criticized for
its piecemeal approach of funding many little projects in many areas. In fact, many of these little
projects turned out to be much bigger later after
they had a chance to grow. The kibbutzim in Israel
have been free to start new enterprises and have
used this freedom to start many highly successful
businesses. It is probable that a planning ministry
would never have approved many of these activities
due to the small scale, lack of experience in the
new businesses, etc.

There is clearly a recurring pattern in development policy. Experts urge comprehensive planning. This planning calls for comprehensive new
activities. These lead to organizations that try to
introduce many new activities at once - a complex
job that requires much supervision and training of
others even though the agencies are new, short-
staffed and undertrained themselves. The result is
failure that is only concealed by the financial resources of the government or of an international
assistance agency.

Successful cases have taken a very different
direction that is more of a problem-solving ad hoc
approach. Policy steps are taken one at a time as
particular problems arise. This is the approach
that succeeded particularly well for Israel and
Japan. Where programmes have been introduced, the
more successful ones have often been the simplest
but this was not always the case, e.g. marketing
schemes for high value crops have often been both
complex and successful. However, even these have
the simplicity of being single organizations aimed
at supporting a single crop. The many problems of
coordination that have plagued other package programmes have been reduced by putting all elements of
the package into one organization.

Thus a complex solution (a package) may work
for a carefully limited problem, e.g. a single crop.
Or a simple solution may work for a complex problem,
e.g. the very different credit needs of farmers with
widely varying scales, differing crops and different
consumption needs. What is unlikely to work is a

complex solution for a complex problem. The problem then becomes how to simplify the problem, the
solution, or both, and it is desirable to have as
few and as clear objectives as possible, but
simplification is not easy. Experts and planners
will be urging that all aspects of the problem be
dealt with at once. There will often be multiple
objectives that all claim attention as well as political demands. Thus the policymaker faces a hard
task in trying to deal with one problem at a time.

The key to success in these circumstances is to
realize, and to help others realize, that concentration on one problem does not mean neglect of others.
On the contrary, the very act of seeking simple
solutions often releases resources for other activities. For example, a government that attempts to
take over the grain trade is creating a tremendous
administrative burden that will draw scarce manpower
from other activities. If, however, the government
simply tries to deal with the faults of the existing
marketing system, e.g. by passing a marketing law
and providing cooperatives, or other groups, with
standard weights and measures, the costs in manpower
may be minor. In fact, outsiders - in this example,
cooperatives - may be enlisted to assist in carrying
out the improvement.

A. <u>Simplifying policy decisions</u>. It is worthwhile
considering how the very complex problems that face
planners can be broken down into meaningful components.

(i) Pilot projects. Pilot projects are a useful way of testing solutions before they are
attempted at regional or national levels. Where
there is immediate success then expansion to widespread field tests, to a national programme need not
be time consuming. Pilot projects followed by widespread field testing tend to be time consuming mainly
when there are problems with the technology or
approach being tested. In this case, delays are
likely to be a good thing. A further advantage of
pilot projects is that they allow testing of a
number of alternatives at once, provided the total
cost is not high. This greatly speeds up the dis-
covery of successful methods. Administrators must,
of course, be prepared to accept that some projects
will fail. Testing of several alternatives at low
cost is usually practical only if project design and
implementation are decentralized.

A major difficulty with pilot projects is that

project sponsors are so eager for success that they
burden the project with heavy costs. The result is
a project that even if successful could not be replicated on a significant scale. World Bank projects, for instance, are often so complex that the
Bank insists on the establishment of new project
authorities supported by foreign experts, to run
them. This is justified by citing the weakness of
project management in the country. Training of
local staff to take over is usually a part of the
project. Rarely are these projects expanded or
duplicated by the host country. Their high cost is
especially regrettable because the same amount of
money could fund many pilot projects small enough
so that local managers could be primarily responsible for project development and implementation.
    A second difficulty is that to ensure success,
the pilot project is located in a particularly
favourable site or has other distinct advantages.
    Although planners can try to avoid such errors,
it is difficult to guarantee an unbiased pilot project. It is therefore important to plan not only a
single pilot project but also a follow-up with
widely distributed field tests before a national
programme is undertaken. Such a requirement would
do a great deal to reduce the tendency of project
sponsors to oversell their pilot projects.
    A final difficulty, paradoxically, is that what
works on a pilot basis may succeed only too well on
a larger basis. For instance, a wheat growing
scheme may work well in one district and also initially on a larger scale. The more successful the
programme, however, the more wheat will be produced
and prices will tend to fall. If prices fall, the
conditions that made the pilot project successful
may disappear. People who tried the new methods re-
vert to their old methods. The pilot project may
also create problems when replicated on a national
scale by overloading other parts of the system. For
instance, increased wheat output in the Punjab over-
loaded transportation and marketing channels in
North India.
    These difficulties mean that the pilot project
approach, will not automatically solve all problems,
but it is far preferable than rushing into a
national programme that fails because the basic
technology or approach is wrong.

    (ii) Single crop programmes. A second way of
making big problems smaller, and simpler, is to
concentrate on just one part of the problem, e.g. a

single crop. This particular strategy has worked
well for high value commercial crops, which are frequently export crops, and is usually implemented
through a producers' association, marketing board
or other single crop agency. This is an example of
simplifying the problem rather than the solution
since, in practice, this approach has frequently
involved fairly complex organization and several
services as well as relatively complex technical
packages.

However, this approach has not worked very well
for basic food crops such as grain. It may lead to
some crops and many farmers being forever overlooked.

(iii) Decentralization. One of the most frequent reported failures in developing countries is
the incapacity of governments to carry out what
appears to be sound plans. Administrative agencies
cannot or will not implement the plan. But the very
consistency with which administrative failings are
reported, suggests that the flaw is not in the administrative capacity of government agencies, but in
the policymakers and planners who fail to recognize
the limits to what agencies can do.

Planners and other policymakers need to realistically assess the strengths and weaknesses of all
of the potential implementing organizations available, and then select policies which best use the
existing organizations. Often the best organizations will be in the private sector.

As well as by delegation to the private sector,
the decision-making burden of the policymaker can
also be reduced by sharing responsibility for some
decisions with lower-level personnel or organizations. For instance, the budgeting procedure that
was part of the Red book system used in Malaysia was
very successful in simplifying decision-making.
Instead of negotiating a budget with each administrative unit, local units submitted lists of projects, each with a cost figure, in their order of
priority. When the State and Federal authorities
decided on a budget for the year, they drew a line
under the last project within the budgeted amount.
The rest of the projects were scheduled in the same
manner for future years. The remaining projects on
the list could be revised as convenient.

There are many opportunities to decentralize
decisions in developing countries. Instead of trying to develop a standardized type of housing, ware-
house, clinic or school for the whole country, these
decisions can be left to local communities.

201

Generally this will lower rather than increase costs
as it permits greater use of local building materials and familiar, adapted architectural styles.
The Chinese have probably gone the farthest in this
direction by delegating to the counties much responsibility for planning and implementing industrial development. They have delegated to the
communes some industrial and public works planning
and implementation work as well as primary responsibility for health, education and welfare services.

(iv) Simplifying programmes. The importance
of simplifying programmes was underlined in the discussions on land reform and credit. A credit programme that has a minimum of supervision and restrictions is simpler than one that tries to ensure
that the credit is used for production or tries to
force a farmer to do certain things. The simple
programme is more likely to be successful with small
farmers. Land reform can be made much simpler by
confining it to redistribution and providing for few
exceptions. Where land reform laws have many complex provisions they often get bogged down in court
procedures and various types of evasion.
A programme can, however, to too simple. There
may have to be collateral requirements on loans to
assure repayment by large farmers or even some small
farmers. But many of these necessary complications
can be discovered in pilot projects or from operating experience. In practice, programmes rarely fail
because they are too simple. This may mean that
errors of simplicity are quickly corrected. Unfortunately, the corrections often add up to a complex
of bureaucratic red tape that proves fatal to the
entire programme.

(v) Priorities. None of the above recommendations are intended to suggest that complexity is
necessarily a bad thing. On the contrary, development tends to be a process of increasing complexity.
Complexity, however, is difficult to administer and
good administrators are scarce in most countries.
Hence it pays to avoid complexity if simplicity
works. Further, where complexity is unavoidable, it
is best to move into it a step at a time so that
experience and competence can be developed.
Once activities have been reduced to the smallest, simplest elements possible, the policymaker
still has the problem of choosing which of these
elements to include in current policy. Generally
policymakers think of such decisions as ones of

choice between alternatives. This, however, makes the decision harder because the things that are not included are often important.

There is another way of looking at these decisions. This is to recognize that over time a country can afford to do many things it cannot afford to do in one year or so. The budget may only allow three new programmes to be introduced in one year but as many as seven over, say, a five-year plan and even more over the next 20 years.

The decision that the policymaker faces then largely is, which comes first and which comes later rather than what to include or leave out. Often this is a much easier decision to make since the political opposition is reduced and there may be solid reasons why some steps come naturally before others. For instance, the Chinese rural development strategy relied heavily on rural and agricultural public works. This made cement a priority as it played a big role in public works and the relatively low quality cement was adequate for this purpose. But public works improved water control - irrigation, drainage and flood prevention. Improved water control and use increased the returns to fertilizer. Hence, fertilizer was the second small scale industry developed in Chinese rural development. Increased water control and fertilizer use greatly expanded yields and permitted multi-cropping. This meant there was a big increase in labour demand at harvest time. Larger crops had to be harvested and the land quickly prepared for the next crop. The third small scale rural industry was therefore agricultural machinery. Thus the natural sequence was to develop cement, then fertilizer, then farm machinery. Other countries may find other sequences more appropriate. The important point is that it is a choice of which comes first not which gets left out.

The question then is, how far must one step go before another can be taken? In the Chinese example, all three industries developed together even though they were introduced in a particular sequence. It worked in this case because there was considerable local automomy in making decisions about small scale industry. Each commune could start with what it needed most. Working on one step did not prevent more work on an earlier step at a later date.

Not all decisions are of this type. Land reform is an activity that stops when emphasis dininishes. For this reason it is best to complete this step before going on to another. Similarly, marketing improvements may make markets available to more farmers but not to all. If the reforms improving markets stop, then all further measures on behalf of the excluded farmers are likely to be failures. Thus, although other measures can begin before this type of reform is complete, it must be carried on until completed if all farmers are to be reached by later measures.

B. Where simplification is more difficult. Simplification of the kind outlined above will not always work, however. Usually it is not practical to introduce e.g. price supports for a crop in some areas but not others, because there is likely to be relatively high mobility between areas and such a limited application would lead to smuggling and other distortions. Tariff policies must be uniform for the same reason as well as marketing reform. Tax policies should be uniform but in practice often they are not. Regulatory policies must usually be uniformly applied too. Finally land reform policies are usually applied uniformly for political reasons.

It may be impossible, also to try out such policies for a short time. This is obvious with land reform but with price policy, marketing reforms and tax measures it may take several years before farmers come to fully trust the new policy and to adjust to the situation the changed policy creates. The policymaker is therefore left with little choice but to make a big decision. There are, however, two helpful factors in this situation. First, to the extent that the policymaker has simplified where he could in other ways, he has a much smaller number of big decisions to make. Second, to the extent that the situation has been simplified, there are fewer complications in analyzing the probable effects of the new policy.

In the end, however, the policymaker has no choice but to try to determine what will happen before he tries a new policy. Since he cannot know this for sure, the best he can do is gather information from as many sources as possible. The key sources will usually include:

(a) technicians and professional staff. These people can help by providing information on what should happen, e.g. economists can tell you what should happen as a result of a particular change in price policy.

(b) Experienced professionals and managers in the implementing organizations. In successful countries, considerable policymaking power is delegated to or shared with the organizations that will carry out the plan including non-government organizations. Policy planning without close and continuous interaction with implementing agencies ends up producing guide-lines or recommendations which are not accepted by the organizations concerned because the policies are unrealistic. Such policies are not put into practice.

Understanding what is likely to happen, and why, and what can be done about it, are all matters that need to be studied with those with the necessary experience.

(c) Finally, since no country can try every-thing there will be many policy alternatives which have not been tried before in a particu-lar situation. Even experience with rough parallels of a suggested line of policy may be lacking. In this case, the closest experience to the situation in one developing country will be the experience of other developing coun-tries. Thus when faced with a new situation, the policymaker will find it useful to look at what other countries have done in similar situ-ations and what the results were. Although the relevance of others' experience may not always be obvious, any experience is better than none when making decisions that the policymaker and his country may have to live with for many years.

Chapter 11

PROJECTS

Summary
Identifying, preparing and successfully implementing agricultural projects is generally
difficult, particularly in developing countries. Failure is common or only partial
success. This chapter examines why good projects have been so few and how this situation
can be improved. At the outset, a distinction
needs to be made between experimental, pilot,
demonstration and production projects. Then,
a project needs to be identified, possibly
using a sector or a special survey and taking
full account of people's expressed, and often
only half-articulated needs. The project's
formulation comes next when five main aspects
have to be examined - technical, economic,
financial, institutional and managerial, and
commercial. All too often, technical feasibility dominates the discussion. Managerial
and institutional factors are commonly under-
rated - all to the detriment of a balanced
assessment. Nevertheless, regardless of the
quantity of data assembled, its accuracy and
relevance, the whole process of project
appraisal remains more an art than a science.
Success in implementation depends mainly on
good management and organization, and a close
alignment between a project's particular requirements and the facilities provided,
especially at the local level. Special
arrangements are frequently needed to manage
and supervise larger projects either through
expansion of existing bureaucracies, creation
of autonomous units, an organization reporting
to a central, regional or field agency, or the
use of an external agent. A key element in

project management is evaluation - "on-going"
or "built-in", and special. Ex-post evaluation
while useful does not come into the same category. The prime aim is to enable planning and
implementation to be improved. Monitoring
should not be confused with evaluation. It
allows progress to be measured against some
planned scale of achievement. The ultimate
test may be whether or not a project generates
its own continuing and expanding activity.
Immediate and tangible results may be less significant than later less obvious consequences.

1. Introduction
A. Scarcity of good projects. Most developing
countries lack soundly conceived and well-prepared
projects. International lending and assistance
organizations have repeatedly deplored the lack of
projects to fund. In some cases, countries have
been unable to accept available funds from donors
because their projects did not qualify for financing. Reviews of national development plans sometimes show that plans have been drawn up and goals
and targets set, with no indication of how the targets are to be met, that is, what programmes and
projects are to be the means for plan implementation.
Planning which does not make provision for well-
prepared projects is in effect not planning at all.
Even in countries where projects have been identified and formulated, implementation is often ineffective, leading to failure to reach plan objectives.

Why have there been too few good projects
prepared and implemented, and what can be done to
increase the flow of projects, based on approaches
that have proven successful? This chapter attempts
to try to answer these questions.

B. Types of projects. A sequence of project types
each serving an important function, includes experimental, pilot, demonstration, and production
projects. Production projects often receive the
lion's share of attention but other projects perform
important roles, too. Not all projects go through
all phases: in some cases, large amounts of money
and resources have been allocated directly to production without either an experimental or pilot
project having been undertaken. This is sometimes
a proper approach because many projects do not require substantial innovation - except for managerial
flexibility in adjusting plans to changed conditions.

Because a great many projects require adaptation to meet cultural, regional and other needs, however, an understanding of the roles played by experimental, pilot and demonstration projects can help planners and managers to allocate resources more effectively.

(a) Experimental projects. Experimental projects have the purpose of defining problems in new ways and of assessing alternative solutions. In a given country, they may be concentrated on finding the best means of overcoming constraints imposed by local conditions, or transferring and adapting practices successfully applied in one country to another, where they have not yet been attempted.

Successful projects at the experimental stage have often been characterized by intensive research into a small, well-defined geographic area (frequently having qualities of social and cultural homogeneity). Research often continues through pilot and demonstration stages and sometimes into the production stage, especially when data are sparse and it is necessary to build up statistics covering a series of observations over time.

(b) Pilot projects. Pilot projects build on the lessons gained from experimental projects, providing for the testing of the applicability of new methods and approaches in specific situations.

They allow new ideas and methods to be tested under local conditions at relatively low risk, not only to managers but to politicians. If the amount of funds committed and the trial areas are of modest size, even failures need not be threatening or cause lack of political status or support. By contrast, to leave out the pilot stage and move directly to large-scale production increases the chance of loss if things go badly.

Considerable attention has to be given to the design of pilot projects. For example, the current emphasis on equity, income distribution, and delivery services could lead to a situation in which the social overhead components of projects might be so costly as to make them too expensive to replicate on a large scale. A problem, especially for rural development projects, is to design them to be productive enough to cover most if not all their overhead costs. A basic object of such projects is to reach large numbers of small farmers. To do this, it will be necessary to replicate projects or to have them develop into broad-ranging programmes. This is likely to be an expensive operation, and it

would be unwise to have heavily subsidized pilot
projects if they cannot be broadly reproduced with
local or national funding. Experience indicates,
furthermore, that projects in which the ultimate
clients have a share of paying for the effort have a
greater chance of succeeding.

A pilot project should attempt to prove on a
reduced scale what can later be applied and tested
more thoroughly on a larger basis. Many theorists
and practitioners have argued that the idea or
product being tried out in the pilot project should
be tested away from the eye of the experimenter,
under normal or representative conditions. The
basis for this argument seems to be that if anything
goes wrong under normal conditions it is best to
catch it on a small scale; and further, that because special attention will not be possible during
the production stage of a project, it is best to
have standard or normal supervision during the
smaller, pilot stage. The need to select an average
or representative area is also based on other
factors. There have been many instances of research
into improved crops in which special plots of land
were used, inputs were plentiful and controlled, and
constraints such as pests and insects were excluded
or minimized. The agricultural research stations
were prime examples of this. Under such special
conditions, extraordinary crop yields were possible.
When new seeds or plants so developed were transferred to normal areas for growing, however, yields
dropped dramatically, sometimes even falling below
yields from traditional or unimproved seed. Further,
farmers' practices could not be controlled or
strictly supervised; in some cases no one knew what
the farmers were doing. In light of this, the need
to run pilot projects under more representative
conditions became obvious.

There is a need, however, to distinguish among
the components of a project those which should be
handled under representative conditions, and those
which require the best conditions which can be
created. The community or ecological area selected
should not be one which enjoys extraordinary conditions of soil, rainfall, or other natural conditions. It should conform to the areas where production will be taking place. A rural community,
for example, should have about the average percentage of people employed in agriculture, average
landholdings, per capita income, road networks and
infrastructure. When considering the management
needs of pilot projects, however, traditional

practices have not proven to be acceptable. Project personnel, for example, are one of the most important stimuli which the project brings to an area. Rapport with local people and attention to the peoples' needs have proven to be essential factors in gaining acceptance of new practices. In some cases this approach has contrasted with a more formal and distant attitude held by extension workers and other agency officials.

Pilot projects do not normally yield significant results in a short time. If crop cycles are involved, the period of testing can hardly be shortened, although more crops may be grown by increasing the number of cycles in a given period through irrigation. When social and cultural patterns and long-held individual beliefs are involved, patterns are slow to change. Farmers have in some cases clung tenaciously to traditional husbandry and cultivation techniques, even when their neighbours have experienced sizeable increases in crop yields.

(c) Demonstration projects. Although the terms "pilot project" and "demonstration project" have sometimes been used interchangeably or in combination, there are differences between them, both in scale and objective. Whereas pilot projects are normally small-scale attempts to test new methods and approaches under specified conditions in one area, demonstration projects are usually applied in a larger area, or sometimes in several locations at once. And while pilot projects are more concerned with testing, demonstration projects are intended to exhibit new techniques and approaches and to diffuse practices which promise wide applicability leading to increased output, superior quality, or both.

The scale of operation is significant for demonstration projects as many problems do not become fully apparent until a large scale of operations has been reached. In effect, more of the system is tested in demonstration projects because logistics and support mechanisms, a full range of personnel, and other needs must be met to integrate all of the orgainzational and physical inputs for a full province-level project. Knowledge, services, credit, and other materials must be made readily available to generate farmer and village support.

(d) Production projects. Projects which have gone through one or more of the preceding stages

ordinarily move on to their final stage of full
production. By virtue of having made it this far,
a number of serious implementation problems will
have been worked out, and the strengths of the
project should have been identified. The technology
used in the project will have undergone testing and
evaluation, and be fairly well proven. Other
problems continue due to the scale of operations
and the number of organizations involved in implementation, often including governmental, private
sector, and donor or lending organizations.

In the earlier stages, most projects have needed the skills of research and a painstaking analysis
of alternative possible solutions. In the production stage, and even in some of the larger demonstration projects, the quality of entrepreneurship,
of working with, exhorting, and coordinating
multiple organizations to achieve production-
oriented goals becomes of key importance.

2. Project Identification and Preparation
A. Project identification. Project identification
is the preliminary assessment of the nature, size,
and number of potential projects, and the establishment of some order of priority among them, in relation to a country's overall development plan. It
begins with an idea, progresses to roughly defined
projects, and moves toward more fully developed,
better defined investment proposals. Throughout the
process, administrators, planners and managers must
make a sequence of decisions about which problems
are most pressing, which objectives must be met and
which ideas for projects seem most promising as
possible answers to the problems faced. As the
identification-selection-formulation moves from idea
to completed project proposal, risks will decrease as
more complete and detailed information is collected
and redefined to shape the design of the project.

In practice the impetus for identifying new
projects comes from a number of sources. Within
countries, these include existing technical
ministries or agencies, legislative bodies, political
parties and leaders, private entrepreneurs and the
public at large. External sources include bilateral
and multilateral donor and lending organizations,
political agreements, private entrepreneurs, and
private voluntary organizations such as CARE, Oxfam
and others.

(a) Sector surveys. A variety of techniques and
approaches has been used to identify projects. One

of the most effective is carrying out a sector study. This is an analysis of a sector which provides the basic information for a coordinated development pro- gramme, including a preliminary identification of the most promising projects. Drawing on all avail- able sources of information, these studies provide a good indication of the types of projects needed to meet future requirements, and may also indicate the priorities among these projects.

Sector surveys have identified regions and areas of the country with a high potential for rapid expansion of output. In many cases, they do not spell out projects in detail, and they may only re- commend that more specific studies be conducted. In Zaire, for example, sector surveys emphasized the importance of improving the transportation network as a precondition for large-scale agricultural development. Prospective projects which were iden- tified included opening and repairing access and feeder roads and river crossings, strengthening the existing network in order to accommodate expansion of agricultural exports from the Cuvette Centrale, and in the longer term, to supplement the present export-oriented system with links that would make possible a fuller exploitation of regional pro- ductive potential.

Where possible, the sector study is the pre- ferred way to identify projects because sector programming based on the study is the most logical link between the national plan and projects. How- ever, not all countries are prepared to conduct a sector study at any given time. Further, a number will recently have completed studies, and even if these were not comprehensive, countries cannot con- duct a new study often, or on short notice. Where this is the case, planners have to rely on currently available data and special studies until a more de- tailed sector study can be undertaken. In most cases, the major part of existing sector studies concentrates on economic and financial analysis. However, organizational, managerial, and social aspects may be equally important in determining pro- ject success, so it is often necessary to conduct feasibility studies which take all of these factors into account.

Countries should aim to establish a continuous generation of projects so that some projects will be in the idea stage, when others are in more advanced stages of preparation. It is possible through this process to impart realism to national plan formula- tion, which does not exist when plans are drawn up

with little or no idea which projects will be undertaken under the plan.

(b) Special surveys and studies. The process of
identification and selection often leads straight to
a set of project proposals. For some small-scale,
relatively simple, projects there may be enough
information available to prepare a preliminary project. More often, however, design has begun before
adequate research has been undertaken, and key
issues may have been omitted. Organizers of land
use schemes in one country, for example, began a
project utilizing low-value land without checking to
see who owned it. Once the land became productive,
the owners came forward to claim it, reaping the
benefits of land improvement brought about by the
project. Evaluations of projects in many countries
cite the lack of basic data to plan projects
properly, and the need for more thorough studies to
prove whether they are feasible undertakings. For
more complex projects, therefore, detailed studies
are often necessary before the project design is
attempted.

Frequently, the next step following a sector
study is to conduct a special inventory of selected
areas of the country where projects seem likely in
order to gain a more detailed idea of problems and
potentials. In Guyana, for example, this was done
as part of a study of foodcrop production. A
survey of nearly 350 farms in four sample localities
was completed in order to classify and describe
foodcrop farms, with a view to evaluating production
potentials, identifying constraints, and proposing
actions to overcome them. In some cases, surveys
and studies at this point may result in a recommendation that a project should not be undertaken. In a
survey of Sri Lanka's agricultural sector, some
types of projects recommended in the development
plan were found to be important for implementation
in the longer run, but not of sufficient priority
to demand immediate investment. Recommendations
were made, therefore, for projects and programmes
which promised a relatively quick response rather
than those which had a long period between investment and benefits, such as irrigation. Whether or
not a project results from a preliminary enquiry,
the study is not necessarily a waste of time and
effort. If a project does result from the study,
its design is likely to be well thought-out. If a
decision is made not to go ahead, wasteful allocation of resources may have been avoided. If it is

postponed, it may still prove to be useful later.

(c) Assessing people's needs. Rural people are often a first-class source of information for project ideas. It is essential, therefore, for planners and managers to assess the information which can be supplied by them in possible or proposed project areas. In some areas, farmers have been described as lacking the ability to state clearly their own needs. In such cases, there is often a need for officials to facilitate expression of farmers' needs and objectives - being careful not to supplant farmers' objectives with their own. At this stage, large-scale socio-economic surveys are not called for, but a more general assessment based on a sampling procedure.
These measures suggest a "bottom up" aspect of identification which in some cases has generated ideas for projects to supplement those coming from sector studies. Both are valid sources of information and should be used as fully as possible, supplemented by ideas gathered elsewhere, particularly from political sources.
When enough relevant data have been gathered, and ideas for projects drawn up in rough form, more detailed but still tentative project proposals can be prepared. The objective at this stage is to assess a wide range of possible projects, and to select for further development those which offer the best known solutions to the set of priority development problems.
In some cases, individual projects are so obviously needed that there are few questions about their priority. For example, where large portions of crops are ruined by spoilage, storage facilities are clearly needed. Where export trade expands, port congestion is likely to become an acute problem calling for the construction of more warehouses and better harbour facilities, and so on.
In other areas, compromises may be necessary between projects ready for financing but which rate fairly low in priority, and those of greater importance but needing considerable preparatory and pre-investment work before sizeable investments can be made.
Some planners argue that it is a serious error to limit project choices too much at this point. If irrigation, for example, is seen as the way to increase productivity, other important elements may be ruled out for later consideration, such as projects to provide drainage, farm to market roads, or

credit. Others point out that the projects which
get most attention and the bulk of resources are
often those with the greatest visibility, rather
than projects with high economic payoff and low
capital intensity. In practice, investment decisions are often made on the basis of prejudices
for a certain type of project, or for political
reasons, because well-prepared projects are hard
to come by. This makes it all the more important
to put forward enough good proposals at this stage,
so that a worthwhile investment programme can emerge
from the projects which survive early screening.

B. Project formulation

Finding the best way to achieve the project objective is no easy task since what is the best project
in a technical sense, may not be the best in an
economic sense as it may not fit in with the available resources to finance it. Compromise is required to find that formulation of a project which
has a high economic return, is technically feasible,
is institutionally and managerially adapted to the
country and is within the resources of the country
to finance.

One of the major troubles with project formulation in most countries, and this is by no means
confined to developing countries, is that this compromise is not sought for and technical experts are
left to prepare the project on their own. As a
result they produce merely the best technical
solution, and, if they are trained technicians, the
least-cost best technical solution. Rarely are
economists employed in project formulation and preparation and rarely are projects drawn up to take
account of budgetary or institutional limitations.
Another trouble is that, more often than not, these
technicians are drawn only from the department
responsible for preparing the project. As a result
the project becomes confined to fulfilling the objective as far as it lies within the scope of the
particular department and not to achieving the
objective in full. An example of this was found in
India in irrigation projects which, until recently,
had been prepared only by irrigation engineers and
irrigation departments. Projects which were
magnificent engineering achievements were built but
since the construction activities of the irrigation
department did not extend to the farm level no
arrangements were made to take the water from the
canals to the farmers' fields. The utilization of
the engineering works is thus delayed interminably

and the project's viability becomes seriously threatened.

Thus the first golden rule in project formulation is to ensure that all the factors necessary to the achievement of the project objective are included within the scope of the project.

This rule means that e.g. in an irrigation project the scope of the project, including the arrangements for financing, must be expanded to cover not only the irrigation works such as control structures and canals, but also watercourses and farm channels, arrangements for land levelling by the individual farmer and if necessary: farm credit, provision for drainage, farm to market roads, regional research stations, agricultural extension services and so on. If a project to produce high quality seeds, for example, was confined to enhancing the farmers' ability to produce without attending to the linked problems of field inspection processing, grading and marketing, it would probably be worse than useless. Such a project ought to be as much an institution-building project as a production project. It is not possible to lay down any general hard and fast rules about what to include. Provided the project's purpose is carefully defined, the steps needed to achieve that purpose can be thought through carefully.

Having determined the scope of the project, five main aspects must be taken into account in project formulation: (a) technical feasibility; (b) economic viability; (c) financial requirements and resources; (d) institutional and managerial requirements; (e) commercial aspects.

(a) Technical feasibility. Only technical feasibility is taken into consideration in most projects. Manuals on project preparation tend to concentrate on this aspect to the detriment of the others. For this reason one need not go into great detail here.

By technical feasibility is meant, for example, that the proposed scale of the project is adapted to the resource, area or product to be developed, that the location of the project is technically and/ or economically the best available, that its layout and design are appropriate and so on. In the case of an agricultural, particularly an irrigation, project, technical feasibility involves a careful examination of the availability and quality of the physical resources to be used, particularly water and land: for instance, detailed knowledge of the quantity, quality and reliability of an irrigation supply is essential to its sustained and optimum development. Similarly the capability of project lands to yield a sustained level of production during the life of the project, with an adequate return to the farmer, requires a technical assessment of land resources. It usually involves some type of soil survey and land classification study on which to form a judgement about the quality of the soils, and perhaps their drainage characteristics.

Different types of agricultural projects involve different types of studies to establish their technical feasibility. Groundwater projects require a quantitative assessment of groundwater availability to indicate the safe level of exploitation as well as the water quality. Livestock projects require studies of herd composition and productivity. The number of examples can be multipled but the point should be clear. Establishing the technical feasibility of a project requires much detailed work and is by far the most time-consuming aspect of project formulation. It is also the aspect which requires most care and without which none of the other aspects can be formulated. Indeed preinvestment studies of various kinds are prerequisites to almost any form of project planning. For instance, until a soil and land classification study has been carried out, in conjunction with a contour survey, one cannot tell how much land is potentially irrigable from a particular water source. In turn, without knowledge of water availability, water requirements and cropping patterns, one cannot assess how much water is needed per unit area of land nor can one design the canalisation system. Interlinked relationships between physical resources and their use are complex and subject to a wide range of variation.

Invariably, however, once a project is identified there is an urgency to move on to the next stage and formulate it. Thus the second golden rule proposed here is that pre-investment study requirements should be identified as far in advance of project formulation as possible to allow it to be carried out thoroughly, without pressure to produce answers before the study is finalised.

Pre-investment studies permit an assessment of what is technically feasible. As already mentioned, however, in project formulation, the best technical solution does not always make the best project. On the one hand, by widening the scope of a project to include within it everything that is necessary to

217

achieve the project objective, one has already
brought in many non-technical considerations, e.g.
the speed of project development of an irrigation
project may not be determined by the technically
fastest method of canal construction but by the
speed with which the average farmer can level his
own land to make use of water once it arrives. On
the other hand the best project formulation is
always a compromise between technical, economic and
financial considerations.

Thus the third golden rule of project formulation is 'be flexible'. While no project will
succeed if it ignores the technical realities that
exist, success does not depend upon technical perfection. A good project formulation is one in which
the technical, economic and financial realities are
all considered and a balance is struck in which,
though no individual optima may be reached, no individual constraint is violated. For those concerned with the technical formulation of the project
this means willingness to look at alternatives and
to weigh these in the light of economic and financial restraints.

An example is an irrigation project in India
where, as originally formulated by the irrigation
department, the project was to irrigate about
600,000 acres at a total cost of Rs. 700 million
(figures rounded) in the plan period. This was the
technical optimum and probably also the economic
optimum. Unfortunately, however, such a cost ex-
ceeded the state's financial resources, although
those who had prepared the project could not have
been aware of this since it was formulated before
the plan was drawn up. The state concerned allocated only Rs. 390 million in its Fourth Plan budget
for this project. The project had to be reformu-
lated with two alternatives. One was to stretch
the construction period to ten years and thus reduce the annual demand on the budget. The other was
to reduce the size of the project and construct it
in phases. Owing to technical restrictions only two
other sizes of project could be considered, one of
350,000 acres and one of 250,000 acres. Calculations of the economics of each alternative were
then made. These showed the project to be uneconomic if its construction period was stretched to 10
years, but economic if its size was reduced. The
rate of return was higher for the 350,000-acre
reduced project than for the 250,000-acre version
(18% versus 12%) since much of the cost had still to
be borne even for the smaller project (e.g. the

barrage over the river. Nevertheless the return on
the smaller project was still acceptable. The deciding factor was financial. The 350,000-acre project would still cost Rs. 570 million whereas the
250,000-acre version cost only Rs. 460 million.
Although this was still above the plan allocation
the difference between this cost and the Rs.390
million originally allocated was a gap which the
state financial authorities felt they could meet.
Thus a 'best' project was formulated, which was
technically feasible, economically viable and within the limits set by financial constraints.

(b) Economic viability. A relatively standard type
of economic analysis is available for calculating
the rate of return on capital invested in a project.
This has two main variants. In one, the benefit-
cost ratio benefits and costs are discounted to
their present worth at a discount rate which reflects or ought to reflect the marginal return to
capital in the economy. The ratio of benefits to
costs is then calculated and as long as this exceeds
unity the project can be considered economically
viable. (Very often the rate of interest on government bonds or loans is used as the discount factor.
This should not, however, be done if one is
interested in the economic viability of the project
since the government loan rate rarely reflects the
marginal return on capital.) In the other variant,
the internal rate of return method, the discount
rate which equalises the present worth of benefits
and costs is found by trial and error. So long as
this exceeds the marginal return to capital in the
economy the project can be considered economically
viable. The internal rate of return method is preferred on a number of grounds.
  The calculation of either the internal rate of
return or the benefit-cost ratio can be no more
accurate than the estimate of benefits on which it
is based. A vital part of project formulation and
one which is more often than not badly neglected is
therefore the preparation of a realistic estimate
of project benefits. While this estimate tends to
be subject to a wider margin of error than the
estimate of costs, careful consideration of the
likely variables can at least produce a realistic
estimate of benefits. Recently more sophisticated
benefit estimate techniques have been evolved using
probability analysis. These allow for probable
variations in benefit parameters and give a range
of probable net project benefits, and hence a range

of probable rates of return. The accuracy even of a range of estimates still turns on the use of realistic assumptions.

In calculating project benefits one is trying to estimate the difference between the level of production expected to occur if the project is undertaken with what it would have been if it were not undertaken i.e. with and without the project. However, many estimates of project benefits are subject to a major conceptual error, since they end up comparing the expected results of the project not with what would have happened if the project had not existed but with the situation as it exists at the time the project is formulated. This is a "before and after" comparison and not a "with and without" comparison. An illustration may help to explain this. In many parts of the world, average crop yields of most crops are rising at rates ranging from 1% to 3% per annum. Thus over the life of a project, which may be anything from 20 to 50 years, yields can be expected to rise "without" the project, by anything between 22% and 80% (in a 20-year period). If in the "with" project situation gross output is compared with the situation as it exists at the time of project formulation, all the likely growth in crop yield will be included as part of the project benefit, grossly exaggerating the return on project investment. A better calculation of net project benefit requires a careful evaluation of the likely course of output within the project area as it would probably be if nothing was done, and if the project is carried out.

Difficulties of benefit estimation are particularly large in agricultural projects. In the first place many of the benefits are diffuse and occur over a long period of time. The difficulties, for instance, of trying to predict the growth of crop yields that are likely to result from improvements in drainage or irrigation are acute. They are also very important since the calculation of the internal rate of return is highly sensitive to the level of benefits in the first few years of a project. Take, for instance, the following example. A project costing Rs. 1,000 per acre is expected to produce annual benefits of Rs. 300 per acre once yields reach their maximum expected level. If the assumption is made that this maximum level is attained in three years the internal rate of return is 20% over a 15-year project life. If, however, it is assumed that maximum production is not attained until the sixth year, the internal rate of return falls to 16%.

Secondly, the economic benefits include many
items difficult to forecast, not least because one
is forecasting a condition which has not yet pre-
vailed and one must hypothesize what may happen. The
sort of benefits are: (i) increased acreage of
crops or numbers of livestock; (ii) increased yields
of existing crops or livestock; (iii) lower production costs; (iv) increased employment for agricultural labour force; (v) reduced damages to crops
from flooding or poor drainage.

Not all of these items need to be calculated
for each project. Take, for instance, an irrigation project to increase the supply of water to a
partially developed area. The "without project"
situation involves deciding first how the area
would develop without additional water. Would crop
yields remain at their present levels, or increase?
What would future crop production costs be: could
technological improvements be adopted? Would the
existing pattern of crops change? Would the level
of management efficiency change? What level of
crop and livestock product prices should be used to
value output? For the "with project" situation one
must estimate first the area on which the new water
supplied can be used. This will depend on the
amount of water available in each month and the
amount which is lost between the point of storage,
or diversion, and the farm. The next step is to
make assumptions about which crops will actually be
grown. Except where farmers have to follow a fixed
cropping pattern the farmers' response is difficult
to predict. Assumptions must be made about the
level of yields these crops will attain, how this
will change over time, at what level of production
costs, farm inputs and managerial efficiency the
farmer will operate; and so on. And, again, the
critical issue of input and output price levels
must be faced. The eventual outcome of these
assumptions is an annual stream of benefits to set
against the annual stream of costs. This benefit
stream is based on judgement, experience and feel.
The calculations are more an art than a science.

(c) Financial requirements and resources. Unrealistic estimates of project cost are an almost
invariable characteristic of project formulation in
every country of the world, and for every conceiv-
able type of project from digging a tubewell to
putting a man on the moon. There is little that can
be done about such a universal failing. However, it
is a factor in project preparation one should be

well aware of. Deliberate underestimates of costs, in order to bring them within a specified financial ceiling, should never be resorted to. It is one thing to attempt to find the cheapest technical solution to achieve a project objectively and quite another to understate costs to deceive those concerned with financial allocations. To find the best cost solution within given financial constraints may involve a compromise with the technical optimum e.g. by extending the project implementation period, but this must be done in conscious agreement with all parties to the project. Where the implementation is extended piecemeal for lack of finance, the economic viability of the project is threatened.

The exact financial constraints may not be known at the time of project formulation. Often, perhaps usually, they are only imposed after the initial project formulation has been carried out. When a number of different projects are being put together to form a plan, typically the sum of costs will exceed the sum of the sector allocation. An across-the-board cut is then often imposed on each project. This action has a much greater impact on some projects than others and is an entirely inadequate way of dealing with the problem. Given the inflexibility of most project formulations, however, it may well be the only possible solution.

Two suggested improvements might help to ease this problem: to involve the finance departments of government in the project formulation from a much earlier stage, and these sectoral allocations are to provide at least one alternative project outline involving a different implementation period, and hence a different annual project cost, together with the economic implications of changing this period.

(d) Institutional and managerial requirements. When a project falls within the responsibility of an individual department and is relatively small, institutional and managerial requirements impose little additional strain on the department. If, however, the project is large it is essential to think through in detail the manpower requirements for carrying out the project and ensure that the staff are appointed or new administrative units created on time. This suggestion may sound obvious enough but it is so often overlooked.

When the scope of the project becomes wider it is even more important to ensure that its formulation includes proposals for the establishment of some organisation which can coordinate between the various departments. It is vital to ensure that each unit is carrying out its share of the project to a timetable which will not prevent other departments from carrying out theirs.

(e) Commercial aspects. This covers all the arrangements needed for buying and selling under the project. The project formulation should set out the proposed arrangements for buying the goods and services required for the project, discuss their availability and show that materials needed for project operation are also available.

Under commercial aspects, one would also include an evaluation of market demand for the output of the project, the adequacy of marketing channels, etc. A project to produce timber for pulpwood should indicate, for example, not only that there is a demand for wood pulp but also that the pulp can be produced at an economic price and at a profitability sufficiently attractive to induce investors to put money into a pulping plant.

C. Appraisal of the project

When it comes to appraising projects, the basic aspects which must be reviewed do not change, only the viewpoint which is very similar whether the appraiser is a government committee established to approve the project and allocate funds to it, or whether it is an international financing agency such as the World Bank.

The appraisers want to satisfy themselves that what is set out in the project formulation is realistic, and accurate. If the project has been well formulated then the appraisal is a relatively straightforward affair. If not then further preparation work and probably a reformulation of the project is required

The headings under which an appraisal can be classified follow exactly the same headings used in formulation: technical, economic, financial, institutional, managerial and commercial.

An appraisal group looking into the technical aspect of a project will wish to ensure first that all the technical alternatives have been adequately considered. This may range from questioning the need for the project at all, e.g. whether improved dry land farming techniques and better moisture conservation could not increase output to the same extent as an irrigation project, down to a detailed examination of points of design, e.g. the depth and diameter of a tubewell are appropriate to the

aquifier, or the tubewell slot size and pump and
motor characteristics are appropriate to subsoil and
groundwater conditions in the area. The group will
want to be satisfied that the cost estimates are
realistic and the project phasing is attainable.

Appraisal of the economic viability of the project is an opportunity to review the analysis of
project alternatives which should have been carried
out during project formulation, to ensure that the
technical solution chosen has in fact the highest
economic return commensurate with technical and
financial restraints. This appraisal will also be
concerned with analysis of project benefits to ensure that these have been as realistically estimated
as possible. A common failing of those involved in
project formulation is to take too optimistic a view
of the likely outcome of events; the appraising
economist may well take a less optimistic viewpoint
and end up with a lower estimate of the economic
rate of return. This happens with most appraisals
carried out by international financing agencies;
indeed, this is probably true of most agencies who
will have their own funds at risk in the project.

The appraisal of the financial aspects of the
project covers two main items. The first is the
availability of funds for project construction; the
second is the financial viability of the project
once it is in operation. The availability of funds
is not usually known when the project is formulated.
Only at the stage of appraisal does the matching of
project cost and project funds take place. Where
international financing is involved this is the
stage at which the agency, having satisfied itself
on other issues, will determine how much additional
finance, over and above government funds, is needed
for the project.

The other financial issue is whether the project will be able to meet its financial obligations
when it is in operation. Will a farmer, for example,
who has borrowed money to build a tubewell have
sufficient additional income to repay instalments on
the bank loan? Or, again, will the level of water
rates collected from beneficiaries of an irrigation
project be sufficient to cover part of the cost of
capital amortisation, as well as operation and maintenance costs, and interest on capital? This type
of analysis may require detailed cash flow studies
of both the individual beneficiary and of the whole
project. It may well reveal the need to change the
structure, particularly the level of project charges
e.g. water rates, unless the project is to require

continuing subsidies to keep it in operation.

Appraisal of the institutional and managerial aspects is needed to ensure that the administrative structure proposed for the project, including the adequacy of the staffing and the quality of the staff, is designed to enable the project to be on schedule and operated efficiently; that inter-departmental difficulties have been taken into account, the coordination machinery will work, and that there is an organized flow of decisions and allocation of responsibility within the chain of command. This whole organizational aspect often becomes the most difficult one on which to reach agreement, partly because it is the aspect to which least throught is usually given, and because the project organizational structure is as important to the success of a project as any other aspect.

When all that can be said about project formulation and appraisal has been said, however, the whole process still remains far more an art than a science. There are many variables not susceptible to scientific analysis, so that the final project outcome must always remain veiled in uncertainty. Parts of any project formulation have, indeed, must have, a precise scientific foundation. The design of a dam, for example, is based on the precise calculation of mass and stress which it would be disastrous to ignore; even then, a surprising amount of artistic licence is exercised by the design engineer, in the assumptions he chooses to adopt about say the maximum design flood which the spill-way must be constructed to carry. But this degree of artistic licence which the engineer can use is small relative to what the economist can exercise.

Those who are responsible for project formulation are attempting to satisfy two objectives simultaneously, and they may well be in conflict with each other. One objective is to produce an unbiased assessment of what they think will happen as a result of the project. The other is to produce a sufficiently attractive description of this outcome to ensure that the project will be implemented. Since the project justification depends upon a wide range of subjective judgements, the conflict between these two objectives may well be resolved subconsciously, and the project formulator may never realise that these two objectives are in conflict. He will always be convinced that his assessment is unbiased and perhaps even scientific! Yet the more involved he is in the project's formulation, the more deeply concerned to see it in action, the more biased he is likely to be.

3. Project Implementation
A. The project team. Much has been written about
the special qualities needed by team members.
Desirable characteristics of project managers have
been described to include technical competence,
flexibility, entrepreneurial behaviour, unifying
capability, ability to balance off claims of competing interests, knowledge of how to work through
(or around) organizations, and many other factors.
Doubtless it would be pleasant to be able to find
individuals who have most of the desirable characteristics of such a shopping list. The hard fact
remains, however, that few such individuals are
likely to be available and that projects must continue to be staffed with the talent that is available.

The task of a project is to provide the best
possible solution(s) to the problems which the project has been designed to confront and solve. The
composition of a project team, therefore, depends
in great part on the nature of the problem being
dealt with. Research and experimental projects in
practice have generally had a different team composition than demonstration and production projects.
Similarly, problem-solving projects have differed in
team composition from inputs or services delivery
projects.

Projects which are in the production stages or
are basically services or inputs delivery projects
have operated very successfully with an hierarchical
structure similar to that found in small programmes.

A collegial style of staff operation is more
common to experimental and pilot projects. The
project director or manager at this stage has to be
a person who can guide others in research and ex-
perimentation without imposing a heavy authority
which might stifle innovation and learning.

It has been contended by some that project
managers should be appointed for the life of a project to provide for overall continuity to all of the
project's phases, including ex-post evaluation.
Such a proposition should be investigated in the
light of the project's objectives, its length, and
other characteristics. What is essential is that
there be a continuous locus of authority as a project develops. While this has most often been a
project manager or director, some success has also
been achieved with project management teams.
Whether an individual or a team is used, authority

over inputs and a budget to ensure their availability has proven to be essential.

The project manager is the nerve centre of the project during implementation, though he or she may not be directly involved with some of the project's activity. The first requirement for the project is that everyone concerned must know exactly what it is. A primary continuing responsibility of the manager is to keep the staff informed and aware of the project objective, and proposed inputs and outputs, and what their role is in making the project work. In a problem-sharing project, this may mean that the manager joins in a collegial effort to continually define more clearly the nature of the problem, and how it may be solved. It may mean the assignment of staff members to task forces with defined areas of investigation. In some cases, it may mean that the general expertise of the field staff must be complemented by that of experts in various fields. One responsibility of project management in this event is to establish relations with experts in research, administration, technical fields, and other areas as appropriate. These may be experts from ministries or technical institutes from within the country, from donor or lending agencies, or private organizations abroad. When the services of outsiders are necessary, it is the responsibility of project management to arrange for local people to be trained to take their places whenever possible.

Frequently, one agency or organization has had the responsibility for formulating a project which has been subsequently implemented in part by other agencies. In such cases, it has proved valuable to involve the implementing agency to project formulation. Some organizations have appointed a project manager who was involved both in formulation and implementation. There is no doubt that the fuller dimensions of the project are better understood by the project manager when this is done.

What are the abilities required either of the project director or of the project team? On the technical side, there is the need to schedule project activities to provide for smooth delivery of supplies and the coordination of various ministries, agencies, and private organizations. While such activities may be plotted during the planning stage, on-site experience during implementation is required to modify work plans in order to keep abreast of changing conditions. Further, a technical capability in project scheduling and planning techniques

is not alone sufficient. The project director may
have to play the role of trouble shooter. But many,
in fact, most trouble-shooting actions, must be
delegated to leave the director free to assess overall operations, to develop project policy and secure
the favourable attitude and support of participating
organizations. The project managers in some of the
most successful projects have shown a willingness to
do more than to direct from afar. When direct
observation and action have been necessary, they
have willingly participated in whatever task was
necessary to move the project forward. One aspect
of successful leadership by project managers has
clearly been the willingness and ability to serve by
personal example.

Another task of project management is to keep
higher-level managers informed of project progress
and problems. The director should keep responsible
bureaucratic senior officials informed so that they
can properly evaluate progress and consider expanding projects into regular programmes under departmental sponsorship. Experience has also shown the
need to keep other people at higher levels informed.
It has been observed that in India, the upper
echelons have little chance to be in first-hand contact with field situations. The only effective and
continuing channel is with middle or lower-level
personnel whom the higher level officers know inti-
mately. In the absence of a continuing reliable
source of information from the field, the higher
managers have no basis for making realistic decisions about projects. There is also often a need
for both political executives and top administrators
including ministers, the heads of planning and budget offices, directors-general of major bureaux, and
others, to appreciate the analytic and decision-
making process essential to sound project formulation and implementation.

B. Organization and Process
The choice of an organization to implement a project, and development of guidelines and procedures
for running it, have often proved to be critical
factors. Even when projects are otherwise technically well-prepared, they are not likely to meet
expectations when insufficient attention has been
given to management and organization. These aspects
should be analyzed early in the project cycle,
certainly not later than the time of project formulation, to permit evaluation of alternative arrangements, and to allow preparatory steps to begin so

that the project will not be delayed on this account once implementation begins. Some of the questions that have to be answered include whether a project will be implemented by an existing government agency, by a new agency, by non-governmental agents (contractors, voluntary organizations, or others); what will be the role of local people and groups in the project area; and, what role local governmental organizations and officials can play in implementing or supporting the project?

If an existing agency or organization is to be used, it should be decided whether reforms or administrative changes are necessary to increase the chances of success. If a new agency is to operate the project, it must be decided what kind or organization will be established, where it will be housed, from whence it will get the required personnel, and what kinds of training will be necessary. Further, because development is a field full of uncertainties, sufficient flexibility must be built into organizational structure and processes to allow adaptation to changing conditions, which experience shows are certain to occur during implementation. While there is no doubt that the initial design of a project is important, ex-post project evaluations have indicated repeatedly that building a development project is never a self-executing or self-fulfilling process. Uncertainties and contingencies, human and technological inadequacies, and conflicting interests must continually be dealt with. Success can depend much more upon the rate at which project executing agencies develop the capacity to implement field projects than upon the initial design of the project.

In practice, there is seldom total freedom in the choice of organization, and by and large, choices have been limited to one of the following: (1) expansion of existing bureaucracies; (2) creation of an autonomous or self-autonomous organization; (3) establishment of a project organization reporting to the centre; (4) establishment of an organization reporting to field or regional agencies; and (5) contracting for services or relying on an external agent. In addition, some projects use a combination of some of these five basic approaches. The arrangement eventually chosen depends on the characteristics and objectives of the project, the existing organizational machinery in the country, and the extent to which a new organization can be made viable.
(a) Expansion of existing bureaucracies. The

latitude of choice in selecting an organization
varies considerably from country to country and
even in some cases from ministry to ministry. In
India it has been traditional for projects included
within the Five-Year Plans to be executed by the
responsible bureaucratic organization. Because
different projects are administered at different
levels, i.e. national, state, district, block, and
village, and more than one department is often involved in project implementation, both vertical and
horizontal coordination are necessary. If an existing organization is chosen, the maintenance of such
coordination between various levels and departments
depends largely on prevailing administrative
structures and procedures, and on the calibre of
available personnel. A consideration is choosing
an organization for implementation in e.g. India is
to know how far Indian administrative structures
and procedures facilitate or hinder coordination,
and which organizations and different hierarchical
levels may be expected to cooperate to get a project implemented.

One problem sometimes faced in choosing an
existing bureaucratic structure to execute projects
is the fragmenting of tasks. In spite of supposedly rational organization, in practice bureaucratic communication is often deficient. In India's
agricultural structure directives move from the
higher to the lower units in the hierarchy, but the
flow of information in the reverse direction is
not equally well provided for. Within the bureaucracy, status structure is a strong barrier to the
flow of information from the lower to the higher
levels.

A common technique for achieving multi-sectoral
coordination, when an activity involves more than
one ministry, is to establish inter-ministerial
committees. A difficulty with this approach is that
representatives of a ministry act only after close
consultation with the head of their organization.
Such arrangements tend to be unwieldly and slow.
Inter-ministerial coordinating committees have been
more successful when given project responsibility
and authority over the budgetary allocations.

Where activities are, typically, constrained by
time limits, coordination may be speeded by more
frequent meetings among department heads. But even
where there is a need for continued coordination,
department heads, for lack of time, sometimes
delegate the task of coordination to an assistant
or other subordinate who attends interdepartmental

meetings. Such subordinates generally have to refer to their respective department heads before making a decision. Although one may assume that the designated subordinate is acting for the department, his discretionary authority is usually limited. While the climate among departments and ministries varies, a common relationship among bureaucratic departments is a competitive one, so that instead of dealing with actual problems, jockeying for personal and organizational position, or status considerations, often dominate decision making.

There is much to suggest that the assignment of project responsibility to an existing part of the bureaucracy will not be effective unless modifications to the normal processes of the bureaucracy can be made. While some degree of change in existing organizations seems appropriate in most cases, the scale and pace of change is also a factor affecting implementation. Where the scale of change is too demanding, or where the rate of change called for is too fast, institutions are often unable to respond. An evaluation of one donor-sponsored project in Africa concluded that the number of things that can push a project off course is partly a function of the new institutional relationships upon which implementation is dependent. In this case, the project called for the creation and operation of a new division in the ministry of agriculture, a new approach to small-scale lending, increased demands on the land registry staff, a reorientation of extension strategy, and a consequent increase in extension staff responsibilities and workload. In view of the tremendous load this placed on the ministry, a full response was impossible. Those engaged in project design bear a responsibility not to endanger project objectives by overloading requirements beyond the bounds of reality.

In addition to jealousy among ministries or departments, or conflicts of jurisdiction which may arise, problems have sometimes arisen in integrating the efforts of different organizations at the level of the land area covered by the project itself. This has led some experts to conclude that where possible, the land area of the project should coincide with the area of an established administrative unit of government, thus providing a common governmental integrating point. This, of course, may conflict with other criteria such as natural or functional zones which form the base area for some projects. Both criteria need to be analyzed and, insofar as possible, reconciled if integration of

administrative efforts of several governmental
organizations proves to be a problem. Even if the
project area and the administrative unit of government are congruent, there may still be problems of
coordination of local and national efforts.

(b) Creation of an autonomous unit. A second alternative which has often been used is to create
autonomous units to carry out projects. When projects have been assigned to new special or autonomous units, steps have been required to build up the
new organization, to develop operating procedures,
and to recruit and hire new people. Because the
pool of trained people which can be drawn upon is
fairly limited, the establishment of new project
organizations has at times had the effect of with-
drawing qualified personnel from existing agencies
or programmes. Often a new Agency requires staff
with graduate training, and takes them from existing
governmental agencies, particularly the Ministry of
Agriculture, where large gaps are created. To
minimise the chances of this occurring, when projects are listed roughly in terms of priority,
human resources should be analyzed in the same
manner as financial and other resources, and some
attention given to the source from which personnel
will be drawn, especially for large scale projects.
One way of carrying out such an analysis is illustrated in Figure 11-1 which relates given factors
in a project to existing factors which require
modification, and to new inputs and outputs which
are necessary to install the project and put it into
operation.
    Circumstances favour an autonomous agency when
the regular organization - in many cases the Ministry of Agriculture - lacks competency and it appears
impossible to build it up sufficiently to meet the
objectives of an urgently needed project; where the
project is very large in comparison to the regular
organization, or where it is considered unsuitable
for the regular organization. One kind often not
suited for existing organizations is the problem-
solving project, especially at the experimental and
pilot stages during which flexibility and the
ability to respond quickly to local conditions may
be beyond the capability of the regular organization. Land reform projects and programmes have also
often been set up as autonomous units to avoid
bringing controversy to the regular programme.

(c) Project organization reporting to a central

authority. Projects involving large-scale action
involving several or many organizations, or which
operate in different political jurisdictions, have
in some cases been successfully administered by
organizations which report directly to a central
authority, which is sufficiently strong to resolve disputes, and to set policy which will be
recognized as authoritative by all participants.

(d) Project organization reporting to a regional or
field agency. Where project decisions cannot be
made by people who are physically close to the
problems which must be dealt with, and who are
familiar with the substantive nature of the project,
frequent delays in implementation have often proved
to be a continuing handicap. Such delays have often
also been prominent in heavily-layered organizations, in which numerous clearances from upper
levels must precede even relatively routine actions.
To counteract this, some countries have tried to
improve effectiveness by establishing project
organizations at the regional or field level, which
report to a decentralized authority there.

Regional development plans or schemes usually
cut across sectors and aim to improve the overall
development of a region. While they are called projects, they are often in fact a cluster of projects
which mutually reinforce each other. The time needed to implement such projects is often long, though
they may be planned so that sub-units (or individual
projects within the comprehensive or cluster project) may come to maturity in stages. One advantage
of such a strategy is that local people can see the
benefits of some investments in a relatively short
period of time. Another advantage is that some part
of the earlier gains may be used to finance later
undertakings. Finally, such a strategy is consistent with the finding that organizational change has
been more effective in most cases when introduced
gradually.

The problem of finding an adequate number of
trained technicians and managers to implement projects has already been mentioned in connection with
the creation of autonomous and semi-autonomous
organizations for project implementation. It has
usually been a lesser problem, but still a serious
one, in implementing projects where the organizations report to the centre or to a regional agency.
Most of the projects which have been successful in
these categories have called for secondment of personnel from existing organizations, sometimes

Figure 11-1   Roles of Specialists from Different Disciplines in the Design and Operation of Irrigation Systems

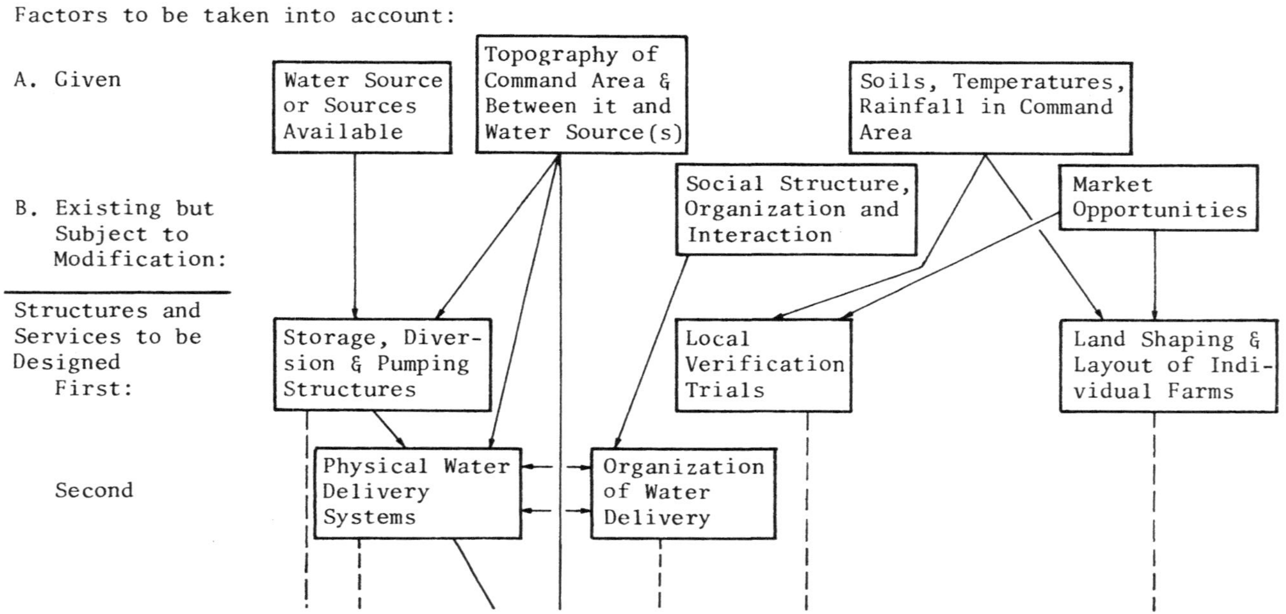

Factors to be taken into account:

A. Given

B. Existing but Subject to Modification:

Structures and Services to be Designed First:

Second

Water Source or Sources Available

Topography of Command Area & Between it and Water Source(s)

Soils, Temperatures, Rainfall in Command Area

Market Opportunities

Social Structure, Organization and Interaction

Storage, Diversion & Pumping Structures

Local Verification Trials

Land Shaping & Layout of Individual Farms

Organization of Water Delivery

Physical Water Delivery Systems

234

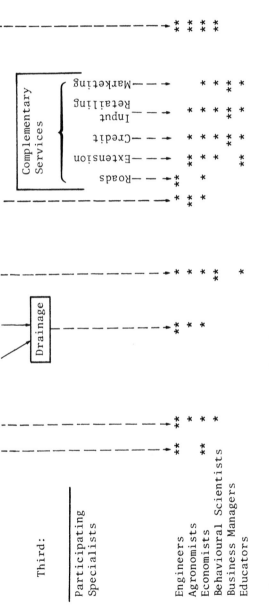

Third:

Participating
Specialists

Engineers
Agronomists
Economists
Behavioural Scientists
Business Managers
Educators

Complementary
Services

Roads
Extension
Credit
Input Retailing
Marketing

Drainage

* Denotes supplementary responsibility
** Denotes major responsibility

235

weakening the conduct of ongoing programmes. The
phasing of project units in regional projects is
one way of alleviating the demand for trained project personnel at any given point in time.

(e) Use of an external agent. Experience shows that
agricultural services are contracted to external
firms and organizations for a number of reasons. The
contracting firm can provide a source of skills
in a client organization. Moreover, contracting
firms are ordinarily available quickly. Because
consultants repeatedly work on problems which may
not routinely confront a given organization, they
develop and maintain valuable analytical skills
which may be uncommon in some countries. Although
the costs for contracted services may appear to be
high when considered in isolation, such costs may
be moderate when compared to the planned-for results.
Lastly, the service - particularly that of an external consulting firm - may provide an objectivity
which cannot be found inside the organization. An
impartial viewpoint, free of pre-set lines of
commitment, may in itself be a valuable service.
    The use of contractors makes it possible for
the bureaucratic organization to tackle a great
variety of tasks on a flexible basis. This is particularly advantageous where the need is intermit-
tent since it avoids staffing for a temporary need.
Execution through a contracting firm makes it
possible to get the best available talents. Many
times the use of contractors is insisted on by
cautious lenders of project funds. The use of
contractors gives greater assurance that the resources allocated will be used for the designated
activity rather than assigned to continuing functions. Where salary levels and conditions of
service of government agencies are particularly poor,
contracting-out services may be the only feasible
way of getting the job done in the short run.
    This practice, however, has a number of disad-
vantages. First, experience in doing the job
seldom remains with the organization. Nor is the
contracting firm likely to consider training for
operational management a high priority. Second,
where an activity has multi-disciplinary content, it
is difficult for the bureaucratic organization to
monitor contracting services. There is sometimes a
strong tendency for one discipline to be over-
emphasized to the exclusion of others. Thus, if
irrigation works are contracted out, in some cases

it has become the responsibility of the engineering department, with little consideration or coordination with related activities.

Contractors and other agency personnel should generally be used sparingly and with discretion. While their use in many countries will continue to be necessary, and while certain tasks will continue to be performed by specialists from external sources, for some time to come, the objective should be to develop capacity within the country, and to a greater degree than exists at present within the major ministries and other agencies responsible for agriculture and rural development. An evaluation of completed projects over a fairly extended period, of at least ten years, would reveal what sources of expertise have had to be obtained from external sources. Those which have consistently been necessary in project works should provide an indicator for training local personnel.

4. Project Evaluation

There are two general types of evaluation. First, there are audits or evaluations conducted to provide accountability of resources. These evaluations are normally conducted by an organizational unit independent from line management. The objective is usually narrowly confined: to determine whether project funds and material were used in accordance with prevailing regulations. These evaluations are not the subject of this section.

The other general type of evaluation embodies what the World Bank refers to as a "learning dimension". The purpose is to determine what went well, and why; what went poorly, and why; and how future efforts can be improved on the basis of the knowledge gained. The primary objective is therefore to enable planning and implementation to be improved. Evaluations which do not fulfill this are of no use from the manager's standpoint.

Project conditions vary according to regional and national characteristics, social and cultural factors, and other aspects. Evaluations need to take into account the aspects of projects which are unique and non-repeatable, while at the same time identifying those successes and problems which have wider applicability within and among countries. There is no guarantee, however, that even evaluations which are conducted effectively, and produce valuable information, will be very useful if there is not a unit which will be able to act authoritatively on the basis of information received from these exercises, or, at least, to formulate guidelines and recommendations for improving projects. Officials of both national and international development organizations are aware of the need to make better use of what is learned from evaluations, but they are often not equipped to do so.

The greatest success in using such findings has occurred when higher levels of authority have: (1) made it clear that evaluation is significant and that its findings will be given serious consideration; and (2) established a sufficiently authoritative unit with the capability for following up on evaluation findings. An analysis of the way they have been undertaken shows that there are three basic approaches: on-going or built-in evaluation, special and ex-post evaluation.

(a) On-going or "built-in" evaluation. Evaluation has most consistently proven successful when it has been an integral part of project design and operation. As this fact has come to be more fully realized, there has been a move towards building evaluation into projects. A major advantage of this approach is that undesirable deviations from project plans can be analyzed and corrective actions taken more quickly. Conversely, the reasons for successes in projects can be determined, and successful practices disseminated to other areas, or other parts of the project, as appropriate.

Monitoring should not be confused with evaluation. The information which is gained from a Monitoring Unit allows project progress to be measured against some planned scale of accomplishment. Evaluation draws on the information gained by monitoring and examines why things went as they did and how future operations could be improved. The connection between good monitoring and evaluation is a very strong one, especially as project-level data have often been either lacking in reliability or completely unavailable. By gathering information keyed to proposed project outputs and objectives, good monitoring systems provide a more solid basis for evaluation, and remove a great deal of the exercise from the realm of speculation.

Evaluations of planned vs. implemented actions are designed to assess reasons for discrepancies in micro-region plans, such as agency inefficiencies or community unresponsiveness. Annual evaluations will make correction possible for the following year's micro-region investment plan. To provide that complementary actions are proceeding as planned, inter-agency coordination will be evaluated. This will facilitate the meshing of interacting elements such as availability of credit, technical assistance for production, physical inputs (seed and fertilizer), and construction.

Just as evaluation is directly related to monitoring, so it is to project design. One of the more comprehensive design schemes developed has been the Logical Framework used by the U.S. Agency for International Development (AID). While not itself an evaluation device, the Logical Framework sets the stage for evaluation. By providing a means of systematically relating the inputs required and the project outputs expected to achieve its purpose, the Logical Framework provides a consistent means by which AID can evaluate projects for which it provides assistance. In sum, it sets standards against which projects can be evaluated. To a large extent, AID evaluations consist of determining and validating whether or not the project outputs are being produced, whether these are in fact serving to achieve the project purpose, and finally whether this achievement is making a significant contribution, as planned, to the higher order goal. Figure 11-2 details the way in which the Logical Framework is intended to operate, and Figure 11-3 is the Worksheet used to summarize the salient aspects of project design.

The Logical Framework concept is a tool for assisting in project design and evaluation. Like any tool, it can be used well or poorly. AID guidelines recognized, for example, the value of the participation of those likely to benefit from the project. Their participation is desirable because: (1) their knowledge of the conditions which are likely to affect implementation in some ways exceeds that of planners and technical specialists; (2) participation eliminates surprises when evaluations are undertaken about the nature and expected magnitude of beneficiaries' actions and resource inputs; and (3) experience indicates clearly that more effective participation is probable during implementation when its participants are involved in the stages of project formulation.

The evaluation procedures built into the AID-sponsored projects and the approaches used in the World and Regional Development Bank projects, are primarily formal and centrally oriented, i.e. designed to feed information to the formal project management. Another approach is directed towards

Figure 11-2   The Logical Framework (AID) of a
Technical Assistance Project

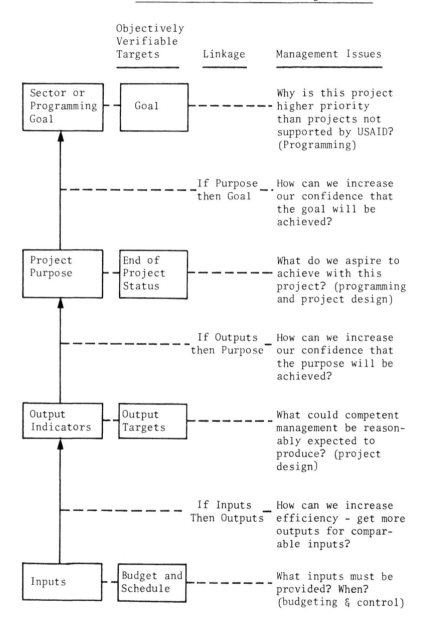

Figure 11-3   Project Design Summary: Logical Framework (AID)

Life of Project
From FY _____ to FY _____
Total U.S. Funding _____
Date Prepared: _____

Project Title & Number: _____

NARRATIVE SUMMARY	OBJECTIVELY VERIFIABLE INDICATORS	MEANS OF VERIFICATION	IMPORTANT ASSUMPTIONS
Program or Sector Goal: The broader objective in which this project contributes: (A-11)	Measures of Goal Achievement: (A-2)	(A-3)	Assumptions for achieving targets: (A-4)
Project Purpose: (B-1)	Conditions that will indicate purpose has been achieved: End-of-Project status. (B-2)	(B-3)	Assumptions for achieving purpose: (B-4)
Project Outputs: (C-1)	Magnitude of Outputs: (C-2)	(C-3)	Assumptions for achieving outputs: (C-4)
Project Inputs: (D-1)	Implementation Target (Type and Quantity) (D-2)	(D-3)	Assumptions for providing inputs: (D-4)

self-evaluation, that is, evaluation by the project
participants and beneficiaries which in itself
serves as a vehicle for transferring management
capability and responsibility.

Neither the formalized built-in or continuing
evaluation system nor the self-evaluation approach
is necessarily a sufficient means of evaluating all
aspects of a given project. For this reason, other
types of evaluation are usually undertaken. Nonetheless, built-in evaluation is the quickest type
of feedback and the best opportunity for effecting
positive changes during the course of project implementation.

(b) Special evaluations. A special evaluation can
be defined as any non-recurring evaluation, excluding audits, undertaken during the implementation
of a project. This kind of exercise may cover all
or some of the same ground as that assessed by means
of a built-in or interval evaluation system, but
special evaluations are usually undertaken by people
external to the project. Their scope may be confined to a specified region or operational sector,
or may cover the entire project. Such evaluations
may ask, and often have, not only whether the project has met or is in the process of meeting its
specific objectives, but also whether those are
indeed the objectives which should be attempted, or
whether more effective ways of pursuing the objectives might have been utilized.

In order to know whether a project has had a
favourable impact, it is necessary to have some idea
of what would have happened without the project in
place. In a strictly logical sense, this is impossible to determine. Project evaluators have
attempted to resolve this problem by designating a
group outside the project area as a "control group".
The control group, in theory, is free of the influences which are brought about by the project. A
baseline study is made of both the "target" population, i.e. the population group which contains both
the proposed project group and the control group.
The purpose of the tests is to ensure that the control group and proposed project beneficiary group
are similar in basic characteristics. Then, in
theory, it will be possible to measure some of the
important aspects of the project by a later test
which would show differences between the project
beneficiaries and the control group. Figure 11-4
indicates graphically an idealized study design for
making comparisons between a control group and a

FIGURE 11-4.   "Ideal" Study Design for
                Making Comparisons (AID)

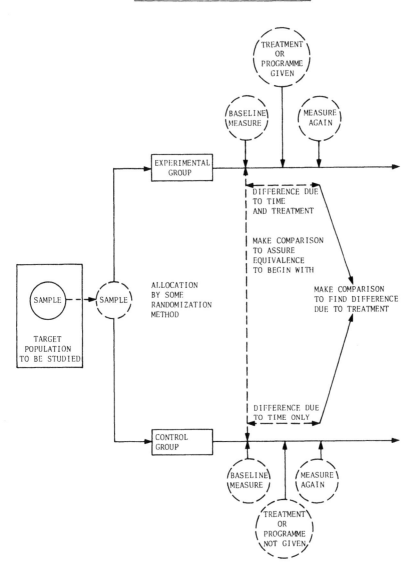

group of project beneficiaries.

Unfortunately, in practice the world does not divide neatly into control groups and groups who will be influenced by projects. Most developing countries have development programmes that reach, in some way, albeit a small one, most areas of the countries. Then, successful innovations have sometimes diffused rapidly, and there is no guaranteed means of confining innovations to a project area in a time of advanced technological means of communication. For some projects which have very limited objectives, it is true that innovations have been successfully applied in delimited areas. In projects such as integrated rural development, which attempts to reach large numbers of people over large areas, measuring project results by use of the control group method has been more difficult and costly.

When circumstances warrant its use, the before and after methodology involving a control group or groups offers a means of selectively testing the effects of different project variables. But when there are doubts about the similarities of control and project groups, where expertise is not available to provide for a high degree of research discipline, or where cost would be prohibitive, another evaluation scheme may be better than the control group approach. Whatever system is used, the means of collecting and dealing with data must be oriented to the specific circumstances, and the researcher must be able to say: "These are the phenomena I am trying to understand; these, therefore, are the kind of data I need". Efficient and reliable methods of data collection can only flow from the terms and nature of the subject being studied.

(c) Ex-post evaluation. Considerable time and attention have been given to evaluating projects after their completion. In theory, ex-post evaluation provides information which allows the project cycle to be closed: from completed projects, data can be gathered and used to plan and implement other projects and programmes more effectively. The following reasons have been given for undertaking ex-post evaluations: (1) obtaining an accurate picture of costs and benefits; (2) determining at what points and for what reasons the schedule for implementation was changed; (3) gathering and maintaining data on changes which were made and which continue to be brought about as a result of the project; (4) documenting results in order to generate political, organizational, and public support for the kind of development effort represented by the project; (5) determining how effective the strategy and operational procedures used were for attaining the specific objectives of this project; and (6) investigating whether the project objectives were in fact proper, in relation to sector objectives.

Some of the factors involved in estimating costs and benefits were discussed earlier. While many of the uncertainties which made cost-benefit analysis difficult at an earlier stage will of course have been resolved when an ex-post evaluation is conducted, some remain. If a reasonably accurate accounting has been kept of the funds, units of worker time, and equipment, commodities, and other materials secured and expended during the project, the costs of the project can usually be ascertained within a relatively short time after the completion of the project. But where project accounts have not been kept well as the project was implemented - which has often been the case - serious problems have arisen in determining project costs.

In a number of instances, participating ministries and organizations, sometimes including the ministry which has major responsibility for a project, have charged support services for projects to a general programme allotment. When a number of different ministries have been involved in one project, this has led to an understatement of project costs. The data requirements for accurate ex-post evaluations can thus be seen to have their roots in the earliest stages of the project. In fact, the basis for evaluation is established, and must be clearly reflected, in the project objectives and work plan. At a minimum, major cost components need to be identified at the point when an accounting system for the project is set up.

A problem which has continuously bedeviled project evaluations is the lack of readily available data. One attempt to solve this problem has been to build into project design the capability to gather, assess, and utilize data as the project unfolds. Where this has been done, ex-post evaluation has been greatly simplified. The most effective monitoring and reporting systems have gathered and reported data tuned to the objectives of the project.

It is even more difficult to estimate project benefits than costs. For one thing, some of the most important benefits may not be readily apparent soon after the conclusion of the project. An AID-supported fertilizer project in the Republic of Korea, which was for a decade considered to be an abject failure, provided training to a considerable number of Korean engineers and technicians. Later, these same engineers and technicians were able to get two large fertilizer plants built well ahead of schedule. The later successes were officially attributed to training received in the earlier project deemed a failure. If, as many people believe, trained manpower is a major factor in self-sustaining development, the final analysis of project success may not be possible for several months, or sometimes several years after the formal conclusion of the project. Sweeping generalizations about project success and failure immediately following their completion have often been inaccurate. Caution is advised when data have not been collected and recorded properly.

The more immediate and tangible results of projects have at times been less significant than later, less obvious results. The ultimate test may be whether or not the project generates its own continuing and expanding activity. Another measure of the likely permanence of 'project-induced' changes is the extent to which project activities have been institutionalized.

The following questions might be some of the ones which evaluators would want to consider:

(1) Have new methods and training been incorporated into the normal life of project participants and do they persist and spread?
(2) Have the people of the project area come to believe that progress is possible?
(3) Have methods of investigation been inculcated so that similar (health, education, farming) problems of new kinds can be solved by the people?
(4) Has an appropriate organizational unit been established and have staff and a budget been provided to continue the activity?
(5) Have communities or groups in the project area incorporated activities into their own local institutions? Do individuals practise new methods within their informal groups?
(6) What unplanned changes have occurred and what are their effects?
(7) What non-project factors have aided project programmes? Can they be drawn on in the future?
(8) Could a different project be designed to

yield similar benefits, but at a lower cost?

If these questions yield positive response, it is likely that the project can indeed be termed a success. These are significant questions to have from the beginning, and they should influence project design, as well as form one basis for subsequent evaluations.

(d) Which type of evaluation should be used? The use of any one of the approaches outlined above does not exclude the desirability or the need to use one or both of the others. In an ideal situation, it would certainly be possible and desirable to use all three. Nonetheless, evaluation efforts bear a price tag, and the careful manager will limit evaluation to those efforts which appear most likely to yield information to allow the project to be managed in the best way possible, at a reasonable cost. From this viewpoint, ex-post evaluation is clearly the least desirable method. Its shortcomings are: (1) that it is ex-post - one cannot improve a completed project; (2) mechanisms to transfer lessons from one project to another are often deficient, or in some cases lacking altogether; (3) there has been a tendency to concentrate on critical findings to the exclusion of carrying forward positive practices for wider dissemination; and (4) highly specific findings are not broadly applicable, and what has been found to be either a mistake or a good practice in one project does not necessarily prove to be in another project.

Special evaluations have proven to be useful, but are often expensive, both in terms of paying for expertise from outside the project, and the time necessary to brief outsiders, which in some cases has cut into the staff time that could itself have been spent on improved implementation. A further drawback has often been the lack of sufficiently detailed recommendations for change. Findings have often been too general, with too little advice on how such findings can be worked into the actual implementation of the project. This is a charge which has often been levelled at external consultants who, for example, find that "extension workers are underpaid". Project personnel are usually quite well aware of problems of this type, but little good has come from such findings when the remedies are beyond reach, or when changes would be required on such a broad scale that a government-wide reorganiation would be required.

The single most effective method is built-in evaluation. Experience suggests that evaluation should be built in from the outset by: (1) seeking consistency among project aims or objectives, inputs and outputs; (2) stating success criteria in terms clearly perceived by all involved in the project; (3) involving beneficiaries early and continuously in establishing and clarifying aims; (4) separating monitoring and evaluating, so that evaluations can concentrate on substantive analysis; and (5) providing sufficient flexibility for managers to adjust the forms of the project to meet changing conditions.

Built-in evaluation supplemented by special evaluation has offered the most effective combination of approaches. Where specialized expertise has been needed, the freshness of an outsider's analysis has been salutary, provided that sufficient guidance on the background, aims, and desired outputs of the project have been provided to the outside evaluator, and that the recommendations of the evaluators have been sufficiently clear and detailed to be implemented.

Evaluations are useful to the extent that the results and the interpretations of the studies are utilized in the planning and decision-making process. The problem arises as to how this analytical input can be fed into the planning process. One method is through training courses and on-site visits. The possibility of creating training centres alongside several of the projects to implement this process has been suggested.

The form of the data, analyses and interpretations must clearly be appropriate to the decisions at hand. One method of providing a useful framework for evaluation is the isolation of critical or casual factors in an activity's success. A system of this type gathers information about present successes, innovations, and new ideas, and looks forward to new objectives and strategies which would be evolved to bring about the adoption and application of these successful experiences. This can be done through evaluations which take care to recognize the successes and to analyze their causes. The contrasting but prevalent practice of focusing on the analysis of project problems gives no clear guidelines for future planning.

The objectives and values of the evaluation team can often become substituted for the objectives of the project. This generally happens when the

evaluator has no clear objectives upon which to
base evaluation measures. In an evaluation of a
Tanzanian beef ranching project, for example, the
statement was made that the most important function
of beef ranching in a country like Tanzania was to
generate a maximum of funds for investment in other
sectors of the economy. However, nowhere in the
assessment of the project could one find any mention
of this objective. In a Costa Rican agricultural
project, a team of evaluators found a discrepancy
between the project objective of increasing rural
incomes and the strategy of increasing production.
This led to inability to evaluate the project in
terms of the project design. These and other experiences have shown that clear and definite objectives are necessary in order to undertake a useful
evaluation study.

While this seems self-evident, tremendous
problems have arisen when area- and situation-
specific factors have not been fully considered.
Evaluations need to note clearly those successes
which seem unlikely to be duplicated elsewhere, or
which could be replicated only if certain measures
were taken, because they depend on a specific set
of local conditions. If any of these conditions are
not isolated, then future project designs may include a set of assumptions inappropriate to the
local project environment.

Chapter 12

FINANCING AGRICULTURAL PLANS

Summary
    Financing an agricultural plan can be a major
    problem. Although foreign assistance can and
    usually does provide an important contribution
    to the total funds needed, the bulk comes from
    domestic sources. It is therefore important
    that a country's financial system, particularly
    in rural areas, can adequately cope with the
    heavy demands of rural development. Mobilising
    rural savings and creating new and improved
    rural credit institutions are not easy tasks
    because of the very nature of agricultural
    systems, and the power structure of land owner-
    ship. Fair and efficient systems of rural
    taxation are only gradually evolving in most
    countries. The decentralisation of fiscal
    authority can be a helpful step in this direc-
    tion. Other positive developments may include
    growth of private rural banks and of local co-
    operatives.

One test of a plan is whether adequate finance is
available to put it into action. If not, the plan
becomes little more than a political gesture. The
development of agriculture requires both fixed and
working capital. Fixed capital is needed for such
investments as irrigation, agricultural machinery
and rural infrastructure, while working capital is
required for current inputs like seeds, fuel, fertilizer and pesticides. The provision of adequate
working capital is as important as that of fixed
capital if agricultural investments are to provide
satisfactory results.

1. Sources of Financing
In the developing world, non-monetized agriculture

250

is widespread. It is characterized by a predomin-
ance of tenant farmers with fragmented lands, who
can rarely save much or build up adequate security.
Under these conditions the financing of agricultural
plans depends to a large extent on public funds. It
is estimated that public investment amounts, on the
average, to about 70 percent of the total agricultural investment in the developing countries, which
indicates the need for a corresponding mobilization
of agricultural savings in the public sector. This
requirement is partly reduced if foreign public and
private investment is available, but domestic
finance has provided the bulk of agricultural
finance in most developing countries.

A. Public funds. Fixed capital needed for agricultural development is generally provided by the
government, at least in the earlier stages of development. However, in order to persuade farmers to
adopt new techniques, the government must either
leave enough resources in their hands to meet the
needs for working capital or provide them with
sources of credit.
      The major taxes on agriculture are land revenue,
agricultural income tax, personal taxes and export
duties. Land taxes yield relatively little in most
developing countries, today. It is sometimes argued
that land tax by itself has an output-increasing
effect. Although this has been true for Japan where
a substantial increase in agricultural output was
obtained not only because of the heavy tax on agricultural land, but also due to the use of fertilizer,
education and other improved inputs at relatively
low cost.
      If land arrangements are such that large hold-
ings are inefficiently used, while there is surplus
labour available on small holdings, a tax based on,
or related to, potential output could force owners
of large holdings to use their land more producti-
vely to meet taxes. Such results have been obtained
in some Latin American countries. If the land tax
is progressive i.e. the rate per acre increases with
the size of holdings and/or the value of land, there
is increased pressure on large landowners to sell
part of their holdings or to improve land utilization. A progressive land tax could also be assessed
on potential output, which would discourage absentee
landlordism and speculative holdings of idle lands,
and promote the sale of such lands to small farmers.
This has been the case in Brazil, India, Panama and
China (Taiwan).

In China, the taxation of land is based on
normal yield; and additional output arising from
good management or weather conditions is exempted in
order to offer incentives to increase production.
The existence of a land tax to be paid in cash is
also important as a way of increasing the marketed
surplus. Farmers must grow and sell more to supply
their increased cash needs.

However, the importance of land revenue has declined in relation to the total tax revenue. The
prevailing systems are generally inequitable as the
tax falls on all lands equally, without any exemp-
tion. The yields from such taxes are fairly inflexible as the tax is fixed and does not grow in
proportion to agricultural income. In addition, the
unwillingness of farmers to pay tax to a distant
government, with which they have little contact,
compounds the problem of collection. The way out of
this difficulty is not to abolish land tax, but to
make it progressive according to the acreage, value,
or presumed output of land. Another important step
is to decentralize both the authority to tax and to
deliver services. Local authorities should provide
services to farmers so that when the farmers see
what they are getting for their money, they are
likely to be more willing to give voluntary labour
as well as to pay more taxes to meet their needs.
By contrast, taxes going for some unseen and unknown
purpose have often been vigorously resisted.

It has been difficult to get sufficient revenue
from agricultural income tax with the poor record-
keeping and difficulties in assessing taxable capacity when income is mostly in kind. If most income
is being generated by large farms, then in theory it
may be possible to obtain most of the agricultural
savings by taxing a relatively small number of large
farmers. This would not apply to many countries
where a large amount of land is in smallholdings.

The key elements in establishing a successful
agricultural income tax system are: the administration feasibility of reaching a very large number of
farmers with low incomes, and the adequacy of determining the level and change of this income over
time. Problems with these elements largely explain
why very few developing countries have, until now,
directly taxed their agricultural sector through
income tax.

Personal taxes seem better suited to countries
with traditional agriculture. They involve family-
by-family assessment of income and income-earning
assets, made by local officials or community leaders,

to determine what is a fair tax for each family. Such taxes would be most effective when tied to local expenditures where benefits are obvious to local tax-payers. By keeping the assessment procedure simple, it is possible to make the personal tax a better substitute for poll tax, as it can be related to crude measures of ability to pay, increasing its revenue potential.

One direct means of taxing agriculture is through betterment levies. Agricultural land often appreciates in value because of irrigation works, the opening up of new roads, or other infrastructures by the state. It is considered legitimate that some of this gain should be recaptured by the government since it has occurred from actions largely unrelated to farmers' own efforts. Betterment levies are often a tax on capital gains, as in India and Pakistan on major irrigation works. Another means of capturing such gains is a road tax on landowners. Sometimes this kind of tax is attached to the agricultural income tax so that payments are proportional to output and to road usage.

Historically, the main source of revenue from agriculture in the developing countries has been taxation of foreign trade, e.g. import and export duties. The chief attraction of these duties is that they are relatively easy to administer. But the combined effect of export taxes on agricultural output and import duties on agricultural inputs can seriously affect incentives for domestic as well as export production. Great care must therefore be taken in devising these duties, to ensure that they do not create adverse incentives for agricultural production, by turning the terms of trade seriously against agriculture. The main purpose should be to capture windfall gains which arise from sudden shifts in international prices. For this to happen, they must be adjusted quickly and flexibly in response to the changing international situation. For commercial agriculture, one successful approach has been to place taxes on a sliding scale for farm exports, which become applicable only when export prices rise above a predetermined level.

Fiscal authorities should formulate and execute a system of taxation which has built-in incentives and disincentives - incentives to those who would take advantage of the resources available to them, and disincentives to those who would refuse to exploit these resources. The tax system in agriculture should be used as a means to ensure that a significant part of increased income in agriculture

is reinvested rather than wasted on ostentatious
consumption. At the same time, the government
should ensure that adequate and judicious subsidies
are provided on major agricultural inputs like
fertilizer, pesticides, improved seeds and irrigation water to compensate for foreign exchange restrictions, tariffs or other fiscal devices raising
the costs of these inputs. Many countries provide
fertilizer at lower than world prices. But these
subsidy programmes tend to benefit large more than
small farmers. For governments to help those
farmers who need subsidies most, it may be worthwhile putting them on a selective basis to benefit
only certain groups or particular regions.

Decentralization of fiscal authority. Farmers generally need better public services if they are to
perform more effectively and, in theory, these could
be provided through higher taxes. The reality in
most developing countries, however, is that farmers
have had little or no voice in what has been done
with the taxes they have paid. They have paid taxes
to support non-farming classes, with the poorer
farmers having to shoulder the heaviest tax burdens.
It is not surprising, therefore, that farmers are
loath to pay taxes to some distant government from
whom they may have little reason to expect any returns. One way of dealing with this problem is to
decentralize taxing authority, and to mobilize, and
use, local resources more effectively; regional and
local governments could be made responsible for
collecting direct taxes on land and personal taxes.
In practice, however, little has been done in this
area.
     At present, the proportion of expenditure on
rural development allocated as a result of local decisions is fairly small - in the range of 10 to 20
percent. Budget authority continues to rest with
the central government in most countries, with a
major part of the funds allocated on a departmental
basis. Funds which provincial authorities can
allocate out of their own resources are generally
inadequate. Even where there is a considerable
degree of local autonomy in spending, reliance on
central governments for funds is very great. Central
governments usually curtail attempts by local
authorities to raise additional revenue directly,
although such actions not only supplement central
government allocations, but also strengthen the
basis for local participation in planning, and lead
to increased local fiscal responsibility.

254

The extent to which resources are raised at
this level depends, in part, on the extent to which
those contributing to the cost directly benefit from
the programmes. The response of the local community
to accepting taxation and making local projects
work, may be quite favourable if they are the major
beneficiaries. If economic power is concentrated,
however, as in some states in India, the rural elite
may be unwilling to pay the financial cost of public
works unless forced to do so.

From the point of view of developing responsible and sound central/regional fiscal relationships, the following criteria should be taken into
account:

(1) The regions should be allowed to fully
exploit their own resources to cover routine expenditures, and to help finance some development
expenditures.

(2) Natural resources such as oil, natural gas
and minerals should be regarded as national assets.
Taxes and royalties earned on such assets should be
put into a national "development pool" for redistribution.

(3) The central government should give regions
a development grant based on one or more of the
following factors: population, growth potential,
backwardness, and local development effort.

The above three criteria can be adapted to a country's particular requirements. The important thing
is to fully mobilize the development resources of
the country with a minimum of confusion, or rivalry
between the regions.

B. Private Funds

(i) Moneylenders and intermediaries. Private finance comes from both informal and capital markets,
and from household savings. The informal market is
made up of a non-commercial and a commercial sector.
The non-commercial sector is represented by loans
from friends and relatives who often charge no
interest, and the commercial sector by loans from
crop buyers, input dealers, landlords and professional moneylenders. It is this source that probably
provides about 90 to 95 percent of the credit needs
of small farmers in most developing countries. The
village moneylenders who are by far the most important source of credit to these farmers, are well-

known for their operational knowledge and flexibility, though they often became a class of exploit-
ers, using the weakness of the borrowers to their
advantage. Since the source of credit is nearby,
and readily accessible, quick adjustment can be
made to changing situations, and generally the size
of the loan is determined by the farmer himself. For
these reasons, farmers continue to borrow from local
moneylenders although they tend to charge usurious
rates, and, in many places, institutional credit has
made no significant inroads into their trade.

Apart from moneylenders, private input or provision dealers have been, on occasions, an important
source of credit. Given proper incentives, such as
liberal imports of certain key agricultural inputs,
they have been quick to respond.

(ii) Private commercial banks. Private commercial
banks can be a good source of credit and have provided this service to large commercial farms in
Latin America. But almost no use is made of them by
small farmers in tropical Africa and elsewhere,
because there are few branches of private banks in
rural areas, and banks are reluctant to lend to
small farmers who do not have title to land which
might otherwise be used as collateral.

There is, however, a network of rural banks of
considerable importance in some Asian countries, e.g.
the Philippines, where the majority of farmers are
tenants with little or no collateral to offer
private banks. Consequently an Agricultural
Guaranty Loan Fund was established in the Philippines' Central Bank. Money from this Fund, together
with insurance against losses, was lent to widely
separated private rural banks, which in turn made
loans to tenant farmers without the usual collateral
requirement, and at reasonable interest rates. It
was largely in this manner that farm inputs for the
high yielding rice varieties were financed in the
Philippines.

The Indian subcontinent has a fairly well-
developed network of rural banks. In India, a
National Small Credit Guaranty Corporation was created to assume some of the risks of lending to farmers by insuring the banks against losses of up to 75
percent of crop loans of 1,000 rupees or less. With
this risk insurance, commercial banks have opened
millions of new farmer accounts, and in the process
they have found that small farmers may be better
risks than larger ones. Small farmers work hard,
farm their lands intensively and pay back loans

diligently. In Mexico, the Government established
a Guaranty and Development Fund for Agriculture in
1956 directed by the Bank of Mexico which, through
this Fund, is able to ensure that an additional
volume of resources from the private sector flows
into agriculture. For the private sector to be an
effective source of funds for agriculture, it is
clearly important for the government to be willing
to assume at least part of the risks involved.
Otherwise, private funds will flow only to large
farmers, leaving the vast majority of small farmers
to the mercy of traditional moneylenders and middlemen.

(iii) Household savings. The assumption that rural
people with low incomes and little economic awareness have very little capacity for voluntary
savings seems to be oversimplified. Voluntary
savings do exist in the rural areas, but financial
markets are badly fragmented. Individuals often use
their savings for operating expenses on the farm,
for purchasing additional land or cattle, or in some
countries for buying jewelry, or other durable val-
uables, as a hedge against inflation.
    Sometimes farmers are forced to save in order
to become members of cooperatives or credit unions.
These organizations require individuals to purchase
share capital and to keep a deposit in order to be
able to borrow. In a few cases, cooperatives also
create forced savings by withholding part of the
sales proceeds from a member's sales through the cooperative. In Kenya, a few cooperatives deposited
proceeds of members' sales through the cooperative
in regular savings accounts. In spite of the modest
rates of interest paid, cooperative officials were
pleasantly surprised by the amount of deposits
which were not withdrawn. In Bangladesh, directors
of the Comilla programme required individuals to
make minimal periodic savings deposits in order to
remain eligible for other developmental activities.
Again, despite a very low rate of interest, large
amounts of funds were deposited in the programme
over the years.
    These are only a few examples of successful
experiments in a limited number of countries. There
are few countries where rural savings have been
vigorously promoted and strong incentives given to
farmers to defer consumption in favour of savings.
Only China (Taiwan), Japan, Republic of Korea and
(formerly) South Vietnam have emphasized mobilizing
rural savings, and they experienced a tremendous

growth in savings through a network of rural banks
and aggressive incentive systems.

In most developing countries, however, what is
really lacking is the institutional structure to
mobilize rural savings.

C. Foreign funds. The shortfall in the domestic
mobilization of savings, both public and private,
can be met partly by foreign aid and investment.
Although difficult to estimate precisely, foreign
aid and investment probably account for 10 to 15
percent of total annual investment in agriculture of
developing countries, with a higher percentage in
the poorer countries. So far, however, official
external assistance to agriculture has failed to
meet the United Nations target set for this purpose.
Apart from large scale irrigation and infrastructure
projects, fertilizer inputs, mechanization programmes, and technical aid for research and extension,
measures to increase farm output and implement rural
development programmes make only a relatively small
demand on foreign exchange. However, foreign funds
can play an important part in other agricultural
development activities if they can be used to
finance local as well as foreign exchange costs, and
working capital as well as fixed capital.

Sources of external finance to developing
countries, whether for agricultural or industrial
development, are bilateral foreign aid and loans,
credit from multilateral agencies, including the
World Bank, regional development banks and the
United Nations Development Programme; and loans and
grants from foreign private investors and some
private foundations.

Analysis of external assistance to agriculture
is based on commitments because there are no data
available on disbursements, which are usually lower
(probably by as much as one-third), particularly for
the project type of assistance which is most common.
Data relate only to official flows (mainly Official
Development Assistance), and as data relating to
centrally planned countries are still incomplete
they have been excluded from Table 12.1, which shows
official commitments to agriculture from 1973 to
1979.

Although commitments in the "narrow" definition
(relating closely to food production) increased at a
relatively high rate in the 1970s, they were in 1979
still 44% below requirements as estimated by FAO and
the World Food Council. To bridge this gap, considerable expansion in total external assistance is

Table 12-1   Official Commitments to Agriculture, 1973-1979

	1973	1974	1975	1976	1977	1978	1979(4)
				.... $ million			
1. Agriculture "narrow" definition(1)							
Concessional (ODA)	1,322	2,111	2,137	2,377	3,257	4,433	...
Total in current prices (2)	1,848	3,110	3,341	3,360	4,760	6,423	6,680
at 1975 prices (3)	2,530	3,494	3,341	3,360	4,367	5,138	4,671
2. Agriculture "broad" definition (1)							
Concessional (ODA)	1,725	2,869	3,258	3,425	4,566	5,853	7,100
Total in current prices (2)	2,320	4,208	5,481	5,199	7,141	9,088	9,971
at 1975 prices (3)	3,178	4,728	5,481	5,199	6,551	7,270	6,973
3. Share of ODA in total commitments to agriculture				.... %			
"narrow" definition	72	68	64	71	68	69	...
"broad" definition	74	68	59	66	64	68	71
Share of agriculture "narrow" definition in commitments under "broad" definition	80	74	61	65	67	71	67
Share of official commitments to agriculture in commitments to all sectors "broad"	12	15	14	14	17	17	...

Sources: The State of Food and Agriculture 1980 F.A.O. Rome p.54.
(1) Agriculture "narrow" definition excludes assistance for such purposes as forestry, rural development, rural infrastructure, agro-industries, fertilizer production and regional and river projects which are included in the broad definition. (2) Official concessional commitments (ODA) plus official non-concessional commitments defined by OECD as other official flows. (3) Deflated by the UN unit value index of the exports of manufactured goods. (4) Preliminary.

obviously required and agriculture needs to receive
a larger share of total commitments. This share
rose from 12% in the "broad" definition in 1973 to
17% in 1978.

Multilateral agencies gave higher priority to
agriculture than bilateral sources in the 1970s.
Agriculture represented 37% of their total commitments to all sectors in 1979 compared to 26% in
1973. The share of agriculture in total commitments
by the World Bank in 1978 was as high as 42% against
only 27% in 1973. On the other hand, agriculture
accounted for only 6% and 9% of total commitments by
bilateral sources in 1973 and 1978 respectively.

The World Bank has been the largest single
source of external resources for agricultural development. Total commitments by the Bank to agriculture more than trebled at current prices during
1973-79 and amounted to $3,416 million in 1979.

Regional development banks as a group have increased their commitment to agriculture at a faster
rate than the World Bank. They committed $1,174
million to agriculture in 1979, more than 5 times
the corresponding level of 1973, and equivalent to
12% of total commitments (9% in 1973).

An important development since the mid-1970s
has been the establishment in 1977 of the International Fund for Agricultural Development (IFAD).
Most of the initial resources of just over $1
billion for its first triennium. 1977-80, had been
committed by late 1980.

Commitments to agriculture from OPEC multilateral sources began in 1974, they represented only
1% of total commitments in 1978 and fell considerably in 1979. However, bilateral assistance from
OPEC countries has been more significant. The
emergence of OPEC as a source of assistance for development financing in the 1970s has led to the
creation of national and multinational institutions
which serve as a framework for its aid (e.g. the
Kuwait Fund for Arab Economic Development).

Bilateral commitments to agriculture by the
Development Assistance Committee (DAC) member countries (Australia, Austria, Belgium, Canada, Denmark,
France, Germany F.R., Italy, Japan, Norway, Netherlands, Portugal, Sweden, Switzerland, United Kingdom
and the United States) on concessional terms increased significantly in the 1970s, reaching about
$4,174 million in 1979 when they represented 57% of
total ODA to agriculture, compared to 52% in 1973.

It is difficult to determine with any precision
what pattern of agricultural investment is supported

by external sources of financing. Crop and livestock production probably accounted for about 35%
of the total, land and water development about 22%
to 25%, agro-industries and manufactured inputs 20%
to 22%, rural and regional development and rural
infrastructure 15% and fisheries and forestry about
2% each. Commitments for research, extension and
training have risen sharply in recent years, their
share rose from less than 0.5% in 1973 to about 3%
in 1979.

Although privately financed programmes like
Oxfam have been small when measured by total funds
invested, area covered, or number of people reached,
they have been important in other ways. These programmes are usually experimental in nature, and by
virtue of their size and relatively direct and
flexible methods of operation, have had the freedom
to explore alternative ways of getting things done
in a way that is usually not possible for governmental organizations. Such private programmes and
projects have often served as innovators in the
development of new techniques, providing insights
and specific methods which have subsequently been
adopted by governments. This has been true in maize
and rice research, development of formulated foods,
and also for rural development, health service and
family planning projects. Governmental agencies
would be wise to maintain continuing contact with
the efforts of private groups, as they have often
anticipated successful measures for more widespread
application.

2. Role of Institutions in Financing Agricultural Development

Efficient financial institutions to extend credit to
farmers are a key factor in agricultural and rural
development. Institutions which deal mostly with
agriculture are: specialized agencies sponsored by
the government, private banks in rural areas and
group credit organizations.

A. Specialized agencies sponsored by government.
Governments have established specialized agencies
such as agricultural banks, land banks, or various
forms of agricultural development guaranty funds to
help channel resources into the agricultural sector.
The main objectives of these agencies are: (a) to
mobilize domestic savings in order to broaden the
resource base of agricultural credit, (b) to assure
reasonable prices for agricultural produce, (c) to
assist the producers with the proper use of loans,

and (d) to improve the rate of loan recovery. Some governments are also seeking to persuade commercial banks and insurance companies to invest in agricultural development projects.

The usual pattern of operation is for the government, or the central bank, to loan money to an agricultural bank which in turn loans the funds either directly or through cooperatives to farmers. The money loaned thus provides a revolving loan fund for the institution, with administrative costs covered by the interest charged. However, this pattern rarely works well for the rural poor, for large farmers are generally the main beneficiaries of institutional credit.

Public credit institutions are under various pressures which bring them to lend primarily to large farmers, including the need to keep administrative costs down, to avoid default, and to use credit to increase production. Administrative costs rise if the emphasis changes to small farmers, especially if they include loan supervision, since the number of loans increase and their average size falls. Moreover, there is a widespread but mistaken belief that large farmers are less likely to default and more likely to adopt new technology. Large farmers have another advantage in that they can offer their more valuable lands as collateral; and, of course, they can, and sometimes do, exert political pressure to get loans.

B. Private rural banks. With few exceptions, private rural banks have performed poorly. This is mainly because of a widely-held but incorrect view of many planners in developing countries that rural savings do not exist. As a result, little thought and effort has been given to having commercial banks mobilize savings and provide farmers with credits. In most countries, rural credit is provided by the public sector from domestic resources or through foreign assistance. These publicly sponsored credit programmes have been in constant danger from defaults, from capital erosion caused by unrealistic interest rates and very high costs of administration and supervision. The heavily subsidized interest rates usually place a low ceiling on savings deposits too, so that the system discourages commercial banks from lending to farmers and gives little inducement to farmers to save.

It is also important for the institutions to provide a safer place for farmers to deposit their savings, and to make sure that depositing and with-

drawing procedures are simple, with suitable
locations for savings institutions fully taken into
account. If potential savers are forced to travel
more than a few miles to deposit or withdraw funds,
then this factor alone discourages farmers' involvement.

A well-chosen set of incentives for banks to
seek voluntary deposits, as well as for farmers to
save, has been adopted by various countries but the
most important incentive is to raise interest rates
on savings. Some have insurance programmes on
savings deposits which eliminate the savers' risk of
agency failure. Several, like Brazil and Chile,
link savings with price inflation. Others have used
mobile banks as a way of reaching rural savers.
Savings institutions in a few countries (e.g. in
Bangladesh, and credit unions in Latin America) have
offered automatic life insurance on savings deposits
so that, in the event of the death of the depositor,
beneficiaries receive a multiple of the savings deposited. In Colombia, depositors are eligible for
educational scholarships which are drawn by lottery
daily from the list of savers in the agricultural
credit bank. Some countries, such as China (Taiwan),
offer tax concessions on income derived from savings
deposits.

If some of the best features of the traditional
rural money market, involving the operation of
private money lenders (including the decentralized
system of credit, flexibility of repayment and
personal relationships between the moneylender and
the client) were incorporated into a modern financial institution, it could make it more acceptable
to the farmers and more effective as a credit institution. Using this approach, lending systems
could be decentralized, so that institutions could
reach small farmers primarily through their agents,
who would operate at the village level with little
overhead cost and paper work. To be effective,
these village-based loan agents should be given full
authority to determine the creditworthiness of
farmers, and allowed to grant loans on the spot,
provided they investigated each situation adequately.
Agents could be rewarded on the basis of good performance (e.g. for low default rates). Even if the
loan agents charged higher than ideal interest rates,
their activities would compete with the monopoly
position which village moneylenders often exercise.
To improve their performance, loan agents would be
likely to make an effort to guide farmers to adopt
the right kind of technologies.

C. Group credit organizations.   The need for group
credit arises for a number of reasons, including
reduction in the cost of distributing credit, greater assurance about repayment, and mobilization of
new savings.   In this system, funds for productive
purposes are extended to groups of farmers joined
together in the form of an association, cooperative,
credit union, users' society, ejido, or similar
group.   The group plays an intermediary role between
the credit-granting authority and ultimate user in
securing, managing and repaying loans.
    Group lending, whether in the form of loose
associations or formally organized cooperative
credit societies, depends on the following conditions for its success:

    (a)   Homogeneity of the members: When the
members have similar income and ownership status,
they tend to distribute the loans more equally among
themselves; otherwise, only better-off members may
benefit from the programme.   For example, in India,
cooperative leadership and management are reported
to be mostly in the hands of large farmers and land
ownership is the most important criterion for extending credit.   Even where fundamental land reforms
have been introduced, as in Mexico and Egypt, credit
programmes have generally helped the middle level
farmers, rather than the poor farmers, because of
many other inequities in the society and the absence
of an egalitarian framework of policies.

    (b)   Social cohesion: Such cohesion may be
produced by religious, racial, political or ideolo-
gical considerations.   Some of the most successful
credit or multi-purpose groups have been run by
those farmers who shared a certain common social
heritage.   For instance, the large Brazilian Cooperative, Cotia, was formed by Japanese immigrants,
whose cultural homogeneity was a powerful unifying
force despite the wide range of farm sizes within
the membership.   Reliance on tribal ties of small
villages explains the success of some African
attempts to organize groups, as in Tanzania and
Uganda.

    (c)   Group responsibility and solidarity:
Another important element for the success of group
lending is the feeling of solidarity which is produced within a group either by political action, or
outstanding leadership.   This is borne out by the
experience of Bangladesh, Uganda and China (Taiwan).

In Comilla, Bangladesh, the credit cooperatives allowed any farmer who deposited some savings in his local society to borrow up to five times the amount of his combined share and savings deposits, with his plot of land taken as collateral. Group solidarity was re-inforced by weekly meetings, and the practice of extending more credit to those who attended these meetings. Also, the entire local community was held responsible for any default by any member of the group. In Uganda, credit is extended to farmers who have been active members of cooperative marketing societies for at least three years. In China (Taiwan), both farmers' associations and the traditional loosely organized cooperative hui are based on strong group solidarity. Farm sizes are generally similar and there are hardly any class distinctions. Both types of organization believe in the benefits of cooperation and in the system of collective responsibility for savings and loans. In contrast, credit societies in India and Ecuador have not been able to mobilize much solidarity. In India the requirement of pledging land as collateral has favoured the large farmers, and in Ecuador individualistic practices are encouraged by the prevailing local power structure.

(d) Careful screening system: Such a system ensures low default rates and is another condition for the success of group credit organizations. The INDAP Program in Chile suffered because credit was given too easily, without establishing careful guidelines for the use of these loans. In Uganda, on the other hand, the rate of default was very low because of rigorous selection of group members. Also group credit systems function better when members are required to deposit some savings of their own as part of the working capital. This encourages them to feel responsible for the success of the group venture.

(e) A strong commitment by the central as well as local leadership is an essential prerequisite for the success of any group credit institution. Government support, both financial and political, is needed, especially at the initial stages of the organization. All the countries which developed strong cooperatives benefitted from firm government support at the beginning. As cooperative groups acquired experience and power, the governments gradually withdraw their primary role and assumed more of a supportive role. The challenge is to find the right balance between the central government's role and local leaders' responsibility. In successful group associations, local leaders generally assume the responsibility for securing and repayment of loans, while supervision and promotional tasks are left to the upper level of organizations.

There are two types of group lending organizations which have achieved much less success than was originally expected: cooperative credit societies and supervised credit.

Experience in many countries has shown that whenever cooperative credit societies were established with the single objective of disbursing agricultural credit to members at low interest rates, they met with little success. Multipurpose societies were far more successful since they also influence planning, processing and marketing of the farmer's produce and, therefore, could become an essential part of his life. The advantage that the multi-purpose cooperatives enjoy over single-purpose credit societies is amply borne out by the experience of Egypt, Japan and Republic of Korea. In these countries, most of the problems of the farmers were taken care of by multi-purpose cooperatives, like giving them access to means of production, finance, marketing and high-productivity technology.

Supervised credit combines the granting of production credit with extension work. The loan is based on a detailed seasonal production plan, prepared by the farmers with the help of an agricultural supervisor, who also visits them from time to time helping them use efficiently the supplies and equipment financed by the loan. While this form of credit has worked well in Israel, in Ethiopia and in some other countries, generally it has also aroused suspicions and hostility toward undue government intervention. The secret of success, which has eluded many countries, is to strike the proper balance between when and how to help the farmers, and when to let them help themselves.

To summarize, then, financial institutions have to take note of the following considerations if they are to prove effective:

(i) They must make an effort to mobilize their own resources. As long as financial institutions consider that budgetary and semi-budgetary funds are limitless and can be obtained at negative rates of interest, they will not make any effort to raise their own resources.

(ii)   Interest rates on savings and credits should be high enough to give incentives both to savers and lending institutions.

(iii) Institutions should either increase the number of branches in rural areas or make use of branches of other institutions (e.g. private banks can use branches of cooperative credit societies) which are already there.

(iv)   The institutions should try to incorporate some of the best features of the traditional money market, particularly their flexibility and operational knowledge.

Chapter 13

ORGANIZATION FOR PLANNING

Summary
     Weak systems of public administration hinder
the preparation and implementation of economic,
and especially agricultural, development plans.
Traditional structures which are able to cope
with mainly routine official business are unlikely to satisfy the demanding criteria of
organizations for development. There are
several ways of dealing with this problem. The
least satisfactory is likely to be wholesale
reform of government administration. Instead it
could be improved, gradually changed and integrated with new organizations. However, this
institution building needs careful watching to
avoid unnecessary conflicts of interest and the
worst excesses of bureaucracy. Its success is
likely to depend on timing - not too hasty or
too slow - but taking advantage of gradually
increasing numbers of better-trained administrators, nearly always in scarce supply.
     The Ministry of Agriculture is likely to
play a key role in development planning and its
form and functions will need to change with the
times. An Agricultural Co-ordinating Council -
of some type - is necessary to bring together
the efforts of the various agencies involved in
agricultural development, assisted by programming units within these agencies. While the
functions of the Ministry of Agriculture will
vary considerably from country to country,
policy, planning and co-ordination are among
its main functions. Its effectiveness depends
to a large extent on strength in the field and
close liaison is vital between headquarters,
the regions and local areas. Local farmers'
organizations can play a very useful participa-

tive role in planning organization. Their
effectiveness may largely depend on official
efforts at de-centralisation, and effective
communications at all levels in both public
and private sectors.

1. Introduction
A. The administrative constraint. The literature on
agricultural and rural development often refers to
ineffective or weak public administration as a major
handicap. Indeed, it has sometimes been referred to
as "by far the most important single factor responsible for poor results in agriculture". Outdated
administrative systems often prove very inadequate
for any operation except the maintenance of the
status quo when the emphasis should be on change and
development. In Africa, particularly, this institutional constraint lies in the low priority, dispersed nature and inadequate staffing of government
agencies "dabbling in agriculture".

B. The problems and their setting. Far-reaching
changes in public administrative systems and institutions are generally needed to meet the challenge
of economic development.

In no sector has this challenge been greater
than in agriculture where problems arise which make
administrative and organizational improvement
especially difficult. In contrast with industry,
agriculture has many, usually widely dispersed,
units and it is much harder for agriculture than
industry to introduce better methods of production.
While there are a great variety of organizational
and institutional units to choose from in agriculture, they are neither easy to establish or
develop.

Different approaches and kinds of institutional
structures are needed for farmers who are still
largely in the grip of traditional subsistence agriculture, compared to farmers in transition to commercial agriculture, or who are already commercially
oriented and technically sophisticated. For many
developing countries, the task of establishing and
operating organizations which meet the needs of
these different kinds of farmers is beyond their own
resources

Institution building takes a great deal of time
even if the commitment is there. Frequently, however, the time required for institutional development and alterations in the distribution of political
and administrative power that it may imply, deter

policy-makers from taking the required action.

It is a truism that organizations and institutions are only as good as their staffs. The formulation of agricultural policies, and implementation of programmes which adequately reflect these policies, require large technical staffs with specialized training and experience, and the sound judgment which comes from long and continuing service. In many countries, factionalism rooted in party politics or other political activity and tribalism makes difficult the institutionalization of a technically expert, efficient, honest and well-coordinated bureaucracy.

Many 'new' countries have inherited legacies of institutional structures which are ill-suited to agricultural development, or are incompatible with their present political organization. Every new African country, for example, has sought to modify its inherited administrative structures to meet the requirements of an independent state. They have concentrated attention on breaking up the provincial administrations which were the chief agent of central control by colonial governments.

For many old countries and some new ones, the main problem is either the existence of outmoded organizations incompatible with development goals, or the lack of clearly defined functions and authority of newly-established departments and agencies in relation to long established organizations. Both among traditional and new organizations, functions may either overlap without design, or supplant one another without coordinated efforts toward solving development problems.

Finally, many organizations have conflicting interest groups, with objectives which may be incompatible with those of their organizations; or there may be political motives, red tape, corruption, paternalism and inefficiency to hamstring operations. Personal rivalries and strivings for personal status and power can also interfere with effectiveness. These attributes exist to a greater or lesser degree in the institutions of all countries and must be taken into account by those attempting to improve relationships within organizations, as well as between agricultural organizations and farmers.

C. Dealing with the problem. There is no universal blueprint which can be used to deal with these problems. However, the search for universal solutions goes on, despite mounting evidence that they have rarely been productive, nor are they likely to be.

The needs and policies of all governments are not likely to be identical nor should they be. Different needs require different solutions for an organization or institution is not an end in itself; its inherent value is based on ability to achieve desired policy and programme objectives.

An organization or institution must take into account existing patterns of governmental authority, as well as the way civil servants operate. The system of authority and the bureaucracy of each country is unique in its history, ability, requirements and organization. Account must be taken, therefore, of the inherent characteristics of the human resources available to staff an organization, and the relationships which exist among the bureaucracy.

The design of an organization should also take into account the personal and social characteristics of the people it is to serve. Since the ultimate focus of most organizations is on farmers, it is their needs which must determine the form and character of institutional and administrative structures. Agricultural development goals can be achieved more easily if they build upon elements of the existing social order instead of attempting to work against it. Experience shows that unless programmes are adjusted to local conditions, serious difficulties may arise. A case in point is the initial failure of the Chinese commune experiment, partly because the authorities ignored or attempted to destroy the traditional marketing structure, without offering a viable alternative. The failure of this experiment, despite the Government's authoritarian powers and propaganda, showed how dangerous it was to replace rather than build on the systems peasants had developed over centuries.

When an organization is established, it should be designed to achieve the purposes for which it was set up, with specific policies or specific programme. This is not a magic formula for institutional building, however, for changing objectives and situations may require adjustments in structure, and administrative procedures. This points to the need for continuing review and evaluation of the structure and practices of an institution, in relation to what it is trying to do.

Institution builders can learn much from the experience of others. A useful principle is to set up organizations reasonably simple to operate and designed to give speedy answers to problems. Such organizations are particularly needed where trained

271

and experienced staff, as well as telephone, secretarial, transport and other resources are limited. Institutions modelled on the pattern of those in developed countries are not likely to be suitable in most developed countries. Those who establish organizations sometimes make the mistake of giving more attention to form than to substance. This may lead to the creation of complicated "tall" organizations, with many levels of administration. The greater the number of levels of administration, the slower the movement of information, either from the top down or from the bottom up. A "flat" organization, where the number of persons reporting to any supervisor is limited to those he can effectively oversee, is likely to be more productive.

Thus, while there is much to learn from others, the starting point must be farmers' needs as well as the cultural, social and political environment in which they work. Organizations designed to carry out specific policies, programmes and projects are likely to be more effective than those set up as catchalls for sundry problems.

2. Organizing the Agricultural Sector
A. The "wholistic" vs. the partial approach. Agricultural development requires a wide range of administrative agencies. Some decisions require action by the central government, others by regional and subregional organizations. Final execution of plans must be carried out at the local level by institutions in both the private or public sector. If in the private sector, their organization can be influenced through incentives or regulation. If in the public sector, they may be established by national or regional authorities, or formed from below by farmers, or others in local areas.

In many countries, the lack of effective agricultural institutions has given rise to questions as to the best way of approaching the problem. Is it better to improve organizations on a piecemeal basis or in a "wholistic" way? There are advocates for both points of view.

Given the magnitude and scope of the problem, especially as it relates to agriculture, there is an understandable tendency to favour widespread reform. However, establishment of new agencies, however well conceived, frequently brings little or no improvement in public administration because they are not immune to the weaknesses which afflict the rest of the body politic.

This is hardly surprising to anyone familiar

with the history of attempts to initiate general
administrative reform in poor countries. Proposals
for reforms, which in the abstract appeared desirable and reasonable, have frequently ended up as
distorted, piecemeal solutions with little resemb-
lance to what was originally intended. Where implementation of a wholesale reform has actually been
carved out, in more or less the intended way, it has
often proved to be beyond the absorptive capacity of
a public service committed to traditional ways.

Administrative improvement is clearly long-term
and difficult. Yet paradoxically far-reaching
changes are essential in political and social areas
as the first step in administrative reform.

The question thus arises whether many of the
attempts to improve administration have not tried
too much. In early stages of development, attempts
at fundamental, across-the- board reform in any
field of activity are likely to be premature and
self-defeating. Pre-conditions for the success of
such efforts, however justifiable in terms of need
or desire, simply do not exist.

On the other hand, partial reform, or at least
improvement, is feasible in selected instances
where preconditions for comprehensive reform do not
exist. Prospects for reform are good where the need
to get something important done arouses in political
authorities an awareness that administrative change
is essential, where the venture is backed by a
powerful person, group or entity and where the proposed reforms are not beyond the capacity of the
governmental unit(s) concerned. These prerequisites
may, of course, exist in some countries, in some
periods, in sufficient strength to permit wholesale
reforms to be carried out; but it would be more
realistic to assume that the lack of one or more of
the preconditions dooms most such attempts. It is,
therefore, prudence, backed by experience, that
counsels necessity for courage and patience to think
small.

The wholesale approach to reform may not be so
much wrong as premature. Partial changes may not be
as neat and satisfying, but the choice between
global and partial reform may not be a real one. The
frequent failed attempts at global reform have made
it clear that many governments are not equipped with
the managerial skills and decision-making powers to
effectively carry out such reforms. Most changes
have really been piece-meal. If effective, they
could have served as models to other parts of
government: if a failure, they could have made it

clear that further reform is required. In either case, partial reforms may have induced further action and prepared the way for a more fundamental, across-the-board advance.

B. The organizational dilemma. Attempts to organize the agricultural sector on a rational basis soon encounter a dilemma: the various elements which together promote development, are frequently so interrelated that a single coordinating body is needed to ensure all the required elements mesh together; yet the scope of agriculture makes it impossible for one organization to deal effectively with all the many aspects of its development. This problem is made more intractible because farmers and agri-businessmen in the private sector - as well as politicians, technicians and civil servants in the public sector - often play important roles in the development process; and in some countries state or provincial governments share considerable responsibilities for agriculture with central governments.

Given the fact that Ministries of Agriculture tend to be among the most traditional organizations, they are generally ill-equipped to deal with development problems. As a result, those interested in promoting development frequently yield to the temptation to ignore such ministries. Moreover, ingrained tendencies found in all governments, often result in the expropriation by other ministries of powers which would normally be expected to reside in a Ministry of Agriculture.

One result is that Ministries of Agriculture have been so greatly denuded of functions that some have become little more than paper ministries, inadequately staffed and incapable of producing viable development programmes. Functions affecting agriculture have often become so widely dispersed among different government organizations that coordination is virtually impossible and agricultural and rural development, whatever the expressed wish of the government, has low priority. Sooner or later, this situation almost invariably produces calls for an organizational review and the strengthening of the Ministry of Agriculture.

Given the scarce administrative resources, and low capacity for coordination, among the staffs of agricultural institutions in many developing countries, it stands to reason that likelihood of failure increases if, instead of concentrating powers in one organization, efforts at development are split among several agencies, all with their own

headquarters and field staffs. This does not mean
that all matters affecting development must be
gathered within a single ministry or agency. There
are inevitably policy matters vital to development
which normally are not the concern of a Ministry of
Agriculture alone, and dealing with all such matters
within one, all-embracing ministry would be far too
great a burden for governments of most countries.

What is needed is not so much a super-ministry
as an integrated approach to development. This
approach is especially important in dealing with the
farmer, because his enterprise is usually a single
unit on which activities of all the various institutions working in the field converge. While an
enterprise which provides farm credit should follow
policies and guidelines laid down by a Ministry of
Agriculture, there is no operational reason why it
should be a part of the Ministry. On the contrary,
there is much to be said for having it lie outside
direct civil service regulations and controls.

Most important is the need to define each
function clearly, and assign it to an organization
with clearly defined limits of jurisdiction. Haphazard collections of organizations, frequent shifts
in responsibilities, assumption by some agencies of
functions not properly theirs, or unplanned duplication of functions, can produce such an administrative hodge-podge that coordinated movement toward
the execution of projects and programmes is virtually unattainable. Where this dismal but not uncommon
situation exists, heroic efforts may be necessary to
disentangle the maze of organizations and functions.

C. An Agricultural Coordinating Council. Given the
probability that many organizations will be in the
field of development, there is need to set up a
single agency or body to plan for, and coordinate
policies and activities for the entire sector (see
Figure 13-1 for a diagram of a schematic organization
for agricultural planning). Ideally, this agency
should be the Ministry of Agriculture, since most
governments look to ministries for sectoral planning
and coordination. However, where circumstances make
this difficult, it may be desirable to set up an
Agricultural Coordinating Council. Such a Council
must consist of the political heads of all minist-
ties, departments and agencies concerned with agricultural development if it is to have the necessary
influence. It should lay down the basic policies,
approve development plans and seek to coordinate all
activities in the sector, under the supervision of

Figure 13.1   Schematic Organization for
              Planning Agriculture

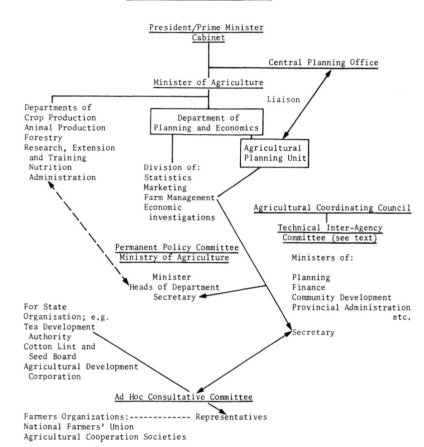

the appropriate governmental authority.

Because members of such a council are almost always busy with many matters, it cannot be expected to meet more than once or twice a year. If more frequent meetings are required, an executive committee, composed of those political heads of ministries departments and agencies most concerned with agriculture, may be authorized to act for the full council for specific purposes.

To provide technical support each council member could nominate a technician from his ministry, department, or agency, to a technical inter-agency committee, which would meet as often as necessary to do all the technical planning required to help the council (or its executive committee) adopt appropriate plans and policies. The technical committee should also be charged with carrying out the coordinative and other functions of the council, including implementing plans and policies. Only high level civil servants (ideally, heads of planning units) should be required to serve on the technical committee and those nominated should attend the committee's meetings instead of sending their subordinates. Substitution of lower civil servants on the technical committee is likely to reduce its importance and, almost inevitably, its effectiveness, given the circumstances existing in most countries. It may also be necessary to set up one or more executive sub-committees of the technical committee, with members from those organizations most concerned with agriculture, or with specific aspects of development. They would carry out specified tasks for the technical committee including the preparation of plans and programmes for the approval of the whole technical committee.

D. Programming units. An Agricultural Coordinating Council, supported by a technical committee (hereinafter referred to as programming units to distinguish them from central planning agencies), is well-suited to the task of coordinating all organizations concerned with agricultural development. A technical committee comprising the heads of programming units in all the organizations represented on the committee (as well as its parent body, the agricultural coordinating council), implies the existence of programming units in each of these organizations. Such programming units are imperative for an integrated approach, not only in the agricultural sector as a whole, but within the spheres of activities of each organization.

The programming unit should be considered by its organization as the virtual equivalent of a central planning agency for a national government. It should set standards and criteria for the operating departments or divisions to follow in preparing and carrying out projects; it should prepare the development (or investment) programme and the recurrent budget for its organization (on the basis of directives from the head of the organization); and prepare alternative investment policies for consideration by the head of the organization (after consulting the directors of the operating departments or divisions); set standards for the operating departments or divisions to follow in reporting on the progress of projects; and on the basis of these and other reports, prepare regular, timely and reasonably complete reports and evaluations, of its organization's overall programme; it should also coordinate the technical assistance programme, if any, for its organization; and act as liaison with the central planning agency of the government, as well as with any other sectoral or subsectoral groups (like the inter-agency technical committee of the agricultural coordinating council).

The existence of a network of programming units not only allows for the formulation and implementation of an integrated approach for agriculture, but also provides for fitting that approach into the planned development of other sectors of an economy through a national plan. When every organization operating in the agricultural sector has its own programming unit, there is need for an agency to coordinate all the various programmes. This can be done by the central planning agency, but as this agency is normally too far removed from the problems confronting each sector, it is better to have this work done by an organization within the sector, most probably the Ministry of Agriculture.

E. The distribution of functions. Given the wide span of control required of a Ministry of Agriculture, a division of responsibilities is inevitable. The problem, where the option exists, is to choose an optimum pattern for dividing these responsibilities. This unavoidably requires detailed study to make sure that the pattern selected actually satisfies the objectives of the country, in its particular stage of agricultural development. There is little doubt that the subject repays careful study.

Since division always introduces problems of coordination, the general bias should be toward

278

retaining in a single organization - i.e. the
Ministry of Agriculture - as many related functions
as possible. Where countries have gone too far in
dispersing functions, the major problem is then,
somehow, to reverse this situation.

The problem most frequently encountered is probably what to do about a Ministry which lacks the
capability to deal with the functions assigned to it.
Sometimes, that capability has been reduced by complex administrative practices which delay decision-
making. Alternatively, the Ministry's poor
performance may be caused by a lack of adequate
leadership and staff. Low salaries and shrinking
real incomes frequently worsen personnel problems.
Career opportunities are likely to be meagre, which
leads to a "brain drain" away from the ministries.

In these circumstances, building up the capability of a Ministry of Agriculture can be a long-
term affair. Improvements may be introduced in the
short-term by the use of expatriates in advisory and
managerial positions.

Training programmes designed to meet specific
needs of a Ministry's staff can also do much to
build up capabilities. Here, again, time is needed,
although training courses designed to meet specific
objectives can often be shortened. A judicious
mixture of outside assistance and special training
programmes can thus make it possible for a Ministry
to deal effectively with more functions, even in the
short run. An to the extent that this can be
achieved (even though functions are sometimes performed in less than the ideal way), it is desirable
to retain functions in a Ministry of Agriculture, if
that is where they belong.

In many countries, however, governments have
tried to avoid these difficulties by organizing new
agencies, each with a special programme, which frequently overlap the functions of existing agencies.

Nevertheless, there are functions which should
be dispersed because certain tasks can be done more
efficiently that way. Some functions are more
easily dispersed than others, including services at
the fringe of agriculture which involve activities
of interest to other disciplines and agencies e.g.
higher education in agriculture, and agricultural
research. In such cases the activity in question
may be, and often is, located in a ministry or
agency other than the Ministry of Agriculture.

A second type of dispersion arises when special
organizations are created to deal with specific
crops or livestock products. These organizations,

public or private, may provide very useful services, and depend for their success on introducing better production and marketing techniques.

A third type of disperson involves establishment of a separate agency for the integrated development of a geographical area or region such as the East Ghor Authority in Jordan, and the Awash Valley Authority in Ethiopia.

Another type occurs where responsibility for agriculture, or part of it, may devolve upon political subdivisions of a central government. Thus, in federal governments like those of India and Nigeria, primary responsibility for agriculture is within the jurisdiction of the states.

A fifth variety collects within a single agency all components relating to a specific subsectoral activity, water resource use and development, especially in arid countries, is a ready example. Piecemeal water control usually hampers efficient use, as well as planning and development, while fragmentation of government control leads to waste and slow progress. Examples in other fields include the Republic of Korea's National Agricultural Cooperative Federation, a multipurpose organization providing credit, farm supplies, insurance, banking and marketing services, created by combining an agricultural bank and cooperatives.

A separate organization may be set up to execute a specific project or programme, sometimes as a condition for a loan from a foreign or international agency e.g. the World Bank. In this way, the Bank, for example, seeks to assure itself that staff, financial and technical resources, separate from those of operating ministries, are assigned to a project or programme. By specifying the qualifications of staff and requiring separate organizations, the Bank aims to increase the probabilities of improving management, and successfully completing the project or programme covered by the loan.

Whether or not this approach is more desirable than the one generally taken by, for instance, the U.S. Agency for International Development (A.I.D.) depends on whether one is more concerned with institution building than with the progress of a specific project or programme. The A.I.D. generally encourages existing ministries and agencies to take responsibility for their projects. If the prime objective is the successful implementation of a specific project rather than building up an organization, there is much to be said for a special agency to implement it. If, for example, an irri-

gation or land reclamation project is involved,
organization of a special, autonomous, agency may
be justified on the grounds of the considerable investment required, especially if full utilization of
the land covered by the project is to be achieved.

A special agency has obvious advantages. It
permits the new organization and its staff to concentrate on the project as first priority, without
being diverted to other projects and programmes.
With an independent budget, it has the finances required to do its job properly. If a staff member
is unsatisfactory, dismissal is much easier than in
a ministry. Staff members can be judged by results,
and promoted on the basis of merit, instead of by
inflexible civil service regulations. Finally, the
agency is more likely to have competent management,
concerned with productivity and cost-effectiveness.

But there is another side to the story. Since
there is generally a shortage of trained personnel,
creation of new agencies has not always produced the
results expected. Technicians may hesitate to join
an agency which has yet to establish a reputation,
and which may demand harder work, with less security
and prestige than does the Ministry of Agriculture.
If, however, the new agency has strong political
support and its future seems assured, it may entice
most of the best personnel from the Ministry of
Agriculture, leaving that organization less able to
do its job, making it more necessary than ever to
create new agencies for every new project or programme. And if new organizations are established
too freely, as they sometimes are, the result may
only be to disperse responsibilities among agencies,
which not only compete for the limited supply of
manpower, but engage in uncoordinated activities or,
worse, in destructive competition.

When there is no practical alternative to setting up new agricultural organizations, it is well
to keep the following principles in mind:

(1) New organizations should be established
only when careful review indicates that the services
they are intended to provide cannot be performed by
the Ministry of Agriculture, or other existing
organizations.

(2) Even when need has been established, the
creation of new organizations should be spread out
over time to ensure that competition for limited
technical staffs does not get out of hand.

(3) Where there is an established need for a
new organization, consideration should be given to

making it temporary until the capability of the
Ministry of Agriculture can be improved, in which
case the duration of the new organization's separate
existence should be clearly limited by the statute
which creates it.

(4) Whenever a temporary organization has completed the task it was created to do, any continuing
agricultural services which it performs should be
looked at to determine whether it can become part of
the normal activities of the Ministry of Agriculture
or another permanent agency.

(5) The responsibilities of the new organization should be defined clearly, and great care taken
to avoid wasteful duplication of functions of other
organizations.

(6) Limit a new organization to carry out one
project until it has demonstrated its ability to
take on more.

(7) Coordination of the new organization's
activities with those of the Ministry of Agriculture
should be provided for when it is created. Make the
organization a part of the Ministry; or have the
head of the new agency report direct to the Minster
of Agriculture; or make the Minister of Agriculture
chairman of the new organization's board of directors. Other suitable ways may be worked out with
coordination in mind.

3. Organizing the Ministry of Agriculture
A. What should be included in the Ministry. Although
the guidelines set out above may assist in determining which functions should be retained in a
Ministry of Agriculture, and which transferred,
there is no list of functions or services which can
be furnished for inclusion in all Ministries of
Agriculture. It could hardly be otherwise, given
the variety of agricultural activities among countries; differences in ecology, climate, national
objectives, stage of development; as well as in
social, cultural, political and economic conditions.
Indeed, it would be safer to proceed with the
assumption that each country must select for its
Ministry of Agriculture those functions which meet
its unique circumstances at a given time, and be
prepared to change them if and when circumstances
require.

Some useful guidelines have already been laid
down and others can be added. Thus, crops and soils
usually form the basis of activities of a Ministry
of Agriculture, and animal production should be

closely integrated with crops in a farming economy. (Animal production is sometimes attached to a different ministry, causing confusion to extension workers as well as splitting the agricultural development effort.) Although forestry can be handled by another ministry, influence on agriculture in matters of soil conservation, watershed development and fuel supplies is usually great enough for it to be included within the Ministry of Agriculture. Inland fisheries, as opposed to marine fisheries, can also usefully be attached to the Ministry.

Because there is an intricate relationship between prices of different agricultural products which requires close coordination with credit policy, the ministry should also control the formulation of price and credit policy. Since execution of these policies often involves the resolution of many technical factors, this particular area need not be a function of the Ministry. However, in some countries, execution of price controls are of such importance that they may need to be carried out by the Ministry. In other countries, production and marketing boards have been set up to implement official policy.

Whether or not irrigation development should be a part of a Ministry of Agriculture depends on the importance of irrigation in a country's agriculture and economy. A country which heavily depends on irrigation may need a separate ministry, particularly if irrigation projects involve large-scale mechanization. If only small-scale mechanization is involved, however, irrigation might be placed within the Ministry of Agriculture.

Where land problems take on a highly political aspect, the organizational structure to deal with them might best be separated from the Ministry. But while the separate organization should be concerned with the technical and fact-finding aspects (e.g. the making of cadastral and soil surveys), executive powers to alter the existing situation should normally be retained by the Ministry of Agriculture.

Industries processing agricultural raw material and, to some extent, industries which provide inputs to agriculture often fall between two stools in that the Ministry or ministries concerned with industry generally deal with strategic industries, while the Ministry of Agriculture often excludes agro-industry. This situation can be avoided by including in the Ministry of Agriculture a unit which deals with industries related to agriculture in cooperation with the ministries responsible for industry in general.

B. The Ministry's structure. The trend from subsistence to commercial agriculture has been accelerating in developing countries. Yet, in many, the structure of their Ministry of Agriculture has not been sufficiently adapted to meet changing conditions; many are survivors from another era. Even if they were suitable in their time, they often need streamlining if they are to respond to present needs.

Generally, the structure of the Ministry has evolved in a haphazard manner, so that coordinated development efforts are difficult to achieve. The organization chart of the Ministry is unlikely to portray its actual structure and relationships. Too often, the chart is more impressive on paper than in practice. Faulty communications lead to uncertainty about who reports to whom.

There is no one ideal form of organization for a Ministry of Agriculture. Different ministries have devised different structures, depending on their particular needs and history.

The functions which a Ministry of Agriculture should perform are probably more important than the form of the organization chart, since function should determine form. They may conveniently be divided into five groups: (a) Policy, planning and coordination; (b) Research and implementation; (c) Education and extension work; (d) Direct services and assistance to producers; and (e) Enforcement of regulations.

Policy, planning and coordination are of particular importance and require the creation of a policy and planning unit within the Ministry. The general outlines of such a unit have already been discussed, but it would be well to identify the tasks which such a unit should perform: it should prepare agricultural programmes for the Ministry; assist the technical units to prepare and appraise projects, in accordance with a set of standards and reporting forms which it formulates with the co-operation of these units; submit and defend the programmes it has prepared before national planning and budgetary authorities; recommend policies, instruments of policy, administrative and other measures, as well as machinery, required to implement the programme it prepares; and lastly, review and evaluate the progress of the Ministry's demand for, and use of, outside technical skills, including consultants and consulting firms.

The work of a policy and planning unit transcends organizational lines in a Ministry of Agriculture, and as it must issue directives to which operating units must conform, it is desirable that the unit be established as a staff unit headed by an official who has a higher rank than the heads of the operating units. He should report directly to the Minister (or the highest civil servant in the Ministry) and have the confidence of the one to whom he reports.

Because the establishment of a policy and planning unit, and the training of its staff, is no easy matter Ministries of Agriculture sometimes turn to international agencies for technical assistance. The Ministry of Agriculture in Zambia, for example, sought the assistance of the Food and Agriculture Organization of the United Nations (FAO) in setting up such a unit. Responding to the request, FAO made available an experienced agricultural economist as planning adviser to the Ministry, and with his assistance the Ministry established an Economic Planning Unit, headed by an Assistant Secretary who reported to the Under Secretary (Planning) of the Ministry.

Some Ministries have also found it useful to set up a policy and planning committee composed of the Minister as chairman, the head of the policy and planning unit as vice chairman and senior officials of the Ministry, including the heads of each technical unit as members. This committee can be a useful forum where agricultural policy proposals can be discussed prior to adoption; and it can develop a coordinated approach in the application of policy, in monitoring progress, and, where necessary, making changes in policy or its application.

It is also desirable for a Ministry of Agriculture to establish an Ad Hoc Consultative Committee composed of representatives of all important agricultural interests outside the government. The Committee should have advisory rather than executive functions, and be convened, as required, to provide a sounding board for, and give advice and counsel on, matters of policy, plans or programmes which the Ministry is considering. It should also be an educational medium, called upon to cooperate in disseminating information about adopted policies, etc. While the membership of the Committee should include all the most important representatives of agricultural commodity and regional interests in the country, it should not be so large as to be ineffective. If this threatens to be the case, it might be best to supplement the council with advisory

committees to deal with individual problems affecting e.g. research, credit, marketing, water
control, etc., which could report their recommendations to the whole Committee or, if desirable,
directly to the Ministry. The policy and planning
unit should be the secretariat for the Committee and
for other advisory committees which are established.
The head of the policy and planning unit should be
the secretary of the Ad Hoc Committee and other members of this unit, as designated by the head, should
act as secretaries to the different individual
advisory committees.

In the last analysis, the effectiveness of a
Ministry of Agriculture depends on its strength in
the field. It is well to bear this in mind in setting it up. There should, of course, be close
liaison between headquarters and the staff of the
Ministry at regional, subregional and local levels.
Senior officials from headquarters should visit
regional and subregional areas periodically, to
learn at first hand what problems need to be resolved. These visits should be more than inspections; they should be seen as opportunities to
assist and encourage the field staff, improve conditions of work, cultivate team spirit, and build up
staff's enthusiasm and morale. It is also useful to
have annual, or even more frequent, conferences of
regional and subregional staff at headquarters.

But perhaps most important, headquarters'
officials should undergo training in the principles
of open management to lead them toward bringing
field staff into active participation in planning.
Too often, field staffs have a far greater capacity
for good work than their superiors at H.Q. assume;
the field situation is often grossly misread from
above and, too often, these superiors do not understand that participation by even the lowliest field
staff in planning their work, and setting their work
targets, has considerable potential for improved
performance. Agricultural plans and policies are
often made at the top of the official hierarchy with
little participation by men and women in the field.
After the plans are drawn up, orders are passed down
and the field staff expected to show results. Since
these orders make little or no allowance for difficulties in the field, and often have no logical relationship to the actual situation, field workers
find it difficult to achieve the targets set for
them. Faced with a threat to their security, field
workers may take recourse to manipulating records
and making exaggerated claims. Actual achievements

become of secondary importance to satisfaction of
superiors at headquarters, who may not trouble to
follow up progress in the field. Since the field
staff have to employ considerable ingenuity and
effort to satisfy superiors, it is likely that a
similar expenditure of imagination and time on improving agriculture would be far more productive.
As it is, this failure in official communication between farmers and field staff is likely to lead to
weak and wasteful relationships.

In setting up the field services, it is better
to start with the situation in the field and build
from there, rather than to start at the centre and
build outwards to the field. Too often, when the
structure has been set up from H.Q. outward, an imposing array of officials, sitting at headquarters,
keep in touch with the field staff only by mail or
telephone with an inadequate number of staff in the
field. As between H.Q. and field staffs, therefore,
the primary effort should be to build up an adequate
number of field workers with H.Q. staff being added
as the need for greater support for the field staff
becomes apparent.

4. <u>Regional, Subregional and Local Organization</u>
It should be obvious but not always apparent that no
one can sit in the capital of a country and carry
out, or even formulate, plans for agricultural development. Soviet agriculture has long been hobbled
by Moscow's attempts to impose throughout the country, farm methods or crop patterns which happened to
strike a political leader's fancy. Thus, the grass-
lands system of crop production was made mandatory
under Stalin. Then it was ordered abolished, again
everywhere; corn, which Khruschev called "the queen
of the fields", had to be grown throughout the
Soviet Union. Only recently, after a series of disappointing grain harvests, and continued wasteful
methods of livestock production has there been any
attempt to delegate managerial authority to lower
levels.

Centralized control has generally proved to be
unworkable for a number of reasons. Planners tend
to give priority to national rather than local objectives for instance, and to allocate available resources accordingly. Even when they intend to take
local conditions into account, planners seldom
possess enough knowledge about such conditions, and
farmers' needs, to prepare and carry out plans, etc.
at the local level. They may well have been exposed
to local conditions before moving to the capital but

it is still too easy for them to get out of touch with problems as the local people see them. Not only is this viewpoint necessary, it is also essential that local people are made to feel that local plans etc. are "ours" instead of "theirs". Otherwise, they will make little effort to implement the plans or programmes.

Ways should therefore be found to encourage local participation in the planning process, however small that contribution may be, at first. To the greatest possible extent, plans should be drafted by those who are to be responsible for their implementation. Technicians and planners should contribute judgments for inclusion in plans, programmes and projects but these should not replace or radically modify the views of local people. Planners should thus present the elements of plans in terms which local people can understand, and use, to achieve their own ends.

They would do well to remember that agriculture is an enormously variable production and distribution process, requiring minute local adjustments, within narrow timing tolerances. Generally, farmers and other local people make these timing decisions and adjustments better than anyone else; and will make them only if flexible ways are provided to make it worthwhile for them to do so.

Neglect of local cooperation has almost always had an unfavourable effect on the performance of agricultural and rural development. In contrast, farmer participation often accelerates growth of output and development; for example, price stabilization and support programmes are usually more effective if farmers themselves play an active role in carrying them out. Governments should therefore seek ways of getting farmers themselves to take appropriate steps. Regrettably, most developing countries still need to find ways of bridging the often considerable gap between the views and needs of national planners and of farmers. It is clearly impossible for central planners to deal directly with multitides of farmers scattered throughout a country. Occasional contacts between government officials and farmers must, however, be continual. An additional factor to be borne in mind is that farmers are usually able to provide government officials and planners with a clear picture of their common needs and views, only after they have an opportunity to deliberate on, and discuss, their ideas among themselves. While central ministries and agencies can do much, through their field staffs, to ensure the free flow of information upward and downward, as well as to provide incentives and opportunities to farmers to improve production and marketing practices, these entities are usually inadequate for farmers to arrive at collective decisions. Organizations designed to work closely with farmers, or largely consisting of them, are likely to be more effective.

One of the hardest tasks of administration is the creation of organizations which can respond flexibly to attitudes and changes in local situations, and provide means of conveying to central government accurate and timely information about these attitudes and changes. Governments which have succeeded in creating such organizations have done so, not by applying a pre-conceived formula, but by adapting organizational principles to locally-accepted administrative and behavioural modes.

Countries have used a variety of organizations to achieve these ends: production teams, farmers' clubs or associations, cooperatives, kibutzim, moshavim, panchayats, village development committees, self-help groups, etc. What matters most in each country is not so much the name or form of the organization as the extent of government commitment to whatever kind exists.

However, if this criterion is used as a test, the outlook is not promising for local government and field services of Ministries of Agriculture, and other organizations concerned with agricultural and rural development, are typically the most neglected parts of the public sector. Local governments and field services are usually resource-poor, tradition-bound, and talent-starved. In these circumstances, it is difficult to see these agencies as capable agents for the acceptance of new ideas, stimulation of local action, amd mobilization of resources for development.

Moreover, the environment in which local governments and field services function is often un-promising. It not only makes these jurisdictions and services unlikely agents of change but also provides few incentives for farmers to increase or improve production.

Creation of effective units of local government, and field services of central ministries and agencies, is bound to be a difficult and time-consuming task. This is all the more so if they are expected to develop farmers' organizations with broadly-based participation of their members. Yet, success in this area may well be the key factor in reaching development objectives.

Governments have often been slow to recognize the need for participative farmers' groups. In fact, one can still find governments which claim that they can, with detailed central planning, convince farmers that the central planners know best what is good for them.

The best that can be said for this approach is that at least it represents progress from the time, not many years ago, when governments believed that they could achieve satisfactory results through coercion over farmers. To an increasing number, it has become clear that the best results are obtained from procedures which associate farmers with the formulation, as well as the implementation of planning at the local level.

It is worth considering some of the conditions which make for the success of farmers' organizations, which as stated earlier are not always easy to create. One reason for this is that in stagnant rural societies, these institutions usually do not come into existence except as a result of state policy and initially Government officials generally must spread the idea among farmers, start the organizations and guide them after they have been created. And it is difficult to do these things in such a way that a surge of movement comes from below, strong enough to give the institutions an independent life. Yet this is what must be done.

One way of promoting the establishment and growth of producers' organizations is to provide them with credit. A great deal also depends on the use which a government makes of these organizations. If it endows them with sigificant functions, it can provide them with the status and income they need to make them viable. For example, if the government designates farmers' associations as agencies for distributing fertilizers, seed and other farm inputs or as official agencies for buying farm products, it not only provides them with status and important functions, but also assures them a regular source of income. Such advantages may be decisive where small, struggling farmers' associations often find it hard to compete with private traders who sometimes possess greater resources than are available to farmers.

In China (Taiwan), for instance, the government guaranteed farmers' associations a certain income by providing them with a fixed percentage of local tax collections and by appointing them as distributors of fertilizers. While this did not make the farmers' associations rich, it made it possible for them to operate effectively by providing them with a sufficiently strong financial foundation to engage competent staffs. However, the provision of government resources also runs the risk of making producers' associations no more than government agencies, with the result that farmers may hesitate to make known their true feelings, for fear of reprisal. This can be avoided only if the organizations are permitted a great deal of autonomy.

This conclusion is also relevant to China which has many organizational problems similar to those in mixed-economy countries. In China, producers' co-operatives have given way since 1962 to production teams, which have about half as many farmers as the producers' cooperatives had. Production teams were selected as the basic unit of organization in Chinese agriculture because they were found to be large enough to make the management of a unit of land viable, and small enough not to stretch very much the connection between individual rewards and work. The effectiveness of the production team as the basic agricultural unit and the organizational stability in agriculture, along with increased use of modern inputs, go a long way toward explaining the steady improvement in agricultural production in China in recent years.

The members of a production team elect their own leaders (including the head, accountant, treasurer and watchman) for a one-year term at a general meeting. When election time approaches, the team members draw up a list of potential candidates. The work brigade, a higher level organization of farmers which has jurisdiction over a series of production teams, uses the teams' list to prepare nominees. The work brigade may nominate seven people for four posts. Members of the production team then each have four votes. The four top vote getters become the team's leaders and decide among themselves who will have which job.

Production teams hold general meetings of all adult members about once every month to make major decisions, e.g. approval of the production plan, determination of a system for distribution, amount of income that should be devoted to investment and welfare, etc. These meetings tend to be free and democratic. Not surprisingly, however, a core group of leaders (the team's management committee) often discuss matters beforehand and comes to the meetings with proposals. These are often approved with little discussion, but their proposals are sometimes rejected. While local Communist Party leaders play an important role in harmonizing the goals of the production teams with those of the government, production teams have enough autonomy to allow members a considerable voice in the team's activities. In this sense, the government appears to have realized the importance of permitting team members to exercise a considerable participative role in local decision-making.

A. Cooperatives. The term "cooperative organization" covers a wide range of institutions, as different as the Soviet kolkhoz, the Israeli kibbutz, and the Mexican ejido. The term may also be applied to independent producers anywhere, who associate themselves voluntarily to obtain benefits from group provision of farm inputs, marketing farm products, storing and financing farm products, etc. In western countries, such cooperatives, usually based on small family farms, have enabled farmers to benefit from modern technical developments through the establishment of a common basis for marketing, supplying agricultural machinery, and providing services of various kinds to its membership. The cooperative, whether it consists of small farmers or a large collective settlement, acts as a link between local initiative and national plans, programmes or policies. Regional or national cooperative unions which include a number of cooperatives have been found to be effective in securing the interests of farmers in relation to the government.

Where cooperatives are prominent, they have proved to be such efficient agencies for implementing national policy that many agricultural experts have become strong advocates of this sytem of organization. Denmark and the Netherlands are frequently given as examples of what cooperatives can achieve. The Israeli experience is also frequently cited. In the Republic of Korea, a highly developed system of farmer cooperatives has enabled the government to carry out successful programmes for supporting prices of farm products, distributing fertilizer and other inputs required to expand crop and livestock production, and increasing commercial marketings of agricultural products.

Farmer associations in China (Taiwan), which some purists might claim are only quasi-cooperative arrangements because of the government's involvement, fulfil members' needs from the cradle to the grave. These organizations, besides being concerned with credit, marketing, farm input supplies, joint utilization of equipment and facilities, processing of commodities, and insurance, also deal with members' education, family guidance, health clinics, child care nurseries, weddings, and even furnish members with cars for funerals.

There is little question that cooperatives have been successful in certain technical and social situations. But there is also plenty of evidence of failure and there is a good case for giving particular attention to past experience before embarking on the establishment of cooperatives. There is need to distinguish between situations where farmers still have a high degree of dependence and where they are self-reliant. Thus, while farmers in India have often shown themselves slow to act on their own, those in Japan accepted independence easily. Among the elements which made agricultural cooperatives successful in China (Taiwan) was the all-encompassing nature of these organizations, so that membership was virtually a pre-requisite to farming. There was also a long tradition of cooperative effort.

Another area where attention is necessary is the character of the leadership in farm communities. If the leaders are large, rich farmers and moneylenders, as was true in India, cooperatives cannot be expected to serve small and poor farmers. Leadership in a cooperative designed for small farmers must come from them. They have demonstrated time and again their leadership qualities and ability to improve cooperative efforts in agriculture.

Finally, the type of organization established must fit the members; different kinds of cooperatives may be needed for different places. Where, as in Bangladesh the people in a locality are likely to be fairly similar, the kind of cooperative which will work well there is likely to differ from one where, as in Israel, cooperation must be based on pluralism. Problems affecting cooperative organization must therefore be thought through in the context of the local situation. Foreign models or methods, developed and designed for a different environment, can rarely be transplanted directly. Foreign expertise can play a useful role in bringing the experience of other parts of the world to bear on the problems of cooperatives in a particular country, but that experience must be only one factor in what is essentially adaptation of many factors to a local situation.

B. The devolution problem. Much has been made in recent years of the need for "democratic decentralization" of activities associated with agricultural and rural development. Cogent reasons can be given in support of this point of view, primarily that development must be varied to fit different conditions in the various localities in a country. However, even someone partial to this view must concede that devolution of authority to regional and local levels cannot be made lightly. Premature, or excessive, decentralization can be harmful and wasteful if it is made to jurisdictions that lack the personnel and funds to perform their new functions. Clearly, there are circumstances when it may be fruitless, or even harmful, to devolve substantial operations to local organizations before they are technically and managerially equipped to take on new responsibility.

But decentralization need not be an all-or-nothing affair. It should be seen as a matter of kinds and degrees, extended gradually, and at different rates to the various localities, as circumstances warrant.

In determining whether to delegate authority it is necessary to remember that some tasks are better handled at higher and some at lower levels. Centralization operations are generally required the more complex the technology involved, the more capital-intensive it is, the slower the payoff or return or the more specialized and scarce the technical and managerial skills involved. In contrast the more commonplace the technology, the more people involved, the simpler the management skills required, the more quickly results can be achieved, the more local "feedback" required to guide operations, the stronger the case for decentralization. It is not always possible to identify which activities should always be carried out locally, but some obviously fit into this category; the following are so dependent on local conditions, and on each other, that they need close coordination in each locality: (1) the availability of farm supplies and equipment; (2) local testing of these inputs; (3) extension education; and (4) production credit.

Where local communities have limited ability to assume responsibilities, but where devolution is seen as desirable, decentralization might be made more effective if it is controlled rather than complete. This could also be true for jurisdictions where there is reason to expect that abuses of power, misappropriation of resources, or even honest mis-

takes may occur. In these instances, effective
decentralization can be constrained by firm policy
guidelines, and centrally established standards, enforced by periodic inspections, and other forms of
audit and control, leaving operations in the hands
of locally based personnel.

China uses a unique approach, a "responsibility" or "guarantee" system (pao-kan chihtu) to
provide a mixture of control and decentralization
that apparently works. A local unit (it may be
farmers in a village or another kind of group)
guarantees performance in a specific sphere to
authorities at the level immediately above, in return for which the local unit is allowed wide
latitude in carrying out its operations without
interference from higher authority. So long as the
unit fulfills its obligations, it is free to carry
out its operations as it wishes. Although this
"responsibility system" is a deeply-rooted tradition
in China, it may be adaptable in other less developed countries as a workable arrangement, where
direct administration down to the grassroots is
impossible or undesirable.

Decentralization goes beyond the mere delegation of power; instead, it involves a transfer of
power from the centre to the field or local
authorities. In practice, however, what passes
for decentralization in many countries, is a partial
or temporary delegation of power from the centre,
with the final authority remaining firmly at the
centre. In such circumstances, "decentralization"
cannot be expected to work well, unless, in fact,
only powers to be decentralized have indeed been
transferred.

Finally, decentralization does not involve the
devolution of all powers from the centre - only
those which it wishes to yield - and never does it
involve a devolution of power over policy, which
must continue to be decided at the centre.

5. The Need for Efficient Communication

There is often a tendency for local and central
organizations to work in isolation, without effective communication or understanding between them.
Central authorities pursue their objectives without
adequately informing local authorities, while the
latter follow their objectives independently, often
at odds with central plans and efforts. Communication between localities is even worse. There are
things being done in one locality which are unknown
20 or 30 miles away, because different people are

in charge, or because e.g. physical barriers stand
in the way. To find, support, link and expand
these initiatives involves the establishment of
lines of communication which are often difficult to
create.

A. Communications in the official sector. There are
two parts to the communication problem. The first
relates to within the government sector, the second
to public and private sectors. Within the public
sector, a host of factors can impede communication;
some of these have already been mentioned. Improved
contact between the centre and the field has been
seen to involve a degree of trust, a delegation of
financial and other powers, which is often appal-
lingly difficult to extract from officials in the
capital. Directives usually move from higher to
lower units in the hierarchy, but the flow of
information in the reverse direction is not equally
provided for. With bureaucracies, status is often
a strong barrier to the flow of information from
lower to higher levels. Many officials at the upper
levels do not have sufficient tolerance for suggestions coming from below.

Other obstacles may arise because of the form
which bureaucracies take. For example, in civil
services which distinguish between "generalist"
administrators and technicians, good communications
depend on close collaboration between the two. In
India and elsewhere, where such a distinction is
made, communication between them often becomes
difficult. The traditional structure of administration in these countries is highly compartmentalized.
Each department has a distinct line of command.
Inter-departmental links are few. As a result, the
weakest linkages are the "diagonal" ones, i.e.
between officials in different departments and at
different levels.

Yet another impediment to the free flow of
timely information may be found in the systems used
to communicate. In India, for example, members of
different departments are often close enough to
communicate with each other by meetings or by
personal contact. But the preferred method is
writing - accompanied by the movement of files from
office to office and from level to level. This procedure has proved to be cumbersome, time-consuming
and inefficient. A file may remain on a busy
official's desk for a week or so before he deals
with it and passes it on to the next person. Any one
person in this chain may become a bottleneck. More-

over, in this system, there is little chance to
present different viewpoints, and even less to
settle misunderstandings to arrive at a solution
based on mutual agreement.

These problems, and others, make it clear that
the communication problem is much more complex than
the mere absence of suitable mechanisms. Considerable resources are sometimes devoted to the establishment of such mechanisms But they cannot be
expected to work at all well in the face of bureaucratic and administrative obstacles which result
from deeply entrenched, traditional patterns of
behaviour. Where it seems impossible to revise administrative or bureaucratic systems in the short
run - and it often is - the task is to find ways of
getting around them. Favourable results have been
obtained by holding more frequent meetings or by
increasing personal contacts in other ways.

In contrast with many other countries, China
has such a large amount of communications between
different levels of authority that the volume of
work involved sometimes threatens to be disruptive.
However, frequent meetings of officials of three or
four different levels do provide excellent opportunities for face-to-face communication among
managers of institutions. China has also introduced
a more radical procedure to ensure that higher
officials understand and communicate with lower
level officials. All senior managers of agencies,
and other institutions, are required, as a matter of
course, to be transferred periodically to lower
level positions for a year or two. An official in
the centre may be "sent down" to the commune level;
a commune member may be sent down to the work brigade or to the lower production team level. The
official generally retains his salary, seniority,
fringe benefits and other prerequisites of his
original organization. Yet even while he retains
his connection to that body, he is expected to perform, during the "sent down" period, as a member of
his new organization. One purpose of this procedure
is to ensure that lower levels get proper leadership
and do not deviate from the correct line, but an
equally important reason is to provide for higher
level officials to have a clear understanding of the
economic, social and political situation at lower
levels.

B. <u>Communications between public and private sectors</u>
If communications are frequently less than adequate
within the public sector, one cannot expect them to

be any better between public and private sectors.
In many localities, the only real contact between a
village and the government (and its development
plans) may be limited to the tax collector. In
others, communications may come down to the village
by local government officials or the media, but with
a lack of channels by which the wishes and needs of
the villagers can be expressed to the government.

But there are other villages in which the in-
habitants feel free to talk to officials or political leaders, confident that the conversations will
be passed along to higher levels of government. This
last situation, of course, provides the best soil
for economic and social improvement. A good example
is found in Tanzania, where TANU, the government
Party, plays an important part in providing that
downward communication is accompanied by discussions
to generate comment by rural people, and provide for
changes in plans and programmes. People not surprisingly, seem to consider plans and programmes
their own when they embody the results of their own
efforts.

Chapter 14

MONITORING, REPORTING AND CONTROL

Summary
    Monitoring of planning activity can be a very
useful management tool, it continues to get
little attention in many agricultural programmes and projects, however. Efforts in this
whole area have often, unfortunately, not been
very successful. Too frequently, observation
and recording of events has not been followed
by appropriate management action. Relatively
new techniques are now available to help
managers check progress, or otherwise, towards
planned objectives; but emphasis tends to be
placed too heavily on causes of failure than
success. Monitoring requires a reporting
system to select, analyse and present relevant
material. This system should meet several
criteria such as generating the minimum information necessary for management to take
timely and appropriate action, report both good
and bad results and not require excessive preparation by line and staff managers. Control
of plan or project activity, based on the
reporting system, may involve not only traditional management tools such as budgeting and
auditing but new procedures to take account of
a project's special characteristics. Practical
difficulties in monitoring commonly arise from
poorly-designed or inappropriate systems, inability to undertake base-line studies early
enough, delays in preparation and analysis of
reports, etc. Costs of monitoring are not in-
significant, amounting to as much as 4 to 5
percent of total project costs, so an efficient
system is needed to justify them. Finally,
care is always needed in selecting the projects
(or part of each) which are to be monitored.

Monitoring is part of a system of observation, reporting, and control which responds to the fact that development takes place under uncertainty. Programmes and projects, no matter how well planned and apparently rational, are implemented in this environment, and it is the task of management to translate plans into reality. One aspect of planning is to establish milestones against which progress will later be measured. Monitoring attempts to assess how much progress has actually been made, and to identify problems in moving toward particular targets or milestones.

It is only one step to bringing about necessary changes during project and programme implementation and is not sufficient in itself, since observation of events in no way guarantees that appropriate management action will follow. Yet even only a first step, and despite wider recognition of its importance, monitoring continues to get little attention in many agricultural programmes and projects.

A reporting system is necessary, in addition to monitoring, in order to inform project managers, higher-level officials, and others as appropriate, of the salient facts that have been observed.

Lastly, control results from management decisions taken to move a programme or project in a desired direction during implementation. The addition of control to monitoring and reporting closes a loop, which makes corrective or additional action possible. Control not only includes management decision-making based on data provided by monitoring and reporting, but also an interrelated set of factors which includes motivation, the setting of sub-objectives, scheduling, participation, replanning, budgeting, and accounting. While several theorists exclude some of these practices from control, in practice each of them has been used successfully.

Earlier, it was observed that programmes and projects differ in some important respects. Projects are normally one-time efforts to deal with problems that often require innovation, rapid response, and cohesive structuring of personnel to do what is necessary to meet project objectives. In practice, it has been found necessary to design special means of handling the requirements for project monitoring, reporting and control because the approaches and techniques used in more routine, ongoing programmes simply proved to be inadequate. Programmes, how-however, nearly always have from one to many

projects as major components, and individual projects often form the basis for ongoing programmes.
There are thus links between programmes and projects
which make continuity between separate reporting
systems very desirable.

A. Monitoring
Monitoring is carried out to provide the project
manager, other members of the project team, higher-
level personnel, people in supporting organizations,
and in many cases project participants, with interim
reports during implementation, on progress being
made toward meeting planned objectives. The more
clearly the objectives of the project have been
stated, the more precise the measurement of progress can be, as long as objectives remain constant.
Project design systems such as the U.S. Agency for
International Development (AID)'s Logical Framework
thus emphasize the relationship of both the elements
within the scope of the project (inputs and outputs)
and factors outside the project which will influence
project outcome (assumptions regarding project environment, sectoral and higher-level events), with
an eye toward progress evaluation. However, the
Logical Framework is drawn up before implementation
takes place, and does not always include current
field-level data. By itself, it does not generally
serve as a sufficient means of project monitoring,
nor was it intended to.
    The Logical Framework has been used by AID in
projects which it helped support since 1968.
Additional techniques have since been adopted to
supplement the Logical Framework and serve as a
better guide for monitoring specific project activities. These include the Project Performance Track-
ing System (PPT) and the designation of Critical
Performance Indicators (CPI's). These techniques
(PPT and CPI) are variations on the more widely used
PERT (Programme Evaluation Review Technique) and CPM
(Critical Path Method) scheduling approaches, with
slight modifications to meet AID's requirements.
CPI's, for example are similar to those activities
which fall on the Critical Path of a project, that
is, those activities which form the longest chain
of activities necessary to complete the project. One
difference is that under the AID system, "critical"
indicators also seem to include activities not on
the critical path, but otherwise of great importance
in completing the project. Performance indicators
are "strategic control points where performance can
be measured". Project personnel with an under-

ing of PERT/CPM should have no difficulty in becoming familiar with the AID approach if they should be working on AID-supported projects in their country.

Such techniques as PERT/CPM have been in use a long time and have aided in project monitoring and reporting in many projects, both complex advanced projects and smaller scale activities involving as few as fifteen or twenty activities. They have the virtue of being fairly simple, and can be learned in a few days. For local-level projects in which there is a high degree of involvement by farmers, peasants and people with little experience in the use of such techniques, however, these may be too complex. The monitoring system chosen should fit the overall needs of the project, and in some cases more simple means have been chosen.

The Programming and Implementation System (PIM) was developed through the cooperative efforts of the Institute of Development Studies of Sussex University, the University of Nairobi, and the Government of Kenya. PIM was developed because area plans were not being effectively formulated and implemented in Kenya. PIM became a procedurally-based attempt to decentralize planning implementation, and to deal specifically with several recurring problems: authoritarian management, wasteful meetings, excessive reports, departmentalism, top-down targetry, inadequate resources, and ineffective work programming. One specific element of the approach developed to deal with these problems was a monitoring system. Experience shows that all good monitoring systems form a link between planning and implementation, and PIM is no exception.

The first stage of PIM calls for a meeting at the local level of all parties who will be responsible for carrying out the project. The meetings are chaired by the Area Coordinator, an officer of the Provincial Administration where the project is to be implemented. First, a discussion of the objectives of selected projects is held to re-examine the desirability of the proposed objectives and to assess the potential of the project for achieving them. After this, the main steps in programming are identified: (1) listing and agreeing to the operations necessary for each project; (2) identifying and agreeing on who is responsible for each operation; (3) scheduling estimated start and completion times for each activity; (4) agreeing on targets and completion indicators for each operation; and (5) checking for feasibility, agreement on, and acceptance of targets.

There are important principles involved in the way in which the PIM programming exercise is undertaken. First, there is the recognition that planning for project activity cannot be done by a technical planner in isolation from those with responsibility for project implementation. Second, the process involves getting agreement at each stage - and recording such agreement in writing to minimise assumptions, and later disagreements, about what was agreed on - thus setting the stage for coordinated implementation, and establishing clearly for everyone what it is that will be monitored to check progress. Implementation and monitoring are made still more likely by agreement on who is responsible for each action and by establishing completion indicators. Far more important is that the graphic display technique which is chosen is the interactive analysis in which each responsible organization can assess its role in planning to make the project go well. This built-up multiple checkpoint system makes it far more likely that monitoring will be more effective later on.

The Annual Programming Exercise is followed by a series of management meetings at monthly or other agreed intervals. Meetings are attended only by those with implementation responsibilities. The original plans are reviewed in light of actual progress. A colour-coded record of progress (e.g. ///// = on time, IIII = behind time or below target) is kept. This is a built-in monitoring system which has facilitated a "self-policing" approach. Decisions are made about what remedial actions should be taken, and these decisions are implemented.

One of the sources which the designers of PIM drew on was the planning and implementation scheme devised and put to use by the Government of Malaysia (then Malaya). Malaya created a Ministry of Rural Development in October, 1959, and a National Rural Development Council in January, 1960. Rural planning through the Ministry and Council came to be symbolized by the Red Book and its associated elements. The Red Book was a standardized plan which was to be executed by state and district rural development committees composed of heads of technical departments, e.g., agriculture, drainage, irrigation, and public works, and also Members of Parliament of respective states.

The Red Book was a large, loose leaf folder about two feet square which contained instructions on project identification and selection. The main part of the Book, however, consisted of twelve sections made up of overlay maps, which included maps on the following:

     I.   Basic District
    II.   Land Use
  III.   Roads
   IV.   Rural Water Supplies
    V.   Minor Irrigation Works
   VI.   River Clearing Proposals
  VII.   Schools, Health Centres and Playing Fields
 VIII.   Rural Processing and Marketing Facilities
   IX.   Rural Industries
    X.   Cooperatives
   XI.   Telecommunications Facilities
  XII.   Rural Electricity

Standard instructions for preparing and coding maps and project proposals were inserted in plastic files attached to each of the twelve sections of the Book. Appedixes provided instructions on conducting committee meetings, instructions for standardized comments on projects, and procedures for informing appropriate officials of the essence of each District Committee (primary action level) meeting. The physical setting for the use of the Red Books was an operations room at the district, state, and national levels. These rooms were equipped with wall maps showing development projects, and charts, photographs, and overlays for projects which were in process, those which had been completed, and those which were planned.

One important aspect of the Malaysian system is that current project status could be checked by examining the Red Book maps. Again, however, this represents only a technique, and while it proved to be effective, it would have meant little without the other elements in the system: the formation of Rural Development Committees at district, state, and national levels, the careful project planning which recognized the need for popular involvement, the participation of both political representatives and technical division chiefs at the state level, and finally, support from the highest political levels. To emphasize his instructions to the committees, the Minister of Rural Development, who was also the Deputy Prime Minister, personally visited all of the district operations rooms, frequently arriving un-announced with members of his immediate staff for a briefing on the current development situation and a half-day or full day tour of the area. The District Officer would begin the session by briefing the

Deputy Minister, and the respective technical
officers for each project area would follow with
more detailed accounts. If projects were found to
be behind their implementation schedules, the
Minister tirelessly sought the reasons why, and
issued appropriate orders or took other actions to
resolve any problems which could be so dealt with.

The briefings were thorough, but not overdone,
as the Minister was careful not to disrupt regular
work unduly. However, his objective was to move a
bureaucracy to actions which were unusual for it,
and he believed that unusual measures were called
for. District Officers who were interviewed about
the briefings stated that they called for a great
deal of hard work, but that they were not arbitrary
and helped them to do what was required to get the
job done.

Like the PIM system, the Malaysian approach
recognized the importance of cultural and organizational factors. Monitoring can only be effective
if there is an organizational spirit which facilitates the job of implementation, rather than one
which stifles initiative and threatens or intimi-
dates people in the performance of their duties.
The positive side of PIM is shown in its decentralization, which allowed targets to be set,
and operational plans to be drawn up, by the people
at the operating level who are responsible for project implementation, rather than being drawn up at
a central level and dictated downwards. Experience
shows that those who are responsible for formulating
their own plans play a more effective role in monitoring and policing a project which they "own" by
virtue of their role in creating it. The Red Book
system, while monitored from the highest levels,
also allowed for planning and objectives formulation
from people at local levels. Further, the knowledge
operating personnel have that genuine interest was
felt at high levels, and that action at that level
would be forthcoming to support their efforts, is
known to have been a strong inducement to improved
performance, and to furtherance of their own monitoring efforts.

In spite of these attempts to concentrate on
positive factors, however, PIM, the Red Book, and
other systems have in common with most monitoring
approaches the primary focus of detecting failure.
It is well known that during project implementation,
the frequency of unforeseen delays and bottle-necks
is a force to be reckoned with. Investigation of
these delays and problems is often undertaken with

the intent of fixing blame, sometimes leading involved parties to "pass the buck", make excuses, or
to hide or inaccurately report data. While it is
important to detect and correct failure, it can be
equally important to detect successes. Positive
feedback is necessary to identify those practices
which are working well, and to disseminate information about success, in order to get a desired
spread effect. The fact that more failures are mentioned on monitoring reports may mean not only that
there are more mistakes than successes taking place,
but also indicates that most people are trained to
detect failure and to analyse the implications of
targets not met. A review of monitoring procedures
usually reveals that few provide managers with a
chance to learn about successes in any systematic or
sustained way. Such principles as the popular
"management by exception," for example, feed information to management on the most significant
problems which occur, so that the manager can take
action on things which are going wrong. Monitoring
based on the principle of detecting problems and
correcting them, if this is the only approach being
used, can have the effect of preventing recognition
of successes. Successes, after all, do not always
come by accident, and may reveal new ways of meeting
old objectives, or of creative ways of meeting new
objectives not previously foreseen.

In addition to the important requirement for
monitoring systems, that they provide information to
keep projects on track, two other purposes have been
identified: they provide positive feedback on
successes to meet current objectives as well as information about changed conditions which call for
re-setting objectives or directing the project in a
new direction. This last set of information is
termed feed-forward.

A feedback system seeks out information about
present difficulties and deviations, looking back to
past objectives and targets as the fixed standards
by which performance is being judged. This information is then used to trigger corrective action to
overcome the difficulties.

Both negative and positive feedback have been
widely used. The difference in them can be graphically illustrated. In Cameroon, brown rot is a
serious disease affecting cacao pods. Plantation
planters given a copper powder from which to make a
solution for anti-brown rot spray, were found to
know how to use the spray, and in fact two out of
three began treatment at the proper time. Research

showed (through negative feedback) that various
obstacles to full use included the following:

> 1 in 4 did not have treatment equipment,
> 2 in 4, who had the equipment, had operating
> problems,
> 1 in 3 had difficulties in finding the water
> necessary, bearing in mind the plantation's
> distance from a water source,
> 1 in 3 had labour problems,
> 1 in 2 received the supplies too late for the
> time he would like to begin treatments.

A positive feedback approach would also have
dealt with those farmers who had applied the copper
solution on time and in sufficient quantity to be
effective. Those farmers who applied the solution
on time apparently had to save some packets of powder
from the year before because shipments the following
spring arrived too late. It follows that if the
powder was delivered on time, more planters would
use it. A recommendation based on positive feedback
would be to deliver sufficient powder to local control and distribution points for two crop seasons.
Thereby, the period of application could be leng-
thened, allaying manpower problems and increasing
total effective usage.

In contrast, a system employing feed-forward
gathers information about present successes, innovations and new ideas, and looks forward to new
objectives and strategies which could be evolved to
bring about the widespread adaptation and application of these successes. The main aim of using feed
forward is to ensure that a project manager recog-
nizes and then builds on the strengths, successes
and constructive ideas already present within his or
other projects.

Feed-forward techniques have been successfully
used, but have received little publicity. Innovation and technical advance in Japanese agriculture
during the last half of the 19th century was often
based on methods developed by farmers and spread by
the government. Ensuisen, a method of seed selection, was used by farmers in the Kyushu district,
then taken up by the chief of an agricultural experimental station and disseminated. Tools such as the
rotary weeder, the treadle thresher, and improved
ploughs were invented by local people and then disseminated. The central and prefectural governments
played an important part in spreading the use of
successful practices. "Agricultural improvement

societies" were formed in many prefectures to promote and exchange successful practices. The
Ministry of Agriculture subsequently encouraged all
prefectures to establish such societies. Leading
farmers were appointed as instructors in some agricultural colleges, and toured Japan to demonstrate
improved techniques.

Organizations such as the Southeast Asian
Regional Center for Graduate Study and Research in
Agriculture (SEARCA) devotes considerable attention
to disseminating research information throughout
Asia through its Agricultural Information Bank. Such
efforts, however, more nearly attain the characteristics of a comprehensive data bank which contains
so much data that specific variables may not stand
out. A feed-forward system is more problem-specific.

Consider, for example, a rural development
project with ten units. Two of these are operating
successfully, while the remaining eight are not. A
feedback project monitoring system would concentrate
on the eight units in difficulty; their problems
would be examined and the causes analyzed. Then the
project manager and his staff would try to suggest
ways of overcoming the problems which they uncovered,
based on their past experience. In contrast, a
feed-forward monitoring system would focus on the
two successful units, and analyse in detail the
causes of their success. The project manager and
his staff would then be able to seek ways of transferring these causes of success to improve the
performance of the less successful units, or to
develop new units or projects based on the successes.

By using feed-forward monitoring, a project
manager and his expert staff need no longer be bur-
dened with full responsibility for providing
solutions. Feed-forward enables them to supplement
their own experience of what has worked elsewhere in
the past, with information about what is working
here and now, in individual units within their project. By spreading these isolated successful practices more widely, the project manager ensures that
they are fully used to improve the performance of
the project as a whole.

To be really effective, a feed-forward monitoring system must first recognize that an original
or unorthodox method is in use in one part of a
project. It then gathers further information about
how it is used, and what effects are produced. This
information is fed to the project manager, who,
along with others as appropriate, uses it to set new
objectives and targets for other parts of the

project to which the new method can be applied. Simultaneously, the project manager and his staff seek to clarify further the causes of the innovating unit's success, and then to communicate this valuable "how to do it" information to those project staff affected by the new objectives and targets.

Most feedback monitoring is conducted through a project's organizational hierarchy: the managers of each part of the project monitor the progress of their staff. Their focus of attention is on potential bottle-necks, hold-ups, hindrances and human lapses, since these, they believe, are mainly the things that require action on their part. Thanks to years of practice in feedback procedures, their skill in picking out error from the mass of generally successful operations is highly developed. By contrast, few examples of monitoring for feed-forward have been located in the literature on development projects. However, the idea is not entirely new, and is frequently found in other areas. For example, the application of feed-forward is basic to the field of intelligence, which has as one of its objectives the determination, and possibly the emulation, of technical and craft practices being used by other governments. Similarly, industries have nearly always attempted to discover competitors' successful practices. In capitalist economies this in fact has been one of the chief methods of diffusing innovations, as one firm's success in creating a desirable product has drawn imitators into the field. What would be strange, then, in purposefully building into monitoring systems for development projects the capability of identifying and building on successes?

B. Reporting

All that is monitored cannot and should not be reported. The essence of reporting is selection, preparation, and presentation. Data requirements are often too voluminous, yet key indicators are not identified or highlighted. Many "accomplishments" listed are not important from a management viewpoint, yet many items of concern to management cannot be dealt with effectively because continuity with previous reports is lacking. Long term trends are not identified, reports arrive late or not at all, and little analysis of report contents is carried out to prepare data for management decisions.

An effective reporting system should: (a) generate the minimum information necessary for management to take timely and appropriate action; (b) establish who is reponsible for carrying out the necessary action(s); (c) not require excessive preparation and review time by line and staff managers; (d) alert management to supporting element needs; (e) have a format that will facilitate its use for more than one purpose; (f) Provide each echelon with the information it needs; (g) provide more generalized, well-selected information on the most important indicators as you go from lower to higher levels of management; (h) report both favourable and unfavourable data; and (i) indicate clearly the current status of the project.

Minimum information necessary for good management cannot be defined as a constant, to apply to all projects at all times. Rather, the project's characteristics determine what is appropriate: its scale, its stage (research, pilot, demonstration, or production), organizational affiliations and structure, and the personality and capability of the project staff.

Three kinds of management information systems cover much of what it is possible to report. At the simpler end of the scale, the "status" system is used to periodically inform management whether the project is on, behind, or ahead of schedule, and the status of the budget. This system gives minimal information on technical details, which must be obtained from other sources. Gantt, PERT/CPM, and similar techniques are associated with this type of system. More detailed is the control system which emphasizes control by exception (i.e. management by exception, in which managers only become involved when performance is either below or beyond established standards). A variant, positive control calls for managers to be more heavily informed about technical details of the project. The most complex approach is found in the comprehensive systems, such as the data banks of technical information which attempt to gather any data which might be relevant. This often requires a high capacity computer.

Status reporting systems have in practice proven to be adequate in relatively simple projects carried out at local levels, and in many research and pilot projects. The scope of this approach can be very broad and relatively unstructured, or relatively narrow and structured.

By comparison, a relatively narrow approach has been associated with progress reporting keyed to specifically defined outputs of the type most

routinely included in PERT/CPM networks, such as:
200 loans made by agricultural credit union; or 150
bags of fertilizer delivered. The latter approach
is adequate if an upper-level manager is merely
being kept informed of schedules that have been met,
but inadequate where innovation and close contact
with new developments is called for.

Put another way, the choice of reporting system
relates to whether the projects emphasize "contract"
or "problem-solving" characteristics. Contract
characteristics are found in those projects emphasizing delivery of a well-defined set of services or
standardized technical inputs (seeds, fertilizers,
pesticides, etc.). Problem - solving, by comparison,
more often relies on working with people to identify
their problems and to respond flexibly to their
needs. It has usually been easier to plan, schedule,
monitor, and report on activities in the services
delivery category; thus a PERT/CPM approach has been
adequate for these projects.

The PIM system provides for selectivity in the
kind of data reported in several ways. First, it
limits reporting to plans agreed to in joint session.
Second, routine or ritualistic reports are thrown
out by changing the reporting focus to problems,
opportunities, and action required. The content of
written reports is re-emphasized by the Management
Meetings, where trivia are simply not discussed.
Every person has a clearly defined area of responsibility, and problems in each of these areas are dia-
gnosed. All parties whose support is needed to resolve the problems are named, and short, simple
functional reports and requests for specific assistance are sent to them. In the PIM situation, a
simple status report is not sufficient, and the
approach used comes closer to a control system, with
one exception: the standards of reference can be
modified by joint agreement during the Management
Meetings. The objectives of projects and programmes
are dynamic variables, liable to change over time.
PIM is designed to deal with specific problems, and
therein lies its success.

Projects do not normally use a comprehensive
management information system because of the expense and time involved in establishing broad-based
data banks, requiring analysis for a good-sized
staff. Such systems are therefore associated only
with very long-lived, large-scale projects, or with
continuing programmes (e.g. those operated by SUDENE
in Brazil's Northeast).

C. Control
Traditional control procedures, which include budgeting, cyclic reprogramming, accounting, and
auditing have long been widely, if not universally,
accepted as management tools. Such procedures,
while necessary, are not sufficient to ensure proper
control in projects which require additional
measures because of their special characteristics.
Major factors influencing the choice of these particular controls include the type of project, the
implementing organization, and the degree of de-
viance from established standards which is considered acceptable.

Considerable differences exist in the kinds of
monitoring/reporting/control procedures which are
found appropriate for different types of projects.
One major category of projects is concerned with
"problem-solving". This includes projects such as
those in the Comilla Programme, in which the technical staff, working with villagers and farmers, provided assistance in identifying basic problems, and
developed projects to overcome those problems. In
such projects, the responsibility of the Comilla
technical staff was not to provide precise production inputs, but to assist villagers and farmers
define and solve problems they considered most
important. This effort required an approach in
which problems were defined step by step, so that
projects were developed gradually.

When the local people had identified projects
and roughly worked out solutions with the Academy
staff's assistance, the Director of the Comilla programme had to have a means of getting information
about implementation. He was mainly concerned with
the economic and social changes taking place, in
terms of acceptance of new agricultural practices,
development of reading skills, rate of formation of
village cooperatives, and rate of acceptance of new
programmes, such as women's education. Observation
of earlier similar programmes, had led the Admini-
strator to conclude that it is not primarily the
outsider who successfully brings about planned
change, but the insider from the village who first
learns about the modern world outside, then returns
to the village to talk about his new experiences.
The Academy faculty had also discovered that while
national development workers (N.D.O.'s) played an
important part in disseminating information, the
N.D.O's had little influence in changing farmers'
practices, because they knew little about the prac-
cal aspects of agriculture. Instead, farmers got

advice on agriculture from friends or acquaintances
who were considered to be good farmers. The Academy
staff reasoned that, because the government workers
were only acceptable as dispensers of information,
while trusted villagers or farmers were turned to for
advice, it was more logical to use an influential
villager or farmer as a teacher to begin with. On
this basis the Comilla Thana Training System began.
This was to be one of the most significant monitor-
ing/reporting/control elements in the Comilla project.

Under this system, trusted, leading local farmers were hired by the Academy and given a short
training session. Then they returned to the
villages near their homes to try to organize groups
of farmers who were interested in bettering themselves. When such a group was formed, an Academy
staff member sent a cooperative organization expert
to help the group organize a primary cooperative
society. The group, as one of the steps in agreeing
to a ten-point programme for organization, agreed to
select from their number a member whom they trusted,
who was then sent to the Academy once a week for
training. This person became the Organizer and
teacher for the group. Regular member education
discussions were held thereafter to disseminate information from the Academy. Conversely, the Academy
modified its plans on the basis of feedback from the
Organizer. The group would pass through a trial
period while it practiced the ten points of the
programme. If it made a good start, it would be
accepted into a pilot cooperative.

A second element of control was introduced by
selecting one member of each village cooperative to
serve as the Business Manager of the organization.
This man became responsible for keeping proper and
complete accounts and ensuring that regular cash and
in-kind savings deposits were made by the group.
Gradually, however, it became apparent that friction
occurred between the Organizer/Teacher and the
Business Manager, and the two roles were combined
into one.

Feedback, and to some extent feed-forward, were
built into the system at Comilla. The ten-point
programme provided both guidelines and a broad way
of gauging progress. Selection of the Organizer by
the people placed a great deal of monitoring and
managing/control authority with them. Yet another
link in the control chain was direct monitoring by
the Academy staff and, frequently by the Director
himself. There is often no substitute for direct

contact, and the size of Comilla thana (about 100 square miles) made such contact relatively easy.

A second major category of project concentrates on the delivery of a package of practices or inputs. These projects often attempt to increase farm income by providing technological innovations which, if applied systematically, are known to result in increased farm yield. Assuming that there is a direct relationship between the visits of extension agents, farmer agents, or others who can provide instructions on the use of the technological package, and farm outputs, and assuming that supplies and equipment are available so that farmers can make use of the technology on time and at an adequate level, it is possible to establish a schedule in advance of implementation, which can provide reporting and control reference points. Most of the projects in this category are ones concerned with cash crop development, an example of which is the Kenya Smallholder Tea Project.

External financing for tea processing in Kenya was possible only if the quality and amount of tea, which would be forthcoming, were to be guaranteed by a planning and organizing body. The Kenya Tea Development Authority (KTDA) was created to fill this role. It was to exercise close control over annual planting, nurseries, field supervision, inspection and collection of green tea leaf, and the sites and operations of factories. This close supervision was necessary because the quality and yield of tea depend greatly on meticulous, specialized care by the grower. Planting, pruning (pegging), plucking, and other steps in the growth cycle must be precise, or both yields and quality of leaf can fall drastically.

The KTDA is governed by a Board, tea committees at divisional, district and province levels, an executive staff, and a field staff. The Board, consisting of governmental executives, growers, and lenders, is responsible for major policy and financial decisions, and it selects the General Manager. Tea committees discuss local policies and disseminate policy decisions to growers. By allocating planting material and by attracting the more successful growers, the committees exert a strong control function over the other growers. The committee members also adopt and influence others to accept production standards. The executive staff located in Nairobi, administers leaf collection, supervises nurseries and growers, and handles most operational matters.

Under such highly technical and supervisory conditiors, control is an ongoing process, measured both by inputs and outputs. Visits by Tea Officers and Leaf Officers come at prescribed times, and techniques of planting, husbandry, and collection are overseen and recorded. It is thus possible to use scheduling devices and periodically to check progress against pre-set schedules. KTDA maintains a tight record over its junior staff, which is required to visit each of its growers about six times a year to grade his growers against established standards, through a field records system. When leaves are plucked, they are taken to a drying centre where each batch is weighed and registered. By all these measures, the KTDA as an autonomous and authoritarian body has proven to be highly successful in improving tea quality and yield, while increasing returns to the smallholder.

Comilla and KTDA represent very different types of projects, yet both have enjoyed more than average success. Each has employed an approach appropriate to the objectives of the two projects, and the monitoring/reporting/control techniques have adequately reflected the objectives and overall operational approach in each case. Looked at another way, Comilla was an experimental project which reached only the pilot stage before being cancelled out by political events. The KTDA, by comparison, reached large-scale production. As projects move along the path from research to pilot to demonstration to production, it is usually possible to monitor and perform control procedures with a greater degree of specificity - although implementation at each stage brings new problems and not a few surprises. Control at all stages must therefore be able to be applied flexibly in response to changed conditions, but this is especially true for projects in the early stages.

The programming and Implementation System (PIM) used in Kenya's Special Rural Development Programme (SRDP) represents an intermediate approach between a problem-solving and an inputs delivery (contract) approach. It was developed to deal with a problem of planning, programming of funds, time, and people through procedural means. The designers of PIM saw a great need to move away from an over-centralized control system in which orders originated at the capital and were transmitted downward, to a system in which field staff, and responsible workers, would respond to a management which gave them a part in drawing up their own work plans and setting their

own work targets. The concentration was not so
much on the ultimate users, i.e., the client groups
in Kenyan society, as on the bureaucracy itself.
There was no guarantee that this approach would
change the target audience itself, for example, by
reorienting the field staff's efforts away from
larger farmers to smallholders and subsistence
farmers who needed assistance most desperately.
Field staff have as often directed their efforts
towards those who are prepared to accept new practices, which mean the more successful, cash-crop
farmers. Nonetheless, the designers of the PIM
approach reasoned that a bottom-up planning/pro-
gramming approach would lead to a more effective
control system for the SRDP, and worked for the institutionalization of PIM procedures with this in
mind. While there may have been many reasons for
this development, the significant consideration
for managers and field staff is that it is more
difficult to assist client groups to identify and
resolve their own problems by planning and implementing projects, if the manager himself has had no
experience with the decentralized effort. PIM
allowed the field staff of the Programme to experience directly what it meant to plan and put into
action their own ideas, under supervision and with
guidance from above.

One effect of the PIM system was the way in
which it changed the role of workers and managers at
different levels. Before PIM, centrally planned
work programmes called for field staff to respond
to targets from above, and to submit fairly detailed
progress reports. When detailed reports are submitted from the field to headquarters, there can be
one of two results: the reports can be read, consuming considerable managerial time; or, they can go
unread, in which case they are of less than zero
value, for they have already taken the time of the
preparing staff. Whichever course is taken, valuable time is lost. With the PIM system, clear
agreement was reached in the Annual Programming
Exercise as to the nature and scope of proposed projects. This clarity and expressly stated responsibility was further developed during the periodic
(often monthly) Management Meetings. As one consequence, an unheard of reversal in communications
began to take place. Whereas before PIM, all orders
were directed downwards, now requests for commodities and resources began to flow upward. Field
staff began to request of Area Officers and Area
Officers of headquarters, assistance to meet project

schedules and objectives as jointly agreed to.
Control had moved down the hierarchy, with concentration on details at lower levels, and more time
for managers at higher levels to concentrate on
broader issues.

Most projects fall between the extremes of
problem-solving (e.g. Comilla), and inputs delivery
(e.g. KTDA). A control system for such projects,
may have to incorporate aspects of both systems.
Project designers and managers should be cautious,
however, not to attempt to use procedures successfully used for problem-solving when inputs delivery
is the major task, not to attempt to impose a rigid
overseer type of control when a more gradual and
open type of problem-solving is called for i.e. adapt
the controls to the particular task in hand.

D. Practical Difficulties in Monitoring
The World Bank and other lending agencies, with much
experience of monitoring and evaluation system of
projects and programmes, have learnt several lessons
from this experience. Most of them are not very
surprising, and have indeed been mentioned earlier
in this chapter. A most common fault is a poorly
designed system with, typically, inadequate staffing,
inability to undertake base-line studies early
enough, more data than are needed or which can be
analysed, delays in processing data, in analysing
them and in presentation of results and, the finish-
ing touch, results which remain unused by project
staff even though they may be relevant. Then, too
much may be attempted too soon, in an ambitious way.
Costs of monitoring and evaluating current activities are not negligible - they can be as high as 4
to 5 percent of total project costs. It needs a
very efficient system to justify such costs, which
have to be met by governments of developing countries, not donor agencies. Costs are easily
identified but not always the gains which monitoring
and evaluation should bring about. Care is thus
needed not to overload a system with costs which
cannot easily be justified.

Caution is also needed in the selection of projects or programmes which are to be monitored. It
may be better to monitor only part of a complex project (involving costly and/or crucial elements), for
example. Pilot projects are invaluable in providing
relatively cheap information about which direction
to take. Projects to monitor should also be influenced by the level of competence of project
managements and their general receptiveness to taking

part in a system of monitoring and evaluation.
Whatever project is adopted, the system used
should be as simple as possible. It may be useful
to pose the following questions - and get satisfactory answers - before arranging to put a monitoring
system into action for any particular project:

(a) What are the main purposes of the monitoring and evaluation?
(b) What kinds of data should be collected?
(c) How will the data be collected?
(d) What methods of analysis will be used?
(e) For whom are the monitoring/evaluation
findings? How will they be used?
(f) How will the system be organized? Which
agency, institute or organizational unit will
be responsible?
(g) How many and what type of staff will be
involved?
(h) What is the likely cost of the system?
How much of the total project costs should be
allocated to it?
(i) How should monitoring evaluation be
financed?
(j) What are the problems and lessons likely
to be learned from implementation of the monitoring and evaluation system?

Finally, one should note that while monitoring
can be a key element in successful project or programme implementation, its benefits can only be
fully realised with an efficient system of management.
The type of evaluation system chosen depends
on:

- what should be measured
- for whom
- for what purpose(s)
- how should it be measured
- how should the data be collected
- when and in what form are the data needed.

Chapter 15

RESEARCH, EXTENSION AND TRAINING

Summary
Agricultural development has been handicapped
by inadequate support for national research,
often misdirected. There are encouraging results, however, from the fairly recent establishment of international research centres, the
latest addition being expressly created to
assist governments to develop and strengthen
their research organizations. To ensure that
more relevant research work is carried out,
there is a clear need for planners, extension
and research workers, and farmers to be in
closer touch with each other. Priority should
be given to farmers' real problems but this is
not always the case. If it were, more emphasis
would be given to the whole farm approach than
to specific parts of the farming economy. A
key role in agricultural research rests with
organization - in the co-ordination of all the
interested parties.
Extension is a logical partner of research
but it has often failed to live up to expectations because major factors are working against
its success. Farmers are not likely to alter
current practices, for example, if there is no
incentive to them to do so - and this is frequently the situation. The nature of extension
work places heavy demands on administration
which, typically, is short of operating funds
and poorly staffed. Yet, good extension
systems can play a very positive role in development. Planners and administrators may need
to look closely at the national extension
system with this objective in mind.
Emphasis in training is gradually shifting
to improvement in quality, a wider coverage of

subject-matter and clientele. Attention needs to be focussed towards more non-formal training systems involving more women and the rural poor. Training programmes, in general, need to be carefully integrated with related developmental and educational activities.

Research

1. Introduction

A general criticism of agricultural research in developing countries is that too little money has gone into it, and, despite very considerable achievements in particular fields, much recent work has been inadequately focused, lacking in continuity, irrelevant to actual needs, and generally suffering from recurrent funding problems. A larger, more clearly defined effort is needed, at both national and international levels, for both export and domestic crops and in some areas for livestock. There is an urgent need for defensive research to support and maintain improved technologies, particularly in disease control. To ensure the relevance of current and future research work, there must be better means of communication between agricultural planners, extension and research workers, and farmers. This is likely to require better coordination, division of labour, monitoring and control, renewed efforts to ensure continuity of staffing and expansion of key programmes.

National research programmes are now able to receive considerable help from the international agricultural research centres financed through the Consultative Group on International Agricultural Research (CGIAR), such as the International Institute for Tropical Agriculture (IITA) at Ibadan. The most recent addition to CGIAR, the International Service for National Agricultural Research (ISNAR), has been created expressly to assist governments to develop and strengthen their research organisations. Such assistance can take the form of preparing international investment proposals for funding by international or bilateral agencies, as well as providing senior research administrators for national programmes.

2. Research Priorities

There are two main groups, besides research workers, who have a major stake in the efficiency and direction of agricultural research: the government or other group which directly or indirectly finances it, and the users of research results, mainly farmers. Users tend to be most interested in the specific results of research, while financiers tend to concentrate on getting the maximum benefits from all the resources used.

The first step in efficient use of research capacities is the establishment of priorities to focus research on the most critical problems. This requires decisions on what commodities and what economic and ecological problems are to be considered when carrying out research. There are never enough resources to do everything, so setting priorities often means deciding what is going to be left out. The Chinese, for instance, decided not to compete with other countries in basic research so they could concentrate on adapting existing knowledge to their own needs. A World Bank sector survey recommended that horticulture and farm mechanization research should take second place in Ethiopia because of resource limitations.

In agriculture, priority problems are usually those faced by the country's farmers. This seems obvious enough, but it is often overlooked as emphasis is placed not on immediate farm problems but on basic, high technology or prestigious research. The result is research which never gets translated into activity the farmer can use, or which fails because it is pushed by extension agents before adequate field and farm economics testing has been done. Thus policy-makers usually find that the steps which provide the greatest return for investment in research are those that focus research on the farmers' problems. This requires an institutional system to bring farmers' problems to the researcher's attention and to provide research results to the farmers. In Kenya, for example, the two-way flow between farmers and researchers was highly developed for tea growers. There was an efficient local organization for providing information to both the extension staff and the growers. Tea committees - local farmers' organizations - not only explained policy to the growers but also presented the farmers' problems to extension agents and the other administrative officers who must act on them.

If research is to be applicable by smaller farmers as well as to improve productivity, extra efforts have to be made. Even though tea growing technology was successfully adapted to smallholder production conditions, thus showing that it could be done, most Kenyan research largely ignored the needs and constraints of the small farmer. Research and extension were poorly coordinated for small farm crops like maize, especially when compared to the service provided to tea growers. Food crops research was neglected and there were no research trials in situations similar to those of small farmers.

In India, at one time 90 percent of the funds set aside for technical assistance to smallholders remained unspent because of various purely administrative snags. There was little research on improving or developing tools for small scale farmers. In Latin America, research policies often led to even worse income maldistribution as findings were appropriate only for the holdings and better lands operated by large owners. Research and extension services lacked effective links and often were antagonistic towards each other. This was also true elsewhere.

In the past, the most effective research was organized on a crop rather than a disciplinary basis. For many years, crop research was concentrated on plantation crops such as cocoa, coconut, coffee, palm oil, tea and industrial crops such as cotton, groundnuts and rubber. Concentration on a crop not only helped to ensure the cooperation of all the skills necessary to solve particular problems but also made it easier to focus research on those crops with the highest priority. The International Rice Commission, for example, had three separate groups working on breeding, fertilizer use and agricultural engineering for twenty years or so. It was not until all basic questions were attacked at one centre, the International Rice Research Institute at Los Banos, that a breakthrough was achieved, within five years, in the form of a high yielding variety of rice. The high yielding wheat variety programmes in Mexico had a multi-disciplinary crop concentration.

One limitation of single crop research programmes, however, is that many farmers grow more than one crop. Where farmers are growing several crops in succession each year, increasing yields for a crop may not help a farmer as much as reducing the growing season, if this allows the growing of a second or third crop. In fact, the farmer may be better-off with reduced yields of particular crops if he can increase the number of crops grown. In many parts of the world farmers interplant different crops together as this system is sometimes more profitable than planting single crops.

Maximizing income on farms may come from reducing the agricultural labour needed. In Japan and

China (Taiwan), for instance, off-farm employment in rural industries is turning most farms into part-time operations often run by women, children and older persons. In much of Africa, farmers seek to reduce labour time used to grow subsistence crops, without giving these crops up entirely, in order to spend more time on cash crops. In most of Asia, much of a farmer's cash income comes from day labour, cottage industries or other activities rather than working his farm. These farmers also find that maximizing income means reducing farm labour needs. Unfortunately this need to reduce labour use in agriculture is directly contrary to the trend of most single crop research, which is to use more inputs which require greater use of labour. Labour saving research often concerns types of mechanization which replace farmers and farm labour rather than help small farmers.

Since subsistence farmers are reluctant to give up food production, it may be better to introduce cash crops that can be grown in combination with other crops. Thus in Latin America, plantain has been planted with coffee. In Costa Rica, the early tobacco harvest allows farmers to grow a second crop on land with some residual fertilization; not only does this lower risks, it grants the farmer some protection against a monopsonistic buyer for his cash crop. Some crops, such as bananas, may not be as easily combined with other crops, however.

Thus it is necessary to seek ways to do more than maximise output of a crop, or income from a particular crop. It is net farm income that must be increased. This may not mean increasing the yields of a particular crop but decreasing the inputs including labour and time that are required, especially for small-scale farming. Small farms, because of the diversity of activities, are often more complex economically than large commercial farms which may concentrate on only one or two crops.

Some research programmes are beginning to recognize the need for a whole farm approach to agricultural research to see if new crops, varieties, practices, or combinations of these, would work in the social and institutional environment of the farmer. This type of research follows the adaptive research needed to show the physical and biological viability of the new practices. It concerns itself with determining the needs of the farmer and the institutional requirements (e.g. credit, markets) if the new practices are to be a success, and has shown the greatest potential in dealing with the diversi-

323

fied type of farming used by small farmers, and in
minimizing the need for purchased inputs which is
particularly important to the poorest farmers.

So that, especially when examining problems of
small farmers but also when dealing with any farm
unit that grows more than one crop, or spends significant amounts of time on more than one economic
activity, it is necessary to concentrate research on
increasing farm income from all activities rather
than just increasing output or income from each crop
individually. Failure to concentrate attention on
farm income has led to the rejection of innovations
resulting in neither increased output or income.

3. Farmers and Research

Unfortunately there are shortages of research personnel in most developing countries, a situation
that will continue for some time. If development is
to proceed as rapidly as most countries would like,
research on a broad front must proceed in spite of
such problems. Ways to expand or supplement domestic research capacity are highly useful.

One way of expanding research capability
already referred to, is the use of international
research institutions or foreign researchers. Many
key breakthroughs in agricultural research were made
by such institutions, e.g. the high yielding
varieties of rice and wheat. Increasingly such research is being organized on an ecological zone
basis and being widened to include more crops which
are specific to certain zones or which make up
smaller parts of food intake, e.g. legumes. Often
such research has special advantages, such as international financing and the ability to draw on genetic resources from all over the world. International work is also beginning to be done on non-
technical subjects such as agricultural policy,
income distribution and rural-urban migration.

No country, however, can rely on this kind of
research for all its needs. New problems, e.g.,
new plant diseases, keep arising which a competent
research service must be able to at least monitor,
even if they must rely on outside sources for
solutions. The process of development, irrigation
and drainage development, changes in soil conditions
due to fertilizer use, and multi-cropping, changes
the ecology of a country and leads to new research
demands. Technologies produced in developed
countries are often inappropriate for developing
countries because of differences in climate and
other conditions, or because the technologies are

mainly labour saving. Even when appropriate, foreign technologies must usually be adapted to the particular conditions in a country and field tested. These steps require extensive research capabilities.

One way of quickly expanding the research capacity of a country is to involve farmers in research tasks. The Puebla Project in Mexico conducted its experiments in farmers' fields using the farmer as the experimenter. Farmers were compensated for any losses incurred. This turned the whole region into an experiment station and meant that experimental results could immediately be interpreted as recommendations for farmers without further adaptive research. This same method has begun to be used to develop specific recommendations for various types of small farm and soil conditions in other parts of Mexico. Coffee research in Costa Rica was also done by experimental demonstrations on regular farms.

Early Japanese agricultural development began in the 1870s and 80s with farmer innovations, many of which were only later taken up by the government and spread to other areas. Initially the government attempted to imitate large scale western methods of cultivation but this failed. Then they turned to promoting the best of traditional technology. Traditional varieties were improved and the improvements were often made by farmers. Innovations originating outside government research organizations included the planting of rice seedlings in rows, a seed selection method using brine, improved plows, the rotary weeder and the treadle threshing machine. The government promoted local meetings and agricultural improvement societies to exchange information and techniques. Some farmers were appointed as instructors at the newly established Komaba Agricultural College. Other farmers were hired as "itinerate instructors" to tour the country, meeting with farmers and demonstrating improved farming techniques.

China seems to have gone farthest in encouraging farmer research and was successful enough so that current trends are towards reinforcing the farm-level research effort although professional research, tied to local problems, is not being ignored.

Often farmers develop new techniques entirely on their own. Japanese farmers moved to the northern island of Hokkaido where, despite expert advice that rice was not suitable to Hokkaido, they experimented with new seeds and practices until they made rice not only a suitable but a prolific crop.

In West Pakistan, farmers in unirrigated areas experimented with high yielding varieties and adopted them in spite of extension and research neglect. In Colombia, a cooperative promoted, tested and financed a series of new speciality crops tailored to the needs of its small scale production units.

Farmers can be integrated into research programmes with the same approach adopted in agricultural extension. Many of the successful demonstration programmes have a large experimental component. This may seem strange to those who see the farmer as ignorant and conservative, but is less surprising when one realizes that adopting a new practice is always an experiment. It is the farmer who must integrate a new practice into the pattern of his economic and social activities. The view that farmers must simply follow the instructions of agents, who already know the right answers, has led to many extension failures. Highly centralized or regimented societies are especially vulnerable to errors in failing to farm-test new practices since they can enforce the use of practices which are wrong. Some of China's early agricultural policies nearly led to disaster before farmer-oriented policies were adopted. The recognition that farmers have to experiment, to adjust practices to their own conditions and that, therefore, farmers and extension agents must work together as collaborators, not just as students and teachers, was the basis of many successful extension programmes.

The use of farmers as researchers also allows combination of local trials and farm economics research into one phase. The same field trials which test the suitability of a variety or practice to a new environment also test the economics of the variety by determining whether the farmer or his neighbour who had done the test are willing to adopt the variety or practice in their own farming. This greatly simplifies the extension agent's job as there is no longer an artificial distinction between farmer and experiment station conditions.

Use of on-farm experiments to test farmer acceptance of new practices can also replace much of the difficult analysis, complicated by social factors and traditions, of farm economics. Farm economics analysis is expensive when done by researchers on experiment stations and is beyond the abilities of most extension agents. Lack of information about the farm economics of new practices frequently leads to failure, e.g. new practices often increase or change the pattern of labour demand in ways that farmers will not accept. The best way to test the suitability of a new practice is to see whether farmers who have tried the practice continue to use it.

In practice, the results of farmer research have been distributed through extension systems just as well as the results of more expensive experiment station research. What farmer research lacks in prestige is compensated for by practicality and relevance to actual farming conditions, and the greater ease in finding a technology that fits local economic and social conditions. Development of traditional practices through use of farmer researchers, and the tying of such research to professional research institutions, helps to avoid the problem of researchers who ignore the situation in which their findings are to be applied.

4. Research Organization

If limited research capabilities are to be fully used, work must be carefully coordinated. The most frequent problem in the establishment of an Agricultural Research Council. Many such Councils have been established. If they are to work, however, they must have the authority to make binding decisions. For this reason, such Councils should be closely connected to the central planning authorities.

The Councils should include members representing the research institutions, financing organisations, extension, farmers and other relevant private, government and parastatal bodies. In countries having federal systems, e.g. Nigeria, the coordination problem will be especially acute. If most research is controlled by the national government, special liaison units will have to be developed to represent the state governments in the research priority-setting process. If much research is state controlled, then the need for a coordinating council, whatever form it takes, becomes more important if the national research effort is to be efficiently carried out.

Another solution to the coordination problem is to put the related activities under a single director, but this approach is not always necessary, feasible or desirable. In some countries, the autonomous status of some research institutions, the universities in Turkey are an example, mean that the looser, more flexibile form of the research council may be preferable. In India, research organizations themselves coordinated maize research. One institute

was selected as a coordinating centre for the programme. Annual meetings were held to report on work
done, and to outline programmes for the next year. In
countries as large as India, separate coordinating
bodies for certain crops or groups of crops are
desirable for work coordination even if there is an
overall council for setting crop priorities and
allocating funds.

A coordinating council and unified direction
are not mutually exclusive solutions to the allocation and coordination problems. An agency might
unify the direction of its own research or research
and extension while a council is established to coordinate with non-departmental research activities.

Extension

Agricultural extension services are generally given
a key role in organizational approaches to rural
development. Their main aim is to spread new technology, and often inputs and credit as well. But
the essential ingredients for success - an appropriate incentive structure, an ability to "deliver"
what the farmers need and the offer of an attractive
"package", too rarely co-exist. So that, inevitably,
extension has often failed to live up to its expectation. Valuable resources have been wasted.

The effort surrounding extension is usually
handicapped by the blinkered approach given to it.
Farmers are not particularly interested in advice
given by extension agents, for example, if the price
of the crop concerned is fixed by the government at
a level which makes that crop unattractive to grow.
This may appear obvious to an outsider, but it is
common for extension services to be facing unfair
odds against low producer prices. Marketing uncertainties work against them to the same dismal
effect.

Then, extension operations by their very nature
put a heavy load on what is frequently a weak administrative structure. Distance from urban centres
handicaps recruitment of capable managers and
middle-level technicians, affecting the quality of
the advice and the farmer's acceptance of the services. The wide dispersal of agents, who must be
physically mobile and capable of adjusting to diverse situations, is costly. Many extension services
are typically short of operating funds which im-
mobilizes staff and undermines morale. There are
usually very few women extension workers despite the
importance of women as heads of household in many

rural areas and as providers of a major part of rural labour.

Generally there are too few technical advisers, many of them inadequately trained, lowly paid, poorly supervised, who try to spread their activities too widely, and in trying to accomplish too much, fail to achieve what a narrower approach may succeed in doing. Extension workers tend to have to give too much time to administrative work when clerical staff could be employed to take over the bulk of this assignment.

Finally, provision of formal machinery for periodic review of the economic performance of extension services is often weak or lacking. Yet apart from its necessity for planning purposes, it could also raise the morale of district-level staff who often feel their efforts are neglected by higher authority. One of the likely findings of such a review is that agents do not give sufficient attention to farm economics and to management of the farm "as a whole", if they did, the reasons for their failure to make a greater impact on economic performance would almost certainly become clearer.

This somewhat depressing appraisal does not, of course, apply to all crops, regions or even countries. Successful extension has most notably been in existence for high-value, often export, crops such as cotton, palm, oil, rubber, sugar cane, tea and tobacco where funds may be provided by commercial farmers and the whole system often managed by them. Here, standards of organization, training, pay and other conditions of employment tend to be much higher than in the general national extension service and agents have clear guidelines for them to follow in carrying out their work. The weak sector concerns traditional food crops where the technological packages are generally poor, especially in climatically unfavourable regions. This situation points to the need not only to improve the general administrative capability of extension in this whole area, but to put together as quickly as possible a package, based on renewed and greatly enlarged research effort focused on food crops. Without such a focus, extension results are likely to remain negligible and morale in the service low.

Generally, then, planners and administrators need to take a close look at the relevance of the existing extension system to determine what kind of information it is giving out, what inputs, and the kind of packages received by farmers. Performance should be judged against rural development projects

329

which are built around a commercially key crop
(cotton, for example) which offers a "tried and
tested" technical package, an assured market and a
means of cost and credit recovery.

Any assessment of the effectiveness of extension has, of course, to take into account a particular country's stage of development. As development
proceeds, the extension agent changes his role from
being a general source of technical information to a
specialist or a liaison officer to a range of subject-matter specialists and finally to a community-
project initiator. In other words, the staffing
structure at the local level needs to move with the
times, reflecting the increase in complexity and
advance in technology of farming operations.

Training

Throughout the 1970s emphasis has generally been
given to improvement in the quality of extension
systems and training institutions, with greater
attention to in-service training. Specialised
training centres and institutions are being established for training on major production problems in
specific regions. Another major group receiving
training continues to be adult male farmers but
rural women are now getting more priority in this
area. And clearly they should, in view of their
importance in farm decision-making and in the supply
of farm labour in many countries.

The establishment of Farmer Training Centres
(FTC) in many developing countries has strategic
value for educational, economic and social reasons.
The FTC provide a learning setting for farmers
where the best teaching materials, equipment and
aids can be provided. It can also make effective
use of the few experts and extension workers. The
FTC can give the trained farmers a sense of identity
with a source of new knowledge, and of belonging and
support among those trained, and the FTC management
staff. A successful pattern which puts together
tested extension principles is used in the "training
and visit" schemes of extension being tried with
World Bank support in India and other countries.

Recent experiences with programmes in agricultural extension and training underline the importance of integrating them with related development
and educational activities. There is also a need
for decentralization - to take account of the great
variation among rural areas. Apart from its technical effectiveness, it can be a way to unlease the

enormous latent resources, human energies and enthusiasm that are vital ingredients in any effective programme for rural development.

Training and extension work has primarily focused on production, leading frequently to a very marked bias toward progressive farmers and more developed areas. Even when this is not a conscious policy, it might be expected that those with the most assets, initiative, and know-how, would be the first to take advantage of any new opportunities be they agricultural, educational or some other type. Although not neglecting production, attention needs to be directed more toward attacking rural poverty and social injustice. In this respect, training programmes should cover a wide range of areas in addition to those concerned with production techniques. A system which covers the village level and trains people in multiple skills, preparing them for various job opportunities or self-employment, is gradually receiving more attention. Clearly, a far broader approach must be taken to the problem of generating adequate numbers of trained rural workers, with emphasis on non-formal skills training systems and maximum opportunities for the active participation of the rural poor.

Chapter 16

CONSULTANCY SERVICES

Summary
Developing countries have for a variety of
reasons found it useful to have the services of
a wide range of consultants, or technical
experts, and this need is not likely to disappear for some time. They provide specialised
skills and knowledge, are generally available
for flexible time periods, can give objective
assessments - and provide a basis for transferring their skills to national counterparts.
They provide no guarantee of improved results.
Much depends on a consultant's terms of reference and the phrasing of their instructions.
In the agricultural sector, consultants work in
four main areas: policy studies; plan, project
and programme analysis; management; and improvement of operating units. Their usefulness
in each of these fields depends to a great
extent on close co-operation with and support
from their clients. Some attention is given in
this chapter about where and how to obtain the
services of consultants and the finer points of
the client-consultant partnership.

1. The Need for Consultancy Services

The process of economic and social change calls for
the application of a wide range of skills. Yet
developing countries have too few trained people to
undertake programmes at the scale required for sustained development. To help find solutions to their
problems, developing countries have called on consultants from a variety of public and private
sources, and the volume of consultancy services provided has increased substantially in recent decades.
Consultancy is rooted in the need not merely to
provide, but to transfer, scarce skills. This is

true whether the consultant is providing services to a firm in an industrially developed country, or to an agricultural organization in a developing country. Several reasons have been given for the use of consultants: obtaining specialized skills and knowledge; conserving funds by having a highly skilled person on the payroll for a relatively short time; obtaining independent evaluations and recommendations; finding or developing fresh approaches to the solution of problems. These reasons are important enough, but one principle underlies them all: that to be successful, a consultancy requires a change in the client's perception of his problem, and an increased ability to deal with it.

The concept of technical assistance, from which modern consultancy services have developed, has changed considerably during the last thirty years or so. During the first stage of technical assistance, it was assumed that most or all of the practices which had been effective in technologically-advanced nations could be transferred to almost all situations without being changed. By about 1950, aid donors became aware that there are significant social and cultural differences between countries. Acceptance of change, it was learned, depended on many factors, including the cultural, social and psychological beliefs and practices of each country. These factors, therefore, had to be considered when providing technical assistance in a form which could be effectively used. This knowledge has led to improvements in the way technical assistance is provided, but it still falls short of what is possible.

Agricultural managers may want to consider using consultants for a number of reasons. Consultants provide a readily available source of knowledge, experience and skills not usually found in a client organization. It is, of course, virtually impossible for any one organization to maintain a staff so large and highly specialized that it can find appropriate approaches, or solutions, tc all problems on a flexible basis. Consultants have often been able to use their specialized capabilities to accelerate the application of technical, economic, and managerial skills to the solution of problems. Further, a consultant who serves many clients frequently works with situations that may confront a client organization only rarely. From this broad exposure, they often learn what problems to anticipate and what actions are likely to succeed.

Another factor to consider is the relative objectivity offered by consultants. Because of their

comparatively independent position, they can often
evaluate a proposed activity or plan in a way which
would be difficult, if not impossible, for an em-
ployee of the organization. Such an impartial viewpoint, free of pre-set lines of commitment, may in
itself be a valuable service in an organization, in
which personal interests and traditional viewpoints
are limiting factors. Further, consultants have at
times been able to express ideas which, though un-
popular, were pertinent and useful. Regular
employees might be loath to express such ideas, or
might even be ignored if they did express them.

Another reason frequently given for using consultants is that their use is necessary to secure
doner funds. This may well be true. The World Bank
for example, has required the use of consultants for
project appraisal, and consultants have been chosen
and employed by borrowing countries with Bank
approval. The granting of Bank loans may depend in
part on consultants' feasibility reports. In other
cases, there may be strongly-held feelings that proposals prepared by expatriates are more likely to
receive funds. African nationals have cited this
feeling as a reason for their low degree of participation in project preparation. Because Africans
sometimes regard foreigners as guests in their
countries, and African customs frequently forbid
criticism of guests, proposals prepared by consultants have at times been accepted without open
criticism, but without deep conviction or support
for the project. Similar feelings have been noted
elsewhere.

2. Effective Use of Consultants
Using consultants to assist in such areas as sector
analysis, feasibility studies, and organizational
analysis should result in more effective operations.
However, consultants provide no guarantee of improved results. The client must first answer the
question, "What is the purpose of this consultancy?"
The client organization will have to define its
problems as clearly as possible and assess the means
available for solving them. This process of self-
analysis is helpful because it requires the client
to attempt to specify work objectives, time and cost
requirements, and the final product expected from
the consultant. Deciding on objectives is the
client's responsibility and not the consultant's,
although consultants may be able to clarify the
choices available.

It is rare that either a client or consultant

can foresee with exactly what problems a consultant should assist. Nor is it likely that a work plan will remain unchanged as a project unfolds. As both the client and consultant learn more about the problem with which they are dealing, the consultant's tasks and work plans often require change. It is therefore important to build into a contract, provision to review and modify the terms of reference, if necessary, during the life of the contract.

At times, the client may be aware that he is unable to define the terms of reference to his own or the donor's satisfaction. In such cases, it may be in the client's interest to retain a consultant to help clarify the issue by preparing a preliminary report or prospectus.

It is said that a client should decide <u>exactly</u> what he wants to achieve before inviting in a consultant. These wants should be stated in terms of cost, productivity, delivery time, or other measurable criteria. Otherwise, the basis for judging a consultant's activities may be lacking, and it will be more difficult to attain a desired objective. In practice, it is not often that the client will be able to define his problems with a high degree of precision. The client more often will state his expectations and objectives in somewhat general terms, and an early task of the consultant will be to work with the client to develop an appropriate approach and work programme. Realistic terms of reference can then be established.

While the terms of reference cannot be complete in every detail, they should include if possible, a statement of the background of the problem; the scope of work, with room for modification; a list of services required; a list of available information, including primary contracts; studies previously carried out; the necessary field surveys; and the responsible organizational element which will monitor the undertaking.

Terms of reference, and especially scopes of work, are often deficient because an inventory of background information has not been assembled. This may mean that a study can be well under way before there is real agreement between a client and consultant as to what is required, and how it can be accomplished. This situation re-emphasizes the need for close and continuing working relations between consultant and client. One pattern is to form an early, tentative approach to a problem, making revisions as more data become available. Developing alternative approaches, and testing them in periodic meetings between client and consultant, will eventually produce a solution, or approach, which satisfactorily passes all tests.

The way in which clients phrase their instructions is also important. Consultants have noted the implications of the following instructions:

(a) "Tell us what's wrong with us". By phrasing instructions in this manner, the client puts himself in a subordinate position. Further, it may indicate that the client will not take part in deciding what is wrong, so he may feel no responsibility for implementing recommended solutions. A client who excludes himself from the process of analysis to determine both "what's wrong," as well as, "what's right" has already begun to limit the possibilities for transferring skill from the consultant to the organization. Another consideration is that the leadership of the client organization may really be asking what is wrong with all of the organization excluding the leaders. Relatively few administrators feel that they should be studied, assuming that most problems exist at other levels within the organization, or outside the organization altogether. Yet bureaucracies and their personnel are a vital element in the delivery system and all levels of their operation must be taken into account.

(b) "Write us a report and recommend this..." It is not uncommon for a consultant to be called on to provide support for a conclusion already reached. Unless the facts call for the requested conclusion, this instruction would subvert the proper role of both the client and consultant. Moreover, if the conclusion has already been reached before the consultancy begins, the facts that are sought may reveal only one side of the picture. A report based on such facts could possibly help an organization in the short run, but more often hides the real problems.

(c) "Do something for us." This instruction assumes that a proper role for a consultant is to perform the work for the client, instead of the client doing it for himself. This procedure occurs in the filling of government positions with expatriates. In some cases, this has been at the advice and with the support of donor organizations. The World Bank, for example, has emphasized the shortage of qualified personnel and the long time required to build up indigenous organizations in its sector

reports for several countries. The Bank has recommended that, as an interim measure, countries
consider employing outside (expatriate) assistance
on a fairly large scale to staff both federal and
state ministries. Most often, for Bank-funded
activities, experts have been recommended in the
areas of project planning, preparation, and implementation, and to provide training. Virtually every
donor organization recommends training counterparts
to replace expatriates as quickly as possible. The
Inter-American Development Bank has stated that,
"The external consultants should not be permanent.
Their assistance should only be given until the
country has prepared its own executing personnel and
no longer needs external assistance..." The World
Bank stresses that training of suitable counterparts
be undertaken both locally and overseas as an integral part of programmes using expatriates.

While there is wide agreement that expatriate
assistance should be as short term as possible, and
counterpart training an integral factor, actual
practice varies. The Israeli technical assistance
programme relies on a team approach, rather than the
use of individual experts, to carry out concurrent
training and demonstration programmes, with early
replacement by local counterparts. In many cases,
however, it has been difficult to assign suitable
counterparts. Often, where expatriates work in the
public sector, no counterpart personnel are provided;
if they are, there is often no programme to transfer
the necessary skills to them.

Short-term assignments allow for critical
shortages to be quickly filled by skilled personnel.
There is real doubt, however, whether this fulfills
the principle of skill transferral necessary for
development, even though its appeal to many clients
has proven to be powerful. It has created at times
a condition of dependence. When consultants leave,
for whatever reason, vacuums are created. Expatriates should be used only in the most pressing
situations, and replaced as soon as possible by
nationals.

(d) "Teach us how to do something." This is a
more positive approach, because it concentrates on
the transfer of skills. Even so, it is incomplete,
because it assumes a one-way flow of information and
skills from consultant to client. At the extreme,
the client is seen as an empty vessel, to be
"filled" from a consultant's vast store of knowledge.
Knowledge is seen as a gift bestowed by those who

consider themselves thus equipped to those who lack this faculty. A better approach is that people must teach each other, and thereby become jointly responsible for a system in which all concerned are able to grow. This is a basic factor in any development and fully applicable to the client-consultant relationship. From the outset, the client and consultant must be partners for learning and getting things done. It follows that consultants should not be hired and then left on their own.

The process of learning together involves more than a flow of information: what is needed is the conversion of information into constructive, purposeful and effective activity. Thus, consulting is directly linked to training, and the creation of sets of tasks which client personnel can carry out to achieve specific results. By the creation and repeated application of such tasks, there will be a transferral of skills from the consultant, which will lead directly to a change in the client's ability to solve problems independently.

Expectations of both clients and consultants should be tempered by a degree of modesty. It will take some time for a client and consultant to work together. There may be many occasions when a consultant will be tempted to do the job himself, because he already knows how, and can do it more quickly. This urge must be resisted. One way to face this problem is to begin each assignment where the client is capable and willing to start. The project must be analyzed to determine where initial inputs will yield the best results with the resources (time, people, funds, commodities) available. If the work is beyond what the client is ready to tackle, or if the changes recommended pose too great a risk for line managers, the chance of failure and frustration may be high. Consultant and client must together develop an approach which will yield early successes, thus laying a base for more advanced work. The design of the programme should be such that efforts will build on early successes, with the pace keyed to what the client can incorporate and use.

3. Areas for Employing Consultants
Consultants have been used in virtually every area of development, exerting vast influence in sector and policy studies, governmental reorganizations, major capital investments, tax changes, land reform and many other areas. Generally, there are four major areas in which consultants work; each has

implications for client governments and
organizations. They are: policy studies; plan,
sector and project analysis; management (including
reorganization and training); improvement of functional operating units, at all levels.

It is the responsibility of the consultant, in
each of these areas, to help the client explore
alternatives and the consequences of each. The
client has to make final choices and implement those
choices. This is especially important in broad
gauge areas such as policy, plan, sector and reorganization studies.

One problem is that consultant's reports may be
so general that they provide enough facts only to
confirm prevailing opinions, or lay the basis for
'further studies'. Clients need more than this:
specific recommendations for shaping policies; projects that are identified and compared with alternative investment possibilities; reorganization plans
whose probable effects are carefully assessed. Again,
what is desired from the consultant should be
clearly identified, so that (unless it is specifically requested) an overview report does not result
from months of work.

In policy studies where high-level advice is
sought, decision-makers must be available to the
consultant. In some cases, consultants have been
asked for policy advice, yet they have been put into
working contact with committees, or subordinates,
who had neither the information nor the authority to
act at the level where the problem existed. If the
consultant's findings are likely to have political
implications which would affect implementation, he
or she should be informed that this is a constraint
within which alternatives must be studied. A technical report which cannot be implemented (for
political reasons) has limited use at best.

When undertaking reorganization studies,
theorists sometimes advise that people throughout
the organization should be consulted about the
effects of possible changes. In reality, the degree
to which people at all levels can be involved in the
early stages of a reorganization study is limited.
The spread of rumours based on incomplete information, especially at the middle and lower working
levels, can be very unsettling. When a few good
alternatives have been chosen and developed, it is a
good idea to check their possible effects with
selected people from different levels. Criticism is
often raised that consultant contacts have been too
exclusively with top level client staff members.

339

Middle level personnel can contribute a great deal, at the proper time, because of their direct, first-hand knowledge of operational problems. When gathering information from middle- and lower-level personnel, questions and explanations should deal with the way in which people at those levels will be able to work effectively with, and be affected by, alternative structures and processes.

Management consultants, as opposed to substantive technical specialists, have generally been used for three kinds of assignments, to work on:

(a) Major policy questions where the organization must re-think its assumptions and convictions about both objectives and means. Strategy developments, diversification, and long range planning are typical areas.

(b) Politically sensitive problems where the internal organization has vested interests and substantial differences in perspective or philosophy. Organization rearrangements and overhead reduction policies are characteristically of this type.

(c) Fact finding analytical evaluation situations where considerable research and analysis is required into complex situations, using specialized techniques and concepts.

4. Obtaining Consultancy Services
A. Sources. Consultancy services have usually been thought of as the flow of technical knowledge and personnel from technologically advanced countries to the developing countries. The major sources of services have been either private organizations or multilateral or bilateral governmental bodies. More recently, there has been a small but increasing amount of consultancy services among the developing countries, and to a lesser extent, within countries. A number now have the capability to export some of their resources. For example, China (Taiwan) can offer expertise in rice farming and family planning; Israel has superior capabilities in arid zone research, regional planning and social services; Singapore has had successes in low cost public housing and family planning; and the Philippines excel in some aspects of tropical agriculture. In some cases, the experience of a consultant providing services from one developing country to another may be more relevant than if a consultant is used from a developed country. The possibility of using consultants within a country should not be neglected. The World Bank encourages the use of domestic firms

when they are qualified, either alone or in combination with foreign firms.

Because funds and foreign exchange are often in short supply, the question of fees will obviously be important in the selection of consultants, although cost is only one of several considerations. The use of a domestic firm in combination with a foreign firm might be considered, as it would serve two purposes. First, total cost to the client can be reduced, and second, if the project is properly designed, some skill transfer from the foreign to the domestically based consultant - as well as to the client - will take place. Since the availability of local skilled consultants is likely to be a problem for some time, the base of such consultants should be expanded when possible.

B. Methods of obtaining services. All major assistance organizations have established guidelines and regulations as to how consultancy services may be obtained. For instance the United Nations has published the Manual on the Use of Consultants in Developing Countries; the World Bank has "Uses of Consultants by the World Bank and Its Borrowers" and the U.S. Agency for International Development sets forth its policies and procedures in a series of manual orders.

The sequence of actions leading to retaining a consultant normally include most of the following: (a) Recognition that a problem exists which calls for a consultant; (b) Appointment of a coordinator or committee; (c) Explanation of the issue and definition of the problem; (d) Preparation of a list of prospective consultants; (e) Preliminary contact and screening; (f) Call for bids (tenders) or request for proposals; (g) Selection of a consultant; (h) Negotiation and concluding the agreement. Each of these steps is discussed below.

(a) Recognition that a problem exists which calls for a consultant. It may seem obvious that an organization would realize when consultancy services are needed. In fact, faced with problems which consultancy might help to solve, organizations may be hesitant to seek help. This could be because the nature of the problem may not be fully understood within the organization; it does not want to admit that a problem exists; or because of previous negative experiences with consultants. In some cases, business will proceed as usual and problems grow in size and intensity, making their solution more

difficult when it is finally undertaken. The ability
to recognize a problem often relates to the progress
reporting systems used (See Chapter 14).

(b) Appointment of a coordinator or committee. The
function of the coordinator or committee is the preparation, and carrying out, of all subsequent steps
necessary to secure a consultant, once a problem has
been identified. This will be the focal point within the client organization, for contacting and negotiating with consultants, and making recommendations
for selection. This job is usually formally
assigned to a procurement or contract office. In
practice, representatives from technical offices are
heavily involved because of their knowledge of the
functional aspects of the project. Previous experience in dealing with consultants should also be
considered when selecting the coordinator, or committee.

(c) Definition of the problem. Before terms of
reference can be drawn up, it is necessary for the
client organization to examine the problems facing
them, and to assess how these might be solved. At
this stage, the outline of the problem and objectives may be rather general, and a shorter, preliminary study for identification of the problem may
be called for, before the major study or consultancy
is begun. The additional money and time spent in
this way is often worthwhile, yielding considerable
savings in the total cost of the consultancy.

(d) Preparation of a list of prospective consultants.
The World Bank, regional banks and bilateral assistance organizations advise client organizations to
draw up a fairly extensive list of firms claiming
expertise in the specific field involved. Some
developing countries have agencies such as national
planning or industrialization boards which maintain
a roster of consultants who have been evaluated on
their legal and financial status and experience.
    In practice, some international consulting
firms will have heard about the proposed activity
and be in contact with the client on their own.
Advertisements in foreign journals and newspapers
are also frequently used to solicit prospective consultants' interest. Whatever method or combination
of methods is used, it is generally the formal
responsibility of the client government to prepare
the list of firms or people from which a consultant
will be selected. However, it is not uncommon for

342

field personnel of international assistance organizations and embassies to offer suggestions about
firms they believe to be qualified. The preliminary
list is likely to have recommendations from several
sources, formal and informal.
  This list may be shortened by studying each
firm's capabilities and experience, and selecting a
few of the best qualified. These firms will be the
ones from which those who will receive invitations
for proposals will be selected. Some organizations,
such as the World Bank, prefer to have borrowers
submit to them the list of consultants who will receive invitations for proposals, so that the Bank
may be satisfied about their quality and general
competence. The Bank indicates approval or dis-
approval of firms listed, but does not formally make
specific nominations or selections.

(e) Preliminary contact and screening. The project
coordinator, or committee, at this stage sends a
description of the project or study to the consultants selected. It is desirable to obtain more
detailed information on the experience and capability of each consultant, including similar projects
which they have undertaken, references who may be
contacted and their availability for the proposed
study of project. When this information is screened
the few organizations which remain are those which
will receive requests for proposals.

(f) Requests for proposals or calls for tenders. It
is in the interest of both client and consultant to
request proposals from only those firms that appear
most qualified. In part, this is because the preparation of proposals by consultants and their
review by clients is difficult, time-consuming and
expensive. Consultant staff time spent on proposals, and related activities, may account for over
25 percent of overhead costs, which will eventually
be passed on to clients in some fashion. Clients
might well consider a pre-qualification system in
which firms would submit a general statement of
qualifications which would involve less work than a
proposal. A selected limited group of contractors
would then be chosen to submit detailed proposals.
  The request for proposal is the first contact
between client and consultant in which the proposed
study or project is discussed in detail.

(g) Selection of a consultant. Many client organizations may either prefer, or be required to use, a

system of competitive bidding. This may require a
consultant to quote a price at the time a technical
proposal is submitted. Cost, although important, is
not the only matter which must be examined. Such
organizations as the World Bank and Asian Development Bank invite unpriced proposals, and the U.S.
Agency for International Development often uses a
two-envelope system, with technical proposals being
considered separately from cost. The trend is now
toward considering first the proposed technical
approach, and weighing the cost factor later since
the main consideration is attaining the objective
of the study or project, which the lowest cost
proposal might not accomplish. In the two-envelope
system, if two firms or consultants appear to be
roughly equally qualified, the one offering the
lower cost is usually chosen. Where a trade-off
between quality and price is necessary, this should
be explicitly understood. A client will need to ask
himself: "How much quality am I willing to trade for
a specified decrease in cost?"

(h) Negotiations and concluding the agreement. When
a client has tentatively selected a consultant on
the basis of both how well he thinks the consultant
can do the job and the cost involved, they will begin a process of negotiation, and possibly refining
the terms of reference. Both have interests to
express during this negotiation phase. Some may
never appear in a formal agreement, but they can be
vital to the success of the study or project. These
factors include functions and training of counterpart personnel, logistical and administrative
support, type and frequency of meetings and reports
which will be used to measure progress as the project unfolds, and the final results expected by the
client in operational terms.

5. Need to Identify the Monitoring Office
Consultants are often financed by one organization
(e.g., IBRD; USAID; FAO) to work for another, such
as the Ministry of Agriculture, in the cooperating
country. In complex studies or projects, several
ministries and donor organizations may be involved.
In either event, it is essential for the parties
involved to recognize any conflicting or different
objectives they hold, and to agree to a working
policy. Otherwise time will be lost and any final
reports or end products may be rejected by the
financing organization, the host government, or
both. To avoid such problems, the terms of reference

should specify the monitoring office and the lines of authority which will decide the consultant's work and reporting arrangements.

In most cases, both the donor and client organizations will expect the consultant to produce recommendations which can be put into practice. This is more likely to happen if the monitoring office is high enough in the organization to implement the recommendations, or to assign this task to others. In complex projects involving more than one ministry, however, no single monitoring office may have the authority to implement recommendations. A common way of dealing with this problem has been to use interministerial committees. Another approach has been to use the overall planning agency as the "referee between claimant sectors." There is no way to stipulate in advance which approach would be better, and the client organization should consider both possibilities.

6. The Client - Consultant Partnership

Once an agreement has been entered into, it is tempting for the consultant to set out to "get the job done." This must be resisted, because when clients participate in problem-solving, two major benefits result: skills are transmitted, and solutions are much more likely to be implemented.

There are several practical ways by which skills can be transmitted. One is to use counterpart personnel, the term most widely used to identify personnel who have been assigned to work directly with technical advisers from foreign assistance organizations or private foreign firms. Some dissatisfaction has been expressed with the terms "adviser" and "counterpart". The terms imply equal status in one sense, but in practice the counterpart is more often a very junior partner, sometimes even directly supervised by the adviser. The relationship should be examined carefully, in light of the objectives of transferring skills and enabling clients to perform more complex tasks independently.

Both consultant and client should look upon their roles as mutually instructive. The consultant brings technical expertise and broad experience with problems similar to those faced by the client. The latter brings detailed knowledge of local operations; the cultural, social, political and psychological environment, and what is likely to work or not work there, as well as something not often stressed: continuity. Neither can make the project work effectively without the cooperation of the other.

What specific steps might be taken to improve cooperation in this area?

Training is an essential part of consultancy,
yet arrangements for counterpart training are usually defined loosely, if at all. More often, the
approach and content of training are left to individual consultants. Few consultant organizations have
established policies for training client personnel.
One can find, on the same project, consultants who
provide excellent training, and others who provide
none. The consultant's time spent on the project
is often short. He wants to launch activities
promptly. In many cases, this seems to conflict
with the process of developing the skills of his
counterpart.

Consultants require capable client counterparts
to work with, but such people are scarce, and unlikely to be assigned to fulltime counterpart tasks.
Junior staff members who are assigned, often lack
the skill and authority necessary to move the project along successfully once the consultant has
departed. To resolve this difficulty, the consultant must work with the counterpart in a phased
series of tasks which will result in much of the
work actually being performed by the counterpart.
This involves every phase from setting objectives
through implementation and reporting. Tasks undertaken by counterparts must begin at the level of
which they are capable and become increasingly
challenging. The consultant cannot impose objectives, but can direct attention to new concepts and
methods most likely to yield answers to the problems
being worked on. Whenever possible, counterparts'
successful accomplishments should be brought to the
attention of their superiors. The transfer of
skills is most complete when it is both actual and
perceived.

The client has the responsibility to make
available the best personnel possible. To do less
will perpetuate a condition in which foreign consultants do the work, with the result that skill
transfer, and thus real development, is negligible.
Consultant reports indicate that counterparts sometimes show little interest in their work with the
consultant. In part, this results from assigning
very junior people and giving them fairly menial
tasks. A further reason is that neither client
governments nor consultants have properly understood
the potential for training which consultancy assignments offer. Consultancy can become a learning and
doing partnership when both client and consultant

346

recognize that they are jointly responsible for the results of projects and studies.

SELECT BIBLIOGRAPHY

Chapters 1 - 5

Chambers, Robert Rural poverty unperceived:
    Problems and remedies (World Bank staff working
    paper No. 400) Washington. The World Bank,
    1980.
Cochrane, W.W. Agricultural development and plan-
    ning: economic concepts, administrative
    procedures and political process. New York.
    1974.
FAO Agriculture towards 2000. Rome FAO 1981.
FAO An introduction to planning forestry
    development. Rome. FAO 1974.
Griffin, K. and Enos, J. Planning development.
    Addison-Wesley. London, 1970.
Hansen, Niles M. (Ed.) Growth centers in regional
    economic development. New York. The Free
    Press, 1974.
Kuklinski, Antoni R. (Ed.) Growth poles and growth
    centres in regional planning. Geneva, UN
    Research Institute for Social Development,
    1972.
Kulp, Earl M. Rural development planning: Systems
    analysis and working method. New York.
    Praeger, 1970.
Lele, U. The design of rural development Baltimore.
    John Hopkins University Press, 1975.
Lewis, W. Arthur Development planning. The
    essentials of economic policy. London. Allen
    and Unwin, 1966.
Mellor, John W. The economics of agricultural
    development. Ithaca. Cornell University
    Press, 1966.
Mellor, John W. The new economics of growth: A
    strategy for India and the developing world.
    Ithaca. Cornell University Press, 1976.

348

Mosher, A.T. Thinking about rural development.
New York. Agricultural Development Council,
1976.

Chapters 6 to 14

Ampuero, Ramos, Luis, A. and Fletcher, Lehman, B.
Planning for rural development with popular
participation. Ames, Iowa. University of
Iowa, 1982.
Baldwin, K.D.S. Demography for agricultural plan-
ners. Rome. FAO,   1975.
Bari, Fazbul Farmers' training program at Comilla.
Comilla, Bangladesh Academy for Rural
Development. 1979.
Bathrick, David D. Agricultural credit for small
farm development: Policies and practices.
Boulder, Colorado. Westview Press, 1981.
Benjamin, McDonald P. Investment projects in
agriculture: Principles and case studies.
Harlow, Essex. Longman, 1981.
Cairncross, J. An approach to food/population
planning. Rome. FAO,   1977.
Casley, Dennis J. and Lury, Denis A. Monitoring and
evaluation of agriculture and rural development
projects. Washington. The World Bank, 1982.
Cernes, Michael M. Measuring project impact:
Monitoring and evaluation in the PIDER rural
development project, Mexico. (World Bank staff
working paper, No. 332). Washington. The
World Bank, 1979.
Clayton, E.S. and Pétry, F. Monitoring systems for
agricultural and rural development projects.
(Economic and social development paper, No. 12)
Rome. FAO,   1981.
Cohen, John M. and Uphoff, N. Rural development
participation: Concepts and measures for project
design, implementation and evaluation. (Rural
Development Monograph, No. 2) Ithaca. Cornell
University, 1977.
Council for Agricultural Planning and Development
Preliminary report on regional agricultural
development planning in the Taiwan area. Taipei.
The Council, 1980.
Council on Environmental Quality and the Department
of State. The global report to the President:
Entering the twenty-first century. (Vol. 2.
Technical Report). Washington. Govt. Printing
Office, 1980.

Deboeck, Guido and Ng, Ronald Monitoring rural
    development in East Asia. (World Bank staff
    working paper No. 439). Washington. The
    World Bank, 1980.
Domike, Arthur L. and Shearer, Eric B. Studies in
    financing agrarian reform in Latin America.
    (Research paper No. 56, Land Tenure Center).
    Madison. Wisconsin University, 1973.
F.A.O. General guidelines to the analysis of
    agricultural production projects (Agricultural
    Planning Study, No. 14) Rome. FAO, 1971.
F.A.O. Income elasticities of demand for agricul-
    tural products. Rome. FAO, 1972.
Gittinger, J.P. Agricultural project analysis: Case
    studies and work exercises. (3 vols) Washington.
    Economic Development Institute, The World
    Bank, 1979.
Hirschman, Albert O. Development projects observed
    Washington. The Brookings Institute, 1967.
Honadle, George and others Integrated rural
    development: Making it work. AID project 936-
    5300. Washington. Development Alternatives,
    1980.
Hunter, Guy Agricultural development and the rural
    poor. Declaration of policy and guidelines for
    action. London. Overseas Development
    Institute, 1978.
Hunter, G., Bunting A. and Bottrall, A. (Eds.)
    Policy and practice in rural development.
    London. Croom Helm for the Overseas Develop-
    ment Institute, 1976.
Imboden, Nicolas Managing information for rural
    development projects. Paris. OECD, 1980.
Islam, Nurul Development planning in Bangladesh: A
    study in political economy. New York. St.
    Martin's Press, 1977.
Johnston, Bruce and Kilby, P. Agriculture and
    structural transformation: Economic strategies
    in late-developing countries. New York.
    Oxford University Press, 1975.
Little, I.M.D. and Mirrlees, J.A. Project appraisal
    and planning for developing countries. London.
    Heinemann, 1974.
Luning, H.A. The need for regionalised agricultural
    development planning: Experiences from Western
    Visayas, Philippines. Laguna, Philippines.
    Southeast Asian Regional Center for Graduate
    Study and Research in Agriculture, 1981.

Miller, Duncan (Ed.) Studies on rural development: Vol. 1. Studies on project design, implementation and evaluation. (Development Centre Papers) Paris. OECD, 1980.

Morss, Elliott R. Strategies for small farmer development: an empirical study of rural development projects (A report prepared for A.I.D.) Washington. Development Alternatives, 1975.

Overseas Development Administration Sector appraisal manual: Rural development. London. ODA, 1980.

Packard, Philip C. Critical path analysis for development administration. The Hague. Institute of Social Studies, 1972.

Robinson, Austin (Ed.) Appropriate technologies for third world development. London. Macmillan, 1979.

Rossmiller, George E. (Ed.) Agricultural sector planning: A general system simulation approach. East Lansing, Michigan. Michigan State University, 1978.

Roumasset, James A., Boussard, J. and Singh, I. (Eds) Risk, uncertainty and agricultural development. New York. Agricultural Development Council, 1979.

Solimano, Giorgio and Taylor, Lance (Eds.) Food price policies and nutrition in Latin America. Tokyo. The United Nations University, 1980.

Timmons, John F. Agrarian reform, agricultural planning and economic development in Peru. Ames, Iowa State University, 1981.

U.S. Agency for International Development Evaluation handbook. Washington. USAID, 1972.

U.S. Agency for International Development Project evaluation guidelines. Washington, USAID, 1973.

Waterston, Albert Development planning: Lessons of experience. Baltimore. John Hopkins University Press, 1966.

Wood, G.P. and Mosher, A.T. (Eds.) Readings in agricultural administration. New York. Agricultural Development Council, 1980.

Chapters 15 and 16

Benor, Daniel and Harrison, J. Agricultural extension: The training and visit system. Washington. The World Bank, 1977.

Boyce, James and Evenson, Robert E. National and international agricultural research and extension programs. New York. Agricultural Development Council, 1975.

Crouch, B.R. and Chamala S. (Eds.) Extension education and rural development (2 vols). New York. Wiley - Interscience, 1981.

Manzoor, Ahmed and Coombs, Philip H. Education for rural development: Case studies for planners. New York. Praeger, 1975.

Ruttan, Vernon W. Agricultural research policy. Minneapolis. University of Minnesota Press, 1982.

For Product Safety Concerns and Information please contact our EU
representative GPSR@taylorandfrancis.com
Taylor & Francis Verlag GmbH, Kaufingerstraße 24, 80331 München, Germany

www.ingramcontent.com/pod-product-compliance
Ingram Content Group UK Ltd.
Pitfield, Milton Keynes, MK11 3LW, UK
UKHW021824240425
457818UK00006B/66